# Delivering Electronic Mail

# Delivering Electronic Mail

### Everything You Need to Know About E-Mail

## Phillip Robinson

**M&T Books**
A Division of M&T Publishing, Inc.
411 Borel Avenue, Suite 100
San Mateo, CA 94402

**Library of Congress Cataloging-in-Publication Data available by request from the Publisher**

ISBN 1-55851-170-9

92-82670 CIP (preassigned)


95   94   93   92      4   3   2   1



**Project Editor:** Sherri Morningstar
**Copy Editor:** Laura Moorhead
**Cover Design:** Lauren Smith Design

**Layout Design:** Margaret Horoszko
**Production Supervisor:** Cindy Williams
**Production Associate:** Jeremy Mende

# Contents

# Acknowledgements

Thanks to the people who write about E-mail in books (Stephen Caswell, Eric Arnum, John Quarterman, and more) and in magazines such as *PC*, *PC World*, *BYTE*, *InfoWorld*, *PC Computing*, *MacWorld*, *MacUser*, and others. They got me started.

Thanks to the people who work for the companies that make E-mail products: Shelley Harrison of cc:Mail, Michele Eddie and Sue Nail of CE Software, Lora Loftis for Microsoft, Darin Richins of WordPerfect, and so many others I'm embarrassed to forget. They took me to the next step.

Thanks to the companies who were kind enough to submit photos and screen shots for inclusion in this book.

Thanks to the people who use E-mail. They topped my knowledge with tales of experience.

Thanks to John Quarterman, Jim Seymour, and Guy Kawasaki for some great insight on good ole fashioned common courtesy and etiquette.

Thanks to Wyse Technology (in the person of Jeannie Low) for the PC I used for E-mail work; thanks to Apple Computer (in the persons of Keri Walker and Doedy Hunter) for the Macintosh I used for E-mail work.

Thanks to the people of M&T Books: Brenda McLaughlin, Christine deChutkowski, and Linda Hanger, who helped me turn all of that reading, testing, and listening into a book.

And finally, thanks to you if you read this book. More thanks if you write to tell me what you liked and didn't like about it, what could be improved, and how your own experience with E-mail has run. Bonus points if you send your ideas via E-mail (MCI Mail: probinson at 327-8909).

# Why This Book is for You

This book is for you if you:

- Want to know what E-mail is and why it is important.
- Need to understand E-mail terms and standards.
- Need to know what kind of E-mail might be best for you or your company.
- Want tips and rules on expanding, upgrading, interconnecting, or extending your current E-mail service.
- Need to know what is coming in E-mail within the next five years.

Electronic mail, or E-mail, is the fastest growing use for computers today. It is becoming vital to individuals and businesses.

This book, *Delivering Electronic Mail*, tells you what E-mail is, how it works, and where it is used today. It also lists some of the most popular E-mail products, mainly software programs that create E-mail systems on various computers. It is not intended as a comparison-shopping guide: program versions change frequently. It is meant to show you how to choose E-mail systems and software by emphasizing the features and foibles for which you should look.

## How this Book is Organized

Inside this book you'll find:

- Definitions of important E-mail terms, so you can converse in "computerese" and read ads and reviews with impunity (Chapter 1)

- Explanations of what to look for in E-mail, on PCs, Macintoshs, work-stations, and minicomputer and mainframe systems, so you can ask the right questions (Chapter 2)
- Suggestions on E-mail set-up and maintenance, so you can avoid some of the false steps others have taken (Chapter 4)
- Further suggestions on advanced E-mail techniques, so you can feel smug about getting more out of the same basic hardware and software that everyone else uses (also Chapter 4)
- Descriptions of popular E-mail products, so you know where to look and what others are using (Chapters 5 through 8)
- A list of company addresses, a glossary of terms, and other such help-ful addenda.

Although E-mail is important, it need not be obscure. Creating E-mail software requires a deep understanding of programming; buying and implementing E-mail does not. This book is aimed at the buyer and user, not the programmer. It provides a good introduction for the novice and a solid reference for the accomplished.

*Delivering Electronic Mail* covers the basics of E-mail and adds both the serious (from routing to censorship and privacy) and light (flaming and Smilies) sidelights.

I hope you enjoy learning more about it as you read.

# Defining E-mail

This introduction tells you where E-mail came from and, briefly, how it works. Electronic Mail, or E-mail, sends messages from one computer to another. It is rapidly becoming one of the most important uses of computers and is immediately beneficial as a fast, secure, reliable, and cost-effective way to communicate. It is also the foundation for some advanced computer programs that could automate much of the paperwork of a typical organization.

E-mail is not the only form of electronic messaging. The telephone is another, as is the facsimile (fax) and telex. Each of these forms can operate independently, but they are also converging. By the late 1990s, their integration may be complete.

Choosing and installing E-mail may seem simple at first glance: You get a computer and hook it up to other computers, you buy an E-mail program, and you're in business. Not so. Think of how complicated moving from paper mail to telephone communications must have been 100 years ago. You would have had to consider which hardware provider to use, where to set up connections, who was going to have a phone and how they would use it, who would take messages when someone called, and so on. Now phones are even more complex, with "800" numbers, "900" numbers, local exchanges, PBXs, voice mail, competing long-distance carriers, leased lines, satellite connections, secure lines, and so on. E-mail messaging is that complex and more.

**Figure 1.
E-mail interfaces
can range from
simple text-only
versions such as
this Cymail
example (top)
to sophisticated,
graphic interfaces
that show icons
and views of
images, such as
this cc:Mail
example (bottom).**

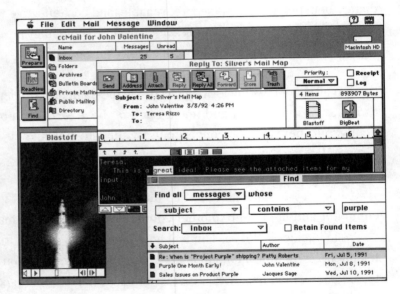

E-mail didn't benefit, as far as simplicity, from the monopoly that held for so long in telephones. It can be as changeable and tumultuous as the quickly evolving computer business and technology. Learning in that climate of rapid change and evolution makes E-mail a moving target. However, some of the basics have survived a decade. Both those fundamentals and the latest trends are profiled here.

E-mail will not be the only form of communication in the future, of course. Nor will it be the only form of mail. Different media have different strengths, so many will survive. Paper mail, or "snail mail" as it is known to E-mail enthusiasts, will still be ideal for conveying a personal, concrete touch. Voice calls and voice mail will carry intonations and emotions that E-mail can't match; fax machines will print a letter even where there is no computer to receive E-mail, and so on.

E-mail won't even fulfill its own possibilities of connecting everyone with a personal computer with instant, multimedia "mailboxes" until lots more work is done to make the various hardware and software components compatible. (Compatibility should be achieved without any extra work or knowledge on the part of the sender and recipient. It needs to be "seamless" and "transparent," popular buzzwords in computing that are truly merited here.)

## Reasons for E-mail

E-mail has come a long way since it was the plaything of bearded researchers working the midnight shift in university computer centers. Companies have adopted it all over the world, to connect people inside the company to one another as well as to those outside the company. In fact, some studies show that the number of business E-mail messages are increasing exponentially.

Imagine a business without telephones. Practically impossible, right? Many analysts think E-mail will become equally as basic to business. Not that every person will have a computer for E-mail. Not everyone has an individual phone in business today, although white-collar workers usually have at least one phone each. Knowledge workers may soon all have PCs and E-mail, and will probably be the first to get it. Blue-collar workers, however, will also be linked to E-mail systems, as the computers that track and support manufacturing and similar tasks are wired into the E-mail network. E-mail could become a main corridor to move information such as job orders, personnel intructions, and engineering suggestions to and from the blue-collar workforce.

As many as 50 to 70 percent of telephone calls don't reach their recipient because that person is away or busy. E-mail eliminates this problem, improving response times and cutting calling expenses. Beating telephone tag also helps improve productivity as people are interrupted less often.

 **Tip:** A key reason to use E-mail is to eliminate telephone tag.

Companies will also be using E-mail to simplify their communications with important outsiders: customers, suppliers, investors, and so on. Some of the communications will be simple text messages, which E-mail makes simpler by permitting quick, inexpensive questions and replies. It can replace the office memo, leaving a stored trail of what the memos were, but moving the information faster and keeping it organized. Some of the communications will be more complex, with spreadsheet or database files "attached" to explanatory messages. These attached files will move from sender to recipient, so the recipient can view and possibly alter what the sender has been working on. Some communications will be interactive, where the sender and recipient will work on the same document at the same time. Both parties, for instance, could view the same diagram on-screen, each pointing to parts of it and able to make changes immediately, and each seeing the changes the other makes.

In other words, for business there are lots of good reasons to use E-mail, from sending simple messages to serving as a foundation for advanced data-sharing applications. Some are:

- more mobility and flexibility for employees
- better communications across time zones
- added value for a LAN (and reason enough to set-up a LAN)
- a consistent interface for communications, with one set of commands for memos, faxes, file transfers, telexes, and so on
- improved and faster decisions and service because of better information flow
- improved meeting plans and preparation

At least, E-mail shortens the memo cycle. Instead of the traditional write, type, edit, retype, copy, address, and send procedures, E-mail requires only the simple write and send. This can have profound consequences when you consider how the cycle adds up through the back-and-forth of typical correspondence. The time saved can be devoted to working on more deals or on improving response to the customer or the quality of the work.

 **Tip:** E-mail could help bring about the "paperless office" ideal, and so be a real force for a less wasteful world.

As the 80s progressed and the 90s dawned, E-mail became a facet of personal life, at least for some adventurous souls in affluent areas such as the U.S., Canada, Western Europe, and Japan. At first these people often used public-service E-mail to contact the office, after hours or from out of town. Then the technology improved, the prices dropped, and some services were tailored to nontechnical personal use. Current personal uses include:

- keeping up with children
- genealogy tracing through E-mail directories
- hearing-impaired communications
- family correspondence with soldiers on foreign assignment
- criminals making deals

Marriages have even sprung from meetings on E-mail.

Individuals use E-mail because it's fast and reliable, and sometimes even because it's cheaper than a long-distance telephone call. A two-page letter can cost as little as 45 cents, anywhere in the country. Try moving that many words for so little with a standard telephone call. (However, to be fair, the E-mail cost mentioned does not include whatever amortized cost there would be of the terminal or computer to send the message, or the portion of the telephone costs that could be shared.)

**Tip:** Remember that although moving information is important, the quality of the relationships for information exchange are more important, in business and personal life.

Link Resources estimates there are 11.5 million E-mail users in the U.S. alone, with 1.5 million of those in homes. Prodigy, one of the most popular services, claims to move 30,000 messages a day.

However, E-mail is not a panacea. For one thing, E-mail in organizations is only practical when most people, or at least most people in the department or workgroup that use it, have computers close at hand. For another, the benefits of E-mail will not be immediately obvious to everyone. Systems people already have, such as paper memos, are known and reliable. Stories about network breakdowns and hard disk crashes may even lead people to think E-mail will be less reliable than paper memos: "What happens if I lose all my mail?"

## History

In other books you can find detailed histories of electronic messaging and E-mail. Not here. History full of "the telegraph was invented in such and such a year" and "the first computer messages were this or that" can be an unaffordable luxury to those who need to understand something and make choices now. But it is useful to know a bit of the background of E-mail, particularly to understand how to integrate it with other messaging technologies.

 **Tip:** You can see E-mail as merging traditional paper mail, which can be read, filed, and forwarded, with the immediate delivery of the telephone.

With traditional paper mail, a sender can create and address a letter, which is routed through a hierarchical organization to the recipient's mailbox. The letter remains there until the recipient chooses to check the box. Upon finding the letter, the recipient may note the sender's address on the outside, then decide whether to read the letter now, later, or never. When read, the letter can be stored, discarded, replied to, or even forwarded to someone else. This "post office" model is used by most E-mail systems today, although the messages are bundles of electric signals sent over lines or radio waves to a recipient.

The first use of electronics in messaging appeared in the 19th century with the telegraph, telephone, and early radio. These contraptions let a person at one end send a message at the speed of light to the person at the other end. Telegraphs carried encoded messages, text transformed at one end into dots and dashes, and then interpreted at the other end back into text again. The first radio did the same, though without the need for a wire in between sender and recipient. Telephones carried a voice, without need for translation into dots and dashes. Radio soon did the same, again without wires.

The telegraph scheme was automated by providing a telex machine to both the sender and recipient. The sender's machine could automatically translate typed words into electronic codes that the recipient's machine could translate back into typed words. The connection between machines was made by typical telephone lines, with dial-up numbers. With a telex, an executive can dictate a letter and give it to the telex department or secretary, who then types it on a telex machine. The letter then appears on the telex machine at the other end, printed on paper, and is delivered to the indicated individual. This is much faster than traditional paper-mail and provides a paper record of the message, unlike a telephone call. Although, it is often more expensive than a telephone call, and certainly more expensive than E-mail, telex messaging is reliable and well-understood.

Sending telexes became quite popular for international messages, for the previous reasons and because it avoids the trouble of immediate language translation. It is often used for money transfer and to check on shipments. You can think of a telex machine as a long-distance typewriter: Type a message locally and the printed version appears across the room or the world.

Most E-mail systems have an option of connecting to the international telex network to send telexes. Integrating the two simplifies creating and sending telexes and lets E-mail get to the more than two million telex machines in the world. (The latest telex machines even have their own disk drives and CRT monitors.)

Facsimile or "fax" messaging became wildly popular in the late 1980s. Fax machines appeared everywhere, turning up even in individual homes and cars. The fax process, however, is much older than that, invented back in the mid 1900s and used intensely in some businesses for decades. Xerox and Western Union developed it in the 60s, then, after Japanese firms pushed prices down in the late 70s and 80s, the market expanded dramatically.

Fax machines also convert messages automatically into codes that move electronically. But a fax is not the same as a telex. It does not understand text that has been typed as "text"—a collection of characters that make up words and numbers—to then type it out again on the other end. Instead, you feed a printed page into a fax machine, which converts it into the code and sends it through the telephone line, and the receiving Fax machine converts the code back into a printed page. You could see a fax machine as a long-distance copier: Feed in a page locally and the copy appears across the room or the world. In fact, the process is merging with copying and laser-printing technology, with some devices now doing all three.

A fax machine can send both text and graphics, unlike a telex, which can only send text. That lets it carry pictures, signatures, and even complete copies of documents with signatures. Faxing is popular in the U.S. because it moves documents instantly, even faster than express services can. Also, it can move legal documents, including signatures, a critical need in most businesses. Sending a fax is quite simple: You don't need to type or know any codes. You just enter the fax phone number of the recipient, feed the document into the fax machine, and you're done. Faxing is wildly popular in Japan because that country's written language of thousands of ideograms is not well-suited to a keyboard. There are millions of fax machines in the U.S., Japan, and the rest of the world.

"Group III" is a standard for sending faxes now, superseding the slower Group I and Group II. Group III needs about 20 seconds to move a page at a resolution of about 200 dpi (dots per inch). Faster speeds and higher resolutions are already appearing.

Fax machines are easy to use, requiring virtually no training, and the latest hardware is cheap and reliable. The result is that many companies have more fax equipment than their MIS (Management Information Systems) officials know— people buy faxes out of departmental funds.

Telegraph messaging has died and use of the telex is fading, though still popular for some international messages. Telephones are everywhere, and fax machines are nearly so. Now we come to E-mail, or as it was first called, Computer-Based Messaging Systems (CBMS). (Western Union first used the term "Electronic Mail" in the 1960s, and even registered it as a trademark in 1974, although it has not been defended.)

E-mail began as a simple way for computer researchers to communicate. A typical company had a number of "terminals": boxes that combined keyboard, screen, and enough electronics to talk to the mainframe through a cable and report the results on a terminal's screen. By using these terminals, a researcher in one room could send a message to a researcher in another room, another building, or just working another shift. At first, researchers were satisfied with an instant message: Type it here and it appears on another terminal screen. Soon, however, that wasn't enough.

Researchers didn't want to be limited to sending a message when both were at their own terminals and both terminals were on. Trying to extend messaging power and to investigate what a computer could do, researchers attempted to implement something more like traditional mail. They also wanted to simulate the typical knowledge worker's setup of a/an:

- inbox, where work to do was received
- outbox, where work was heading out to other workers
- desktop, where work was done
- filing cabinet, where finished work was stored
- trash can, where papers no longer needed are discarded
- mail carrier, who brings memos to the inbox and delivers those from the outbox

A worker checks the inbox for memos, puts them on the desk to read and act upon them (reply, forward, file, or throw away), puts outgoing memos and responses in the outbox (where the mail carrier will come along to scoop them up and move them to the recipients), files those with long-term importance, and discards in the trash can those no longer needed.

E-mail systems have various combinations of these features. The only two features you'll find everywhere are the inbox (with mail waiting to be read) and the mail carrier.

Bringing traditional postal models and the inbox-outbox scheme into electronic messaging would mean the person working on one terminal could type a message to be "stored" in the mainframe computer. The message would wait for the recipient, either quietly waiting in a "mailbox" (just an easy name for the computer memory storage site), or waiting there and sending some notice to the recipient's terminal. The developers of this primitive E-mail system quickly worked to separate mailboxes from particular terminals. (Much of the early work came from the Bolt, Beranek, and Newman Company and from the U.S. government's DARPA (Defense Advanced Research Projects Agency).)

After all, if the message were waiting in the central computer, which all terminals could reach, why should you have to read your mail from a particular terminal? Why should you not instead be able to read messages from any terminal, as long as you identified your mailbox and supplied some password for security? These questions fell in line with the general use of terminals, which permitted anyone to use any terminal as long as they "logged on" with their name and system password. Other features soon followed:

- editors to give word-processing abilities for making messages
- forwarding to send messages on to other mailboxes
- mailing lists to send a message to multiple mailboxes
- replying, to automatically put the sender's address into the recipient's address space on a new message

Commercial mainframe E-mail systems such as IBM's PROFS (Professional Office System) and DISOSS (Distributed Office Support System) appeared. During the late 1970s, mainframe computers with terminals were replaced in many businesses by minicomputers. Minicomputer makers offered their own E-mail in integrated software packages, the likes of Wang Office, Data General's CEO, and DEC's All-In-1. Besides E-mail, these programs had word processing, database management, and scheduling features.

Again, these central systems were connected to terminals, so mail didn't need to change significantly. As more computers infiltrated universities, companies, and government agencies, however, "networks" began to appear. The central computer of a network would be connected by a "bridge" to another computer. The first motivation in most cases was to share printers and hard disks. No single computer printed enough pages or needed enough storage to justify an expensive laser printer or a large-capacity hard disk. A group of computers could justify such expenses if it could share the resources available on the "Local Area Network" (LAN). Soon E-mail became a major reason for networking. In fact, it may now be the most popular reason. In the 80s, companies such as Banyan and 3Com sold networks, and sold E-mail as an option for their own networks. Independent software companies such as Da Vinci, Higgins, Consumers Software, and PCC Systems (later called cc:Mail) began offering E-mail for the most popular networks.

**Figure 2.**
**Host with terminals**
**vs LAN**

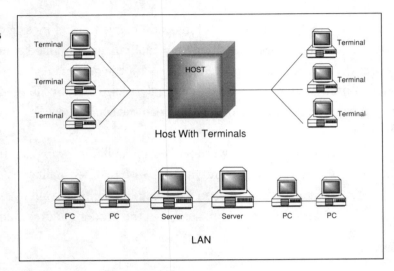

Host With Terminals

LAN

Networks were only possible because personal computers appeared, and were so much cheaper than mainframes or minicomputers. That made the E-mail less costly too—down to $50 to $100 per user in immediate costs. Even the makers of big systems saw the trend; IBM, for instance, offered E-mail in its networked OfficeVision product. By the end of the 80s, E-mail was booming, and so popular E-mail software developers were acquired by the largest software companies. The percentage of white-collar people working with E-mail jumped.

Even LANs weren't enough. People did not want to be limited to communicating only with others on the same computer system. Organizations could be large enough to have more than one computer, especially with minicomputers that were more aimed at departments than entire companies. Why should you only be in touch with those in your department, your division, or even your company? What about other researchers around the world? What about customers, suppliers, consultants, colleagues, and competitors?

Linking computers or even LANs to one another could theoretically transport messages from a terminal on one system, through intervening systems, to a recipient at a terminal on a distant system. This model, called "store-and-forward," proved very popular because of its reach. WANs (Wide Area Networks)

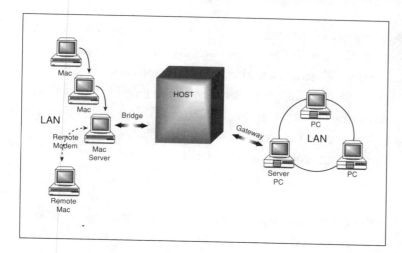

**Figure 3. Simple diagram of a typical wide area network (WAN).**

spread E-mail to people all over the world. They connected islands of E-mail. (Many companies have three, four, or more LANs with varying E-mail packages already installed, and will need ways to connect these to whatever overall E-mail scheme they want for the future.)

Store-and-forward among a variety of computer hardware and software types required some complex translations and conversions. Different E-mail programs used different addressing schemes and different connection signals.

The problem grew larger as personal computers became popular. At first, these only provided E-mail when they were connected through modems and telephone lines to a mainframe or minicomputers, in which case they were basically acting as terminals. Sometimes this E-mail architecture was used inside a particular company or organization, with centralizing that company's mainframe or minicomputer. Other times the central computer offered its E-mail as a commercial service for independent personal-computer users. Commercial-service E-mail systems could be used by a single computer on its own or by a company's central computer, which could call the commercial-service computer to transfer messages to it, depending on that distant computer to then forward the messages to the appropriate mailboxes or other computer systems.

Soon, as the power of personal computers grew, they were able to "multitask." You could be doing one thing with a personal computer while an E-mail checking program ran continuously, watching for incoming mail and notifying you when it was received. You could also run a word processor alongside the E-mail and your other applications, making it easier to craft letters. This was much easier than having to start a specific E-mail program, check for mail, try to create a message with a bare-bones editing program, and then quit E-mail to get back to other computing work.

Connection troubles grew more profound as personal computers were linked to one another in LANs. These LANs could have a connection to a central system to share its E-mail software, or they could, and increasingly did, offer their own E-mail within the LAN.

Connecting the E-mail of one LAN to another meant solving differences between E-mail software, as well as different networking signals, and even different networking cables. The solutions were called "bridges" and "routers" (which made direct hardware connections to other networks) and "gateways" (which used software to translate E-mail messages from one system to another). Routers offer more isolation for connected LAN segments; bridges or repeaters bring the LANs closer together.

Developers have created many such bridges and gateways, but until recently each used its own answer to translate between systems. Now standards are appearing. Some are de facto standards, such as the Message Handling Service (MHS), which has become popular because Novell promotes it. (Novell is the absolutely dominant supplier of network operating system software with its NetWare.) Some are official standards such as the X.400 message-exchange protocol and the X.500 directory-services protocol. Both of these sprang from international committees.

**Tip:** Many, perhaps too many, have said "The great thing about standards is that there are so many to choose from."

## Trends

The E-mail market was once entirely dominated by mainframe and mini-computer programs, by E-mail software that ran on "host" computers. In the 90s that has changed entirely. There are seven big trends now:

- *Decentralization*—New E-mail systems are largely on LANs, not hosts
- *Consolidation*—Fewer LAN E-mail programs have more of the market
- *Integration*—LAN, host, fax, and other messaging forms are joining
- *Infiltration*—E-mail functions are appearing in other "mail-enabled" programs and even in "groupware."
- *Separation*—Transport, directory, and interface services are separating
- *Extension*—E-mail will carry multimedia messages everywhere, aided by portable systems and universal directories
- *Automation*—E-mail will carry messages between programs.

Decentralization means that most of the emphasis now is on the departmental LAN E-mail programs. LAN E-mail is growing at 70 percent a year. IDC (International Data Corp.) estimates that LAN E-mail will grow from 3.3 million users in 1991 to 35.6 million in 1995. These LANs often have only 5 to 20 users. When E-mail needs to cover a wider area than a single LAN can manage, LAN functions are still the heart of the operation, reaching out through gateways to create WANs (Wide Area Networks), and often embracing the host-based mainframe mail that runs over leased telephone lines.

Integration conserves current investments in E-mail. People rarely just dump an older E-mail system. Instead, they look for ways to interconnect their host E-mail with LAN E-mail. As explained later, the costs of LAN E-mail can be much lower than those of host E-mail. Also, the systems built on LAN E-mail can be much more flexible. Integrating today's practical fax services can also save money and time. Sending faxes is much simpler and more immediate with E-mail than with printing and then feeding pages to a fax machine, especially if the fax is going to multiple recipients.

Consolidation is a fact of E-mail life. When the LAN E-mail market was small, there were many contenders selling software. There are still many choices, but a few dominate. As E-mail clearly became a hot new market, some of the largest software companies got into the game either by acquiring or investing in the best prospects from the small companies. The three big examples of this are cc:Mail (acquired by Lotus Development), Microsoft Mail for PC Networks (bought and renamed from Consumer Software's Network Courier), and Da Vinci eMail (large investment by Novell).

cc:Mail and Microsoft Mail completely dominate all others in the LAN software market. cc:Mail appears to be in front as of mid 1992, but Microsoft is challenging that status. (Microsoft actually offers two LAN E-mail programs, quite different but with only slightly different names: Microsoft Mail for PC Networks and Microsoft Mail for AppleTalk Networks.)

Infiltration refers to the way E-mail is becoming part of many computing tools. By creating standard programming methods and by standardizing the way messages move on a network, it is becoming possible to add E-mail functions to most any program. A word processor, spreadsheet, and database manager can all have the ability to send and receive mail messages—they can be "mail-enabled". This trend makes E-mail easier to use and more immediate, and it transforms E-mail from the status of a sophisticated, independent application to a basic function like printing or saving a file to disk. This trend also points toward yet more communicative software, such as the whole area known as "groupware," which is comprised of programs that coordinate the actions of the members in a group.

Separation is a trend in E-mail software architecture. As explained later, there are three major services to do in moving E-mail: transport, directory, and interface. Sometimes the software pieces that handle these are referred to as agents, such as the transport Agent and the user Agent. Historically, each E-mail software company had to provide all of the pieces in the same program. As pressure for standardization increases, however, there is a move to completely separate the services or agents. Quite possibly within the next few years, the transport services will just become part of the network operating system. Directory services will probably follow the same path. That would leave only the user agent or interface function to be supplied by E-mail software firms, a factor that will not diminish the impact of the user agent providers. In fact, there are many new features to add in that arena, such as message management, to give providers ample room to develop and expand.

Extension is the tendency to move more types of information to more people. One extension is in the types of information E-mail carries. E-mail was once only text. Then, "attached files" carried graphics and numbers. Now attached files are being extended to move voice, video, and other media. Some E-mail systems even allow those information types to be part of the main messages themselves, not just as tag-along files. Another extension is moving E-mail out to more sites through portable computers and wireless modems. E-mail will soon be available in pocket-size containers, nearly anywhere in the world. Finally, these extensions will mean many more people using E-mail, a situation only possible with the development of practical universal directories.

Automation describes how E-mail is not limited to people. Programs are using it to communicate with one another, which permits sophisticated program teamwork for people's use—such as a graphics program automatically launching to let a recipient view and edit an attached graphics file. More significantly, however, automation refers to completely program-to-program messages, without direct people participation. For example, a program could monitor the price of a particular stock, then send a message when that price reaches a certain level. Another program could receive the message and follow its own script. That recipient program might use E-mail to send the price to a spreadsheet, which would analyze the price change and return results with an E-mail reply. Then the script program could generate a new message to sell or buy more of the stock, sending that via E-mail to a person or yet another program.

Similar automation could do everything from maintaining performance levels in a nuclear power plant to alerting network administrators to computer troubles. With E-mail connected to other communications forms, the results could even be communicated to a person via a fax machine, pager, voice synthesis in a phone call, or other means.

## How E-mail Works

This brief section describes E-mail operation.

You sign on with your "username" (which may be your full name or some nickname or abbreviation) and your password. You'll often see a welcoming message of general or system news. Then you'll see your inbox, listing mail that has arrived, along with some menu of commands you can use to create your own messages.

You decide to whom you'll send a message by choosing names from a directory that contains the recipient or recipients, as well as anyone to copy it to (carbon copies or blind carbon copies). If you want to send a message to many people, you might find it easier to "broadcast" a message to everyone on the network using a public or private mailing list, or a bulletin board, if your E-mail system offers that capability. If you don't want to just leave a message, but to "converse" with someone through your computer, you can use a chat or conferencing feature, providing your E-mail offers such.

Then you create the message by using either a built-in or separate text editor or word processor. Text editors with E-mail range from rudimentary to sophisticated. They at least let you type and delete characters. At best, they let you move blocks of characters, import text from disk files or other programs, and even check spelling. Few E-mail packages allow formatting of text with font variety, alignment, and the like, but a few do permit underlining and boldfacing of text.

Then you tell the program to send your message. It does so, with that message immediately appearing in the recipient's computer mailbox.

When receiving mail, typically you'll be notified that mail has come in. You may receive notice or when a notify utility (which runs constantly, monitoring the state of your inbox) detects a new message. The alert could be a sound, a flashing note on-screen, or both.

Upon opening your inbox (this could require switching to the E-mail program), some listing of the received messages would appear, typically showing their header information and perhaps the first line or so of the message. With most E-mail systems you could change the order of these messages to sort them by subject or sender instead of the default chronological sorting. If you choose to read a message, it appears on-screen. You could save it in your own folders, print it, or forward it to another mailbox. You could also reply to it immediately: Most E-mail programs allow users to click the mouse or give a

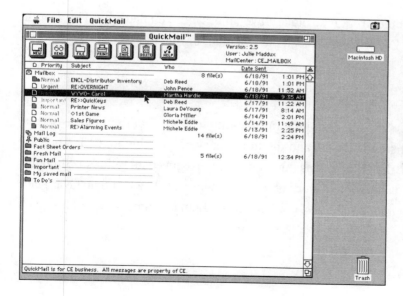

**Figure 4.**
**Most E-mail programs offer an inbox list of received messages that includes the sender, date sent, time sent, subject, and priority level of the messages.**

command to set-up a reply message. In this case, the sender's address is swapped with the recipient's and the subject is listed as "RE:" the previous message's subject. You might also want to repeat part of the previous message in the reply. Some E-mail programs offer commands to cut and paste parts of a message for this purpose.

Before you send a file you may want to attach files to it. Attached files can carry lots more information than you would want to insert into a single message. Some E-mail programs allow only a single attached file per message, while others may set the limit at 20 files, or even allow unlimited number of attachments. Larger limits are sometimes necessary, such as when sending projects that consist of many files. What kind of file you can attach also varies. Some E-mail programs can attach only text files; others can attach any kind of computer file, including sound, video, or program files. (See the comments in Chapter 1 on Multimedia E-mail.) When you receive a message with attachments, you can either store the attached files in your own folders (to access them later with the appropriate application program) or immediately view them (if your E-mail program has "viewer" capabilities). Most E-mail packages can view text files; some can view graphics or spreadsheet files.

Later, you could dredge up old archived messages you had stored by searching for them by key words, subject, date, sender, or other such criteria.

## Summary

E-mail is the latest technology for communications, combining the permanence and precision of letters and the immediacy of the telephone. It is quickly becoming more than that too, as the foundation of a new generation of computer programs for collaboration in work groups. Although it will not completely replace older communications schemes, it will supplant them for some uses and fuse with them in others.

To use E-mail efficiently you need to understand something of its technology, choose the E-mail that's right for you, follow certain codes of E-mail conduct, and manage the E-mail software and hardware well. The following chapters tackle all of those topics.

# CHAPTER ONE

# Understanding E-mail

This chapter details how E-mail works and where it is going. Along the way it defines terms and explains issues. There are lots of these, so the chapter is rather long. Don't feel that you must read it front-to-back, though. You could just skip to the Choosing, Using, and Managing E-mail chapters, referring to this chapter for explanations of the terms you encounter. Or you could leap to chapters 6 through 9 about actual products, and again refer here for explanations (or to the Glossary for terser tellings).

E-mail is a technology, built from several general computer technologies and many particular programmed commands and options. This section describes those underpinnings and features of E-mail.

## Network Technology

E-mail wouldn't exist without computer networks. It is built on computers sharing information, the definition of a network. Networks start with simple modem-to-modem connections between computers and grow through LANs to WANs.

Computers can be connected to other computers by moving floppies ("Sneak-ernet"), by connecting them with cables (file-transfer utilities), by connecting them with cables and operating software (Local Area Networks or LANs), or by attaching a modem and calling another phone with a modem through the telephone network (telecommunications).

Sneakernet is obvious, easy, and limited. File-transfer utilities are great for moving lots of files in short time, but require short cables and don't allow practical, continuous connections. LANs are complex to set-up and maintain, but offer permanent, continuous connections that can move information at very high speeds. They also provide a software foundation for complex, cooperative work between computers. Telecommunications is ideal for distant connections, but cannot match the information transmission speeds of LANs.

### Modem-to-modem connections

The simplest connection between computers is based on the modem, a device that translates computer signals into tones that can travel through a telephone line. With two computers, each equipped with a modem, telecommunications program, and a phone line, you can transfer messages from one system to another. Some bulletin-board systems are based on just this idea (see the discussion of bulletin boards later in this chapter). Such modem connections are also vital to connecting lone computers to commercial-service E-mail. They're also part of many larger E-mail systems as the means for connecting isolated, remote systems to the central E-mail system. However, a two-computer connection with telecomm software alone is not real E-mail. For that you need a LAN.

**Tip:** Today's defacto standard modem works at 9600bps (bits per second), and with compression at up to 38,400bps. Remember when you plan that there are still lots of 1200 and 2400bps modems about being used.

### LANs

The speed at which LANs move information and their immediate and constant connection have made them the fastest growing fact in computing. People are generally willing to brave the setup and administration difficulties to gain the benefits. (Meanwhile, they pound on the hardware and software makers for easier, more reliable, and less fragile network products.)

LAN operation requires:

- clients (also known as "workstations," individual computers or terminals on the network)
- client network software (small pieces of software that run on the client and adapt it to the network)
- network interface hardware (circuits that connect the client to the network physically, typically a plug-in card for a PC)
- a server (a central computer that has a hard disk with software for the clients to share; there could be more than one on the network)
- server network software (a network operating system that handles the client requests for server information or resources)
- cables (the wires connecting clients and the server)

There are lots of books on networks, adapters, network operating systems, and so on. The most important fact to know here is that the E-mail you use is a network application, requiring a server module—that runs on the particular network operating system (NOS)—and a client module for each client.

The server module for E-mail typically contains directory services (the address book for the E-mail system), an E-mail engine (the database that holds the messages), and transport services (the software that moves messages and file attachments). The client module typically contains the user interface—the menus and option lists to let you invoke E-mail engine features.

The most popular network operating system by far is Novell's NetWare. Other popular NOSs include Microsoft's LAN Manager, Banyan VINES, Apple Computer's AppleShare, and Artisoft's LANtastic.

### WANs

LANs can be connected to one another, whether or not they share the same network hardware and software. Such systems are sometimes called "enterprise-wide networks" or "wide-area networks" (WANs).

The hardware method for connecting differing LANs togther is to use a "bridge" or "router," a device that translates the packets of information on one network into a form that another network can understand. If you use a LAN that is connected to another LAN by a bridge or router, you probably won't know the connection is there. It will look like one big network to you, unless you're trying to run sophisticated group applications programs that cannot run on both of the networks. E-mail messages are easily translated by bridges and routers.

 **Tip:** Even with the advantages of WANs, an 80/20 messaging rule of thumb suggests that in practice 80 percent of messages on a system stay local.

### WAN channels—dial-up, leased-line, ISDN, Frame-relay, SMDS

There are many technologies to data information between pieces of a WAN, including dial-up phone lines, leased lines, packet networks (private or public), ISDN, Frame-relay, SMDS, and satellite. These are the physical channels through which the information flows.

Dial-up phone lines are the ones we all use for telephone calls and are often the choice for modem connections. Leased lines typically carry higher-speed transmissions—such as 38.4Kbps (thousand bits per second) compared to dial-up 9600bps—and are always available. However, leased lines also cost more, at least initially, than dial-up lines. (Dial-up lines could be more expensive if you use them enough.)

ISDN (Integrated Services Digital network) moves information as digital signals instead of as analog. The standard or BRI (Basic Rate Interface) ISDN arrangement has three channels, two at 64Kbps for voice or data and one at 16Kbps for control of the other channels. The total 144Kbps seemed quite broad when ISDN was first described years ago, and is still far beyond what today's analog modems can move through a phone line. But 144Kbps isn't that much when compared to what some of the latest fiber-optic and other sophisticated systems can move. It also isn't that much when transmission of video or other multimedia mail is considered. Now there are newer and faster schemes.

Broadband ISDN, which uses fiber-optic cables, can reach 150Mbps (megabits per second), enough for full-motion video transmission. That raises even more interest in phone companies because it means they could become major distributors of information and programming (if given the legal permission to do so). Naturally, such high speeds would also make for potent connections of WANs for E-mail, and able to move any size of information in the attached files. It would allow practical connections of scattered sites over a high-speed *backbone* using phone lines. If ISDN interests you, there are a number of companies making ISDN adapters for network computers, especially PCs.

Frame-relay, SMDS (Switched Multi-megabit Data Service), and satellite connections promise even higher transmission rates than ISDN. These methods package unrelated transmissions together and send them at very high speeds. Such transmission rates will become necessary when E-mail carries multimedia information, where messages and files can easily be megabytes in size and so would take good portions of an hour to move through standard phone lines or ISDN.

Deciding how to interconnect LANs can be a complex task. There are entire books devoted to the ins and outs of interconnection. You need to know the geographical distance and arrangement of the LANs to connect, the costs of phone lines, the size and types of files you want to move, the frequency with which you need to move files, and other such factors. Even if you're only planning on moving E-mail messages across the WAN connections, you can only choose the optimum setup if you know your E-mail users' habits. Do they send large files, lots of files, do they need instant delivery of their messages to distant systems, do they need to connect to commercial-service E-mail networks, and so on.

One essential element in many WANs is the PDN or Public Data Network. These are *packet-switching* services that accept your local telephone call (with a modem), break its information into pieces, and bundle those pieces with others from other calls from the same area, routing the various pieces through high-speed lines to any commercial-service or other computer attached to the PDN. The receiving site collects the pieces back into the original data, even though the various pieces may have followed different routes through the phone system, taking advantage of whatever open lines were available. This lets you make a local call to reach a long-distance computer or network. Telenet and Tymnet are the best-known examples. Many of these PDNs depend on the X.25 protocol for packet-switching, as explained in the following section.

 **Tip:** Ask your commercial-service provider or WAN expert what PDNs you can use to keep calling costs low.

### WAN protocols—X.25, UUCP, TCP/IP, Xmodem, Kermit

When moving information through any channel—dial-up line, frame-relay, or whatever—the sender and receiver need to speak the same language. They will only understand the bits of noise in that channel if they both support the same "protocol."

The UUCP (Unix to Unix Copy) protocol is popular in workstations running the UNIX operating system. Xmodem is popular on PCs and Macintoshs, found in many modem-control programs. You can find Kermit in both mainframes and minicomputers, and on PC programs that hope to connect with those. TCP/IP (Transmission Control Protocol/Internet Protocol) is also popular in Unix workstations, and can be used on PCs as well.

There are a lot of "X." (pronounced "eks-dot") standards from the international committee CCITT. X.400, as explained later, applies to E-mail transport. X.500 concerns E-mail directories. X.25 is more general to networking: It is a protocol standard for connecting to packet-switched networks. X.25 has been around a while and is a popular standard for connecting individual or LAN sites to a WAN. It isn't as fast as leased lines, generally, but is less expensive. X.25 is well-suited to E-mail work, because E-mail typically moves only small files (messages) that fit easily into the packets. X.25 saves you from having to own or worry about the phone lines between the sender and the recipient: The packet-switching network handles that.

### Gateways

"Gateways" are another way to connect LANs and WANs. A gateway is a program that knows how to translate and transmit the messages from one E-mail system to another. Gateways call each other at specified times or intervals to exchange E-mail that is waiting for another system. Most gateway transmissions are over telephone lines, using modems, but they can also work within a network. A gateway could let you send E-mail from one server to another server on the same LAN, from a remote system to the LAN, from the LAN to the remote system, from the LAN to another similar LAN, or from the LAN to a different E-mail system.

Using gateways is typically much less expensive and simpler than using bridges or routers, but it does not yield the "transparent" file transfer that a bridge or router can bring. By using an E-mail program and its file attachment feature, however, you can still move lots of information from one LAN to another. Unfortunately, gateways often cost several thousand dollars just for the software, which isn't as bad as it might sound because you only need one gateway per LAN. If you own and are connecting two LANs, however, you'll need two gateways. You'll also need a separate gateway for each other type of messaging system to which you want to connect. Connecting to MCI Mail is one gateway, to AT&T Mail another, and so on.

Then there's the hardware. Each gateway will need to run on its own PC, at least until you find gateways that run under a multitasking operating system such as OS/2, which could operate several on a single PC.

There are the modems. Generally you'll want high-speed modems that communicate at 38,400bps. Even that speed is puny compared to computer network speeds. Use a standard business modem that runs at 2400bps or 9600bps and your gateway will surely become a tight bottleneck. You might spend as much on longer phone connection charges with a slower modem.

Phone line charges range from inexpensive, late-night charges—if you can afford to wait to send mail until those hours—to expensive leased lines, which might add up to smaller total costs if you need frequent, long-distance transmissions.

Although initial installation may be fairly simple, some gateways require configuration and have access to mailing lists, which help the gateway know how to route messages and files it is translating and sending. They will also need to be set for the times or conditions that trigger calls to other systems that have or need messages.

Gateway options may also require both the particular gateway and a general "gateway preparation" utility. An example of gateway preparation would be the MHS gateway for cc:Mail, which requires both a gateway option and the MHS option. Higgins E-mail needs both Higgins Exchange and the Higgins-to-MHS gateway to communicate using MHS. The Exchange is a WAN mail manager that lets Higgins reference another server's file, directory, and applications resources.

Some gateways are "proprietary," made by just one company to work with that company's hardware and software. That means you'll need another gateway of the same sort on the other end of the line to make a connection.

The gateway to end all gateways comes from Soft*Switch and runs on an IBM mainframe and that supports more than 50 different E-mail programs, from LAN to minicomputer to commercial-service E-mail. Another important name in gateways is Retix, which creates the gateway software that many E-mail companies sell. Touch Communications also makes a variety of gateways, and Digital Equipment (DEC) offers gateways that run on its VAX systems for converting messages for a variety of E-mail systems. Cayman and Alisa make gateways for some popular Macintosh E-mail packages and for connecting Macintosh E-mail to DEC minicomputers.

## Remote systems

"Remote" refers to any network or E-mail client that is not directly cabled to the network. Such a system could be an office with a single PC, a portable PC in a hotel room, or even a hand-held PC in a pocket. A remote client reaches a network through a modem-equipped "access server" PC. There are a number of ways for such systems to do this.

First, they could link through a gateway at the remote site. This is rarely practical or affordable because of the cost of gateways. Few remote PCs require that expenditure for the number of messages they move.

Second, the remote system could use a remote client version of an E-mail package. This would probably have a similar interface to the standard client version of the E-mail system, but, where the standard version would always be connected to the network, the remote version would only be connected when a user calls the network. A standard version sends messages when they are created; a remote version collects them into a queue to send as a batch when a connection is made. At that same connection time, any messages waiting for the remote version would be "downloaded" into the remote user's inbox for reading and handling. Some E-mail packages as well as remote clients offer the user the option to leave copies of these messages in the network inbox, for archiving. Sometimes the remote user client is an extra-price option.

A third way to connect is by using an MHS remote-entry program module, which assumes the E-mail system supports MHS and has an MHS server. Here, the remote PC runs a single-user version of any MHS-compatible E-mail program and dials-in to the server to exchange mail.

A fourth way for a remote system to connect to a network or E-mail is through a remote-control program. This requires a copy of the remote control program and a modem for the remote system, and another copy and modem for a PC on the network. The remote PC's modem connects to the networked PC's modem, and the remote control program then takes control of the network PC, issuing commands from the remote PC and showing the networks PC screen displays on the remote computer's screen. The two PCs work in lockstep, and so the remote PC user could work just as if he or she were physically at the networked PC, reading E-mail and running other network programs. Some of the most popular remote-control programs are Triton Technology's Co/Session, R2LAN from Crosstalk Communications, pcAnywhere from DMA, and Argus/n from Triticom.

Yet another way to connect to a network is to use a special networking modem such as the Shiva NetModem/E. This device gives full access to network resources, just as if the remote system were linked physically and directly to the network. NetModem/E is a modem with an Ethernet connector attached, so it operates as its own node on the LAN. It acts like a logged- in workstation, in fact it doesn't have to be attached to a PC. It can run from 9600bps to 57.6Mbps using compression, so any modem-equipped remote PC or Macintosh can dial-in to the network. It runs a special version of IPX and the NetWare shell on a remote PC, for Novell NetWare networks. It doesn't care if the user interface is command-line or GUI.

### Hub services

Some of the commercial E-mail services (described later in this chapter) and other firms are offering hub services for E-mail. These are computers running E-mail transport software and they can be the centerpiece or an additional gateway for any E-mail system. For example, Immedia Infomatic offers a QuickMail WAN hub that can accept and forward QuickMail messages from any one Quick-Mail site to another. Novell offers an MHS hub, as does CompuServe. SprintMail offers a cc:Mail hub.

Hub services present the same advantages of having a hub built into a system—exchanging mail in batches on a single call instead of with many calls to many recipients. It also has the added advantage of keeping addressing simple-—you just add a WAN address to the LAN addresses on messages. That advantage extends to any attachments and forms the E-mail may send. The hub should support them as well. One more advantage is insulating a LAN or WAN from outside contact: Only messages will pass through the hub service.

### Fax messaging

LAN E-mail programs are sometimes equipped to send and receive *facsimile,* or *fax* messages. When sending, the program converts a text file into the graphic image that is a fax—a set of black dots on a page that make up the various graphics and characters of that page. When receiving, the program captures the graphic image that is a fax page, and continues to hold it as a graphic, not attempting to separate it into graphics portions and text portions.

Only advanced optical character recognition (OCR) programs can translate a fax into text that you could edit with a word processor, and these are still quite rare on networks. Caere and Delrina offer such software, as does Calera, with its FaxGrabber program, which can turn incoming faxes into text or image files that can be edited or file converted. There are more than 20 file conversion formats in FaxGrabber, ranging from ASCII to word processors, graphics, desktop-publishing, databases, and spreadsheets.

Most LANs that want to handle fax messaging will need a fax gateway, which handles the translations and fax transmissions. If you want to fax this way, you'll also want E-mail with a fax viewing capability, so you can see received faxes on the computer screen. Otherwise, you'll need a graphics program to view faxes or you'll have to print them before knowing what was sent.

To send a fax, you may need a third-party fax gateway. Some of these are EZ-FAX from Calculus, GammaNet from GammaLink, LANfax from Alcom, and NET-FAX Manager from OAZ Communications. Some fax gateways let you view the text of your fax before sending it; others can view both its text and graphics. Some fax gateways let you change, forward, and send faxes as files, attaching them to messages on your network just as you would any other kind of attached file.

**Figure 1-1.**
**Having a "viewer"**
**lets you see**
**attachment files**
**that would**
**otherwise only**
**appear as names**
**on a list. For**
**example, a fax**
**viewer such as this**
**one in cc:Mail lets**
**you see a received**
**fax on screen,**
**rather than having**
**to wait for the**
**printed version.**

The integration of fax messaging into an E-mail system gives your faxing some of the advantages of standard E-mail messaging. On top of these advantages is the mailing list: You can address a fax to a single list name, and have that fax automatically sent to all the dozens, hundreds, or even thousands of recipients on the list. The list could mix E-mail and fax recipients, automatically sending the message via the method each recipient desired. The traditional alternative is to send the same fax over and over through a fax machine, dialing one fax number at a time.

 **Tip:** Handling fax messages through an E-mail network helps control faxing, giving a more accurate log of which faxes were sent, by whom, and to whom.

Receiving faxes is more complicated than sending them. The first trouble is in viewing the received fax. It is a graphics file, so you'll need special graphics viewing software. The second trouble is in knowing who the fax is for. If it is received by a fax modem that is connected to the network, the only apparent address is the network's fax phone number. The more precise address will theoretically be part of the fax image, perhaps on a "cover page" that begins the image. This, however, cannot be interpreted by the computer—someone must view the fax and read the address from it, then route it to the intended recipient. That's work for the administrator or some assistant, who will no doubt create an E-mail message to the effect of "here's a fax for you" and then attach the fax graphics file to it.

There are some schemes in the works to automatically route faxes. One is to connect a fax modem with multiple incoming phone lines, perhaps by the work of a PBX. The system would remember on which line each fax came in and use that as an indication of its recipient. Another scheme is to use OCR technology to read the phone number of the fax sender, compare that number to those stored in a database, then route the fax to whomever typically receives faxes from that number. The DID (Direct Inward Dialing) scheme is available in some places, a phone company extra-cost service that lets a fax gateway imitate a PBX switchboard.

Viewing faxes is rarely straightforward, even with a graphics program. Screen resolution is often not good enough for faxes, and many screens are not large enough to show an entire fax at "real" size at one time.

 **Tip:** Sending faxes from an E-mail system is easy; receiving faxes to an E-mail system is difficult.

### Bulletin boards

Bulletin boards are programs that accept incoming modem calls, present callers a list of topics, let them read messages within those topics and respond to the messages with messages of their own, and present them a list of files that can be downloaded (transferred to their computer). Bulletin boards are often devoted to specific subjects, ranging from particular programming languages to scuba diving. Some cover a range of topics. There are tens of thousands in the world, ranging from those running on home PCs to those that are part of commercial services such as CompuServe, GEnie, and Prodigy. Even the Internet has bulletin boards (see Chapter 8 for a description of Internet). Computer magazines often have lists of bulletin-board numbers to call.

Some bulletin boards are just for fun; others are used as a central message site for small businesses, and for sending reports and forms. Many software companies maintain their own bulletin boards for technical support of their programs, with topics on the various aspects of programs, free utilities, and program fixes that callers can download to their own PCs and then run.

Companies such as Mustang Software, Coker Electronics, and SofNet cater to this market. In PCs, the FidoNet bulletin-board system is famous. Many PCs in the world run the FidoNet software, and these systems call one another when phone rates are low, typically in the middle of the night, to exchange comments and E-mail they've gathered during the day.

Bulletin-board systems (BBSs) differ from E-mail in that the messages sent are posted for all to read and comment on. But many bulletin boards include E-mail as an additional feature, although often without many of the sophisticated features found in the latest LAN E-mail packages. Such E-mail on BBSs may let you leave messages on the one bulletin board for others calling in for topics, files, and messages, or they may store-and-forward the mail to other BBSs around the country or the world.

**Figure 1-2.**
**The main menu from a bulletin board will typically look like this example from Mustang Software's Wildcat! bulletin board program. It offers a chance to send private E-mail, as well as options to download files or join conferences.**

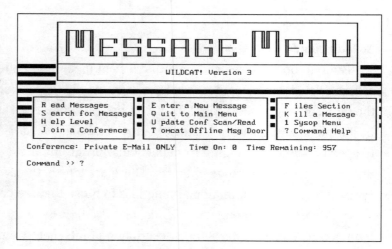

```
       MESSAGE Menu
         WILDCAT! Version 3

 R ead Messages      E nter a New Message    F iles Section
 S earch for Message Q uit to Main Menu      K ill a Message
 H elp Level         U pdate Conf Scan/Read  1 Sysop Menu
 J oin a Conference  T omcat Offline Msg Door ? Command Help

Conference: Private E-Mail ONLY    Time On: 0  Time Remaining: 957

Command >> ?
```

```
From     : RICK HEMING (V.P. Oper.)        Number    : 3109 of 3509
To       : GIOVANNI ZEZZA                  Date      : 05/09/92 2:20p
Subject  : Qmodem license                  Reference : 3101
Read     : NO                              Private   : YES
Conf     : 00Z - QMODEM Support & Info.

-> I've received my copy of qmodem from Gateway2000 with my computer. So

-> for me Your special rate offer ($35).

Sure.  As a registered Gateway customer (we hope you send in your
registration card to us), you can call and order the new Qmodem v5 for
only $35.  Call 1-800-999-9619.

Rick
MSI

Read mode : (3109 -)
Msg Read [3104-3509], [E]dit, [F]orward, [H]elp, [K]ill, [N]onstop,
[P]rint, [Q]uit, [R]eply, [S]ysop, [T]hread, [ENTER = prev]?
```

**Figure 1-3.**
**Since bulletin boards can be open 24 hours a day, they are often used by hardware and software companies to support their customers, as shown in this example of the Mustang Wildcat! BBS.**

Some E-mail programs offer a bulletin-board feature as well. This can be a great way to post messages for all E-mail users to read, rather than having to send a copy to each and every user.

A bulletin board can be a wonderful addition to a messaging system. It can let you offer 24-hour support to anyone with a PC and a modem—you store helpful information on the bulletin board—and it can insulate an internal network from outside callers. They can call the board and read or leave messages, but they don't get actual access to the network, so they can't change files on the server or run programs that could crash any part of the system.

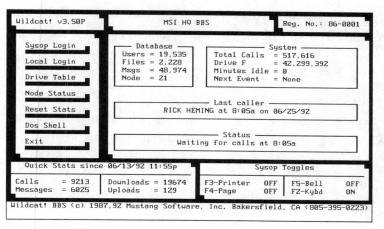

**Figure 1-4.**
**Managing a BBS is similar to managing a central E-mail database—and it helps in both cases to have administrative tools, such as this one for the sysop (system operator) of Mustang Software's Wildcat! BBS.**

### Conferencing software

Conferencing software lets two or more users contribute and read messages at once. Their messages appear in windows, lists, or some other form on each user's screen, indicating who made what comment. Often the messages are also stored in a file so they can be read later by one of those users or by anyone else with access rights to the file. (Sometimes conferencing is known as a "chat" feature.)

Conferencing is like an on-line meeting, with give and take occurring immediately. The difference is that computer conferencing keeps a complete record of the meeting. Conferencing can be used for meetings, suggestion boxes, open forums, bulletin boards, or other communications goals.

 **Tip:** The recorded transcript of a conference may seem like a boon over real meetings, but remember that it can be quite lengthy when compared to the summary notes kept in real meetings.

The immediate nature of conferencing makes it quite different from E-mail messages that will wait for the user. You could think of conferencing as on-line meetings and E-mail as on-line calls. The Efficiency section in Chapter 3 discusses how you can know when to use Conferencing and when to use E-mail.

Ideally, conferencing will be another option on the system that offers E-mail. The hardware and software will eventually permit the conferencees to hear and see each other, making true "telemeetings" rather than just instant text exchange for a group.

The Internet (mentioned in Chapter 7) has a conferencing element called WIDEBAND. The largest conferencing net is the USENET, which also carries global news. VAX-Notes from DEC is a commercial conferencing program.

**Tip:** Conferencing can cut travel costs for meetings among widespread participants.

## Types of E-mail Programs

E-mail has gone through periods based largely on the type of computer at its foundation. At first, there were mainframes and minicomputers, large central systems running a single E-mail program that would reach out to tens, hundreds, or thousands of terminals in a single organization. This "host-based" E-mail still exists, though it is not as popular as it once was. The large systems running similar software were then commercialized to be available either to organizations with many PCs that did not want to own and run their own mainframe or E-mail software, and later yet to anyone with a PC, modem, and money to join. This commercial-service E-mail is still going strong. The latest type is LAN-based E-mail, built around networked PCs.

Although there was once a straightforward question as to which type you might use, the answers have grown muddled as most organizations choose to use some combination of all three, linking them with gateways and bridges to make WAN mail. This section describes the three types of mail in a bit more detail. The last few chapters in this book mention some specific examples of each.

**Tip:** Don't believe that any organization must have only one messaging interface or E-mail system. Different people like different tools, not to mention the fierce devotion people will have to tools they're already using.

There are some companies with a half-dozen users on a private host-based or LAN-based system; others have thousands on commercial-service E-mail. A company's feeling about outsourcing and its analysis of the higher costs of not owning the system versus the lower demands of not maintaining it make the difference.

### Host-based E-mail

Host-based E-mail depends on a central mainframe or minicomputers running E-mail programs. Mainframes have fallen out of favor as the heart of computing because of the numerous advantages of personal computers. Moving

from the mainframe toward the PC is sometimes referred to as "downsizing."
Personal computers are:

- less expensive for computing power
- more easily maintained
- able to run software that is far less expensive
- improving faster than mainframes or minicomputers
- available as incremental options—you don't have to buy them all at once

As mainframes wither as a part of the computer market, so does mainframe-based E-mail. However, mainframes and minicomputers are still quite popular for holding central databases of information, and for acting as the central focus for all the various personal computers and networks in an organization. This too is reflected in E-mail, where mainframes and minicomputers are still employed as gateways, hubs, and other such functions. One growing use of mainframes and minicomputers for E-mail is public-service or commercial-service E-mail.

### Commercial-service E-mail

Commercial-service E-mail, sometimes known as public-service, lets you have E-mail without owning all the necessary hardware and software. Typically, all you need is a PC and a modem for each user. You don't even need to connect them all in a network. Instead, each PC on its own sends messages to the commercial-service computer, which then stores them in mailboxes or forwards them for their recipients.

If recipients are also "subscribers" to the same E-mail service, then all they need do to read their messages is to call up the commercial-service computer. If the recipient is not a subscriber to the same service, there may be gateways and links to some service the recipient does take.

For example, if both sender and recipient are subscribers to the MCI Mail E-mail service, they can exchange messages immediately—just by calling the MCI Mail computer with their PC/modem and sending or reading mail. However, say the sender is an MCI Mail subscriber and the recipient is connected only to a university workstation without MCI Mail privileges. That workstation is probably connected to the Internet, to which MCI Mail has a gateway. By putting the right address on the MCI Mail letter, the sender can assure that it will feed through the MCI Mail system to the Internet system, and finally to the recipient.

Nearly all of the commercial services offer gateways to a fax and telex as well. The gateways are typically transparent: You just enter a fax number instead of an address and the message goes to that fax recipient. (Few commercial services receive fax or telex messages.)

Finally, most offer "hard-copy" delivery, sort of a gateway to the US postal service. To use such a feature, you specify hard-copy delivery of your message and put a regular postal address, a street address, on the message. The commercial-service then routes the message to a printer. MCI Mail, for example, has several laser-printer operations distributed throughout the U.S. That printer puts the message on paper, stuffs it in an addressed envelope, and drops it in the mail. In some cases there's an option for urgent delivery, in which the printed message moves by courier or express service.

 **Tip:** Commercial-service E-mail does not have to be used alone. It can be part of an E-mail mix.

You can use commercial-service E-mail as part of a larger E-mail system, as the route for remote users to contact your in-house E-mail (through gateways from in-house to the service), the route for customers and suppliers to contact in-house E-mail, and as a gateway service for building a WAN from your organization's various LAN and independent sites. Using commercial-service E-mail in these ways has become easier in recent years as the leading services have added

X.400 support and even MHS hubs (so they can transport MHS messages without conversion troubles).

AT&T's EasyLink is the largest commercial-service net, followed by U.S. Sprint's SprintMail, Tymnet's Dialcom, Geisco's Quik-Comm, MCI Mail, and CompuServe. Ranking, however, is by the number of mailboxes, and not by how many of those boxes are within large companies and how many are held by individuals. The number of boxes is approximately:

AT&T EasyLink ......................200,000
Sprintmail ...............................175,000
AT&T Mail...............................120,000
MCI Mail ................................120,000
Dialcom...................................120,000
Quik-Comm ............................100,000

There could be as many as two million people with access to E-mail through information services such as CompuServe, Prodigy, and GEnie.

Most commercial-service E-mail systems offer an interface of typed commands and text menus. That's the interface most likely to be acceptable to the widest range of user computers: PCs, Macintoshs, terminals, workstations, and so on. However, it is sometimes hard to use unless the individual computer owner memorizes a list of basic command abbreviations. For many of the services you can now buy a PC or Macintosh "front-end" program that adds icons, macros (automated scripts), and other helpful touches that save the user from having to learn the menus and commands of the commercial-service. Front ends translate user commands into whatever complex language the service demands. Front end examples are Lotus Express and Desktop Express for MCI Mail, PCTelemail for Telemail, Upfront for Dialcom, or Transend PC for Geisco's Quik-Comm.

 **Tip:** If you use commercial-service E-mail, look for an easy-to-use front-end program.

When commercial service E-mail first appeared it was largely aimed at large organizations. Later some systems beckoned to individual users. Many commercial services now encourage both individuals and companies, pointing out to the companies how they can use commercial services as a link between private systems and telex, courier, postal, and other messaging forms. Most companies interested in E-mail these days have at least a gateway connection to commercial-service mail.

**Tip:** You can find some dial-up MHS hubs for exchanging mail with other MHS sites. Novell runs one of these, and there is one on the CompuServe information service.

### Local Area Networks (LAN)

There are more PCs in the world than all other computer types put together. These PCs can play three roles in E-mail: as intelligent terminals hooked up to host E-mail systems, as independent terminals for commercial-service E-mail, and linked in local area networks for LAN E-mail

E-mail is a key use of LANs; other uses of LANs are sharing printers and mainframe computer access. LANs are often cheaper than mainframe systems because costs are incremental, software is less expensive (because it can be amortized by the developer over so many more buyers), and because the systems are redundant.

There are two kinds of computers on a LAN: workstations (or clients) and servers. The client runs a user-agent program that handles the E-mail interface. The server contains a database for holding messages, the directory services, and the message transport services. The server software is often known as a post office. Some systems use network transport mechanisms such as NetBIOS or IPX/SPX to notify clients of received messages. Others use a small TSR utility to check shared directories for incoming messages.

LAN E-mail advantages include:

- superior user interface
- immediate notification of received mail
- minimal hardware costs (because costs are shared with other computer uses)
- communications cost less (especially for local communications)
- high-speed communications (at 256Kbps to 100Mbps compared to the 9600bps of modem communications)

LAN E-mail disadvantages are:

- it is only available when a LAN installed (may not be cost-effective to install LAN just for E-mail)
- it needs multiple post offices to support a large number of users (and so needs to handle some complex installation and administration tasks)
- it may spread directory administration over multiple servers, complicating directory maintenance compared to central host E-mail.

Most network operating systems (NOSs) have some ability to send messages from one node (workstation) to another. If your NOS has this ability, you don't have to buy an E-mail package. The messaging will just be there, as long as the network is installed (which we're assuming has been done). On UNIX systems, this built-in E-mail is more complete than on PC systems. However, although NOS messaging may be quite simple to use, it is also likely to be very limited in ability. For example, such E-mail can only send simple text messages, not long messages or graphics or other attached files. Even if it has some advanced features, these will probably be obscured by a command-line interface, meaning lots of memorization and typing skills will be necessary to use those features.

There are also a variety of simple peripheral sharing devices that include some basic E-mail and file-transfer functions. These aren't quite networks, and won't allow you to use the latest mail-enabled or groupware applications—explained in the following pages—but they are good enough for quick text messages. Some don't even require standard cabling. For example, Carrier Current Technologies, Datacom Technologies, Intra Systems, and O'Neill Communications make networking systems that offer E-mail and printer sharing through either the power system of a building or through a building infrared or radio-wave communications.

LAN E-mail is clearly the focus for most new E-mail developments. Although gateways will connect it to mainframe hubs and commercial-service fax and postal services, LANs are the place for today's E-mail.

## Components of E-mail (Architecture)

E-mail on any size computer has two basic components: a front end and a back end. The front end, as with all programs, is a user-interface. In the case of E-mail this is often called the user agent, or UA. The back end is the component users never see. This is sometimes referred to as the transport agent (TA) or message transport agent (MTA). More precisely, the back end can be divided into several parts: transport services, directory services, and a message store (also known sometimes as an E-mail engine). Additional services can be added to these, such as authentication services, as explained later.

The user interface, the display and commands offered to the user, should ideally be consistent across platforms. This is the part of E-mail that people see, and so it has the most immediate effects on their productivity and their feelings about E-mail. The UA is often the most-evaluated part of E-mail in reviews, because it is the place you find the options for various carbon copies, blind carbon copies, archiving messages, and so on.

However, the transport services and other back-end services can be more important than the UA. These determine how reliable and scalable the E-mail software is, as explained in more detail in Chapter 4.

The delivery mechanism of an MTA can be fairly simple—just write a message to a central file and then give the message recipient access to that file. Delivery can also be more complicated. To permit different delivery systems to talk to one another, they must share a common language, such as the MHS or X.400 protocols. Message management starts as just storing messages chronologically, but can grow to include smart message sorting and automatic response.

Although E-mail programs once contained all of these agents and services in a monolithic format, they are now being divided into modules. Within a few years this could mean the transport services will be in the operating system software, such as Microsoft's Windows, Novell's NetWare (as NLMs, NetWare Loadable Modules), IBM's OS/2, and Apple's Macintosh operating system, and user agents will be the source of competition of E-mail companies. While some E-mail developers feel OS companies are going to steal some of their sales, OS companies argue that this could lead to better software as companies specialize in either the user agent or in replaceable modules: directory services, authentication services (explained later), transport services, and so on for the operating system.

### Transport agents—proprietary, MHS, SMTP, SNADS, X.400

There are a variety of transport agents in the E-mail world, ranging from some that are proprietary to others that can be found in many programs as de facto or official standards.

cc:Mail and Banyan VINES mail, for instance, have their own transport agents. Microsoft has been working on a transport agent, code-named Spitfire, which will operate without Microsoft's LAN Manager network operating system, and will support X.400. However, because of Microsoft's large investment in LAN Manager, some outsiders are skeptical about its success on competing network operating systems such as Novell's NetWare and Banyan's VINES.

Message Handling Service (MHS) is a protocol translation program initially developed by Action Technologies, which still sells it for network operating systems other than NetWare. Novell now develops MHS for NetWare. (There is some incompatibility between Action Technologies' Version 1.2 of MHS and Novell's version 1.5.) Novell's dominance of the network operating system business has put its MHS on the map as a de facto standard.

MHS runs on its own network PC, known as the MHS server. MHS needs information about the local and remote E-mail users, applications, and connected services—such as a fax gateway and MCI Mail—that it will communicate with. You must set it up with that information.

E-mail programs that support MHS can communicate with each other. Some of the programs even have MHS built-in; others need a separate MHS gateway. OfficeMinder and Futurus TEAM have an MHS gateway as part of the basic package, but they don't need MHS to run. Da Vinci and Syzygy come with MHS, and in fact, need it installed before they can operate at all. Other programs offer MHS gateways as an option, with prices that vary from $500 to several thousand dollars. A few don't offer it at all, limiting their interconnection ability severely. Because of Novell's dominant position in networks, MHS is far more common as an intermediate protocol than the carefully crafted X.400 standard.

MHS can make information portable from one workstation to another on the LAN, even though those workstations are Windows, Mac, DOS, or OS/2 systems. It can also move messages between your LAN and a remote system through a gateway that can run on the same PC as the MHS program. You need to set-up the gateway with the modem connection, phone numbers, and other protocols for calling the distant system through the phone lines (unless you have it set-up to use some other data transmission channel, such as satellite communications). MHS will control that gateway program.

MHS is essentially an in-between step, an E-mail handler that now can be reached by many different E-mail programs. MHS is a de facto standard, useful because it is popular, popular because it is useful and because it has behind it the largest name in networks: Novell. MHS uses the SMF (Standard Message File Format) for its messages.

 **Tip:** Look for MHS compatibility or an MHS gateway for most any E-mail system. It is the de facto standard for translating E-mail messages from one system to another.

Critics have called MHS obsolete and believe it is ready to be replaced (probably by X.400) often, although that hasn't happened. MHS use keeps growing, probably in part because it is so simple (particularly when compared to X.400, of which it is a functional subset). MHS developers don't need to know much about the communication except the address of the message. The commercial-service E-mail network CompuServe now offers an MHS hub, letting anyone with an E-mail system that supports MHS exchange mail with other MHS supporters. Novell also offers such a hub.

 **Tip:** Know what sort of certification standards apply to your E-mail components.

SMTP (Simple Mail Transfer Protocol) is a commonly supported standard in workstations running the UNIX operating system, which makes it the standard for the Internet backbone of workstations across the country. SMTP offers two methods of addressing. In the first, called "Bang" or "UUCP" addressing, the sender specifies the entire path the message will take. That means the sender must know not only the recipient's name but also the names and hierarchy of all the intervening store-and-forwarding systems or "hops." The "bang" is the exclamation mark used to separate these elements of an address, as in "hub1!regionalhub2!recipient," which would send a message first to hub1, then to regionalhub2, and finally to the recipient. If there are a dozen hops, the address can grow quite unwieldy. More confusing yet, there can be a variety of different addresses for a single recipient, depending on how the message will travel.

The other addressing scheme in SMTP is called DNS (Domain Name System) or Internet addressing. This keeps a directory of unique node names so the sender only needs to specify the home machine and user name of the recipient. This system uses the @ symbol, this way: "recipient@machinename."

In more detail this works as "recipient@host.subdomain.domain" where the:

- Recipient is the user name of the person to receive the mail.
- Host is the unique name of the server with which that person works.
- Subdomain is the company, university, or other organization for which that person works.
- Domain is the larger unit to which the subdomain belongs.

The previous elements are separated from each other by periods.

The DNS addresses can be in either uppercase or lowercase. This scheme uses the UUCP protocol to move mail along. Some domain names refer to countries—the Internet is international—but often you'll see them sporting abbreviations that tell what sort of organization the domain is. Here are some examples:

```
com.......................commercial
edu .......................educational
gov.......................government
mil .......................military
net .......................networking organization
org.......................other organizations
```

DNS is growing in popularity in the U.S. and Europe, although it is not as common in Europe. Many around the world still use UUCP addressing, and some mix the two for maximum confusion.

IBM's interconnection strategy in the mid 1980s was DISOSS or Distributed Office Support System. This included its own E-mail. More recently, IBM has been pushing SNADS (Systems Network Architecture Distribution Services) and X.400. SMTP and SNADS have both been pronounced obsolete at times, but you can still find both all over the computing map. They aren't the latest things, but it is hard to root out specifications that are working and helping current systems communicate.

X.400 is a specification created by CCITT (International Telephone & Telegraph Consultative Committee), the standards-setting body of the International Telecommunications Union. E-mail systems that adhere to it should be able to interconnect and exchange messages. X.400 separates the E-mail software into UAs and MTAs. It works within the OSI reference model for networking, another international standard.

Each destination has only one X.400 address, a series of focusing locations, working down from the country to the username. It is stored in the header of the E-mail message.

The strengths of X.400 are that it meets all sorts of needs, it is thorough, and it is an agreed-upon international standard. Its thoroughness means it describes how a message should be structured and how a message should be handled. X.400 also specifies two types of systems: ADMs (Administrative Domains) and PRDMs (Private Domains). ADMs are public mail services operated by authorized telecommunications organizations. In many countries this will be the PT&T (Postal, Telephone, & Telegraph) authority, a governmental agency or a pseudo-governmental monopoly. ADMs keep a directory of all the PRDMs that are registered in their region. A PRDM is run by a private organization, such as a company or government agency. Finally, X.400 is designed to help integrate E-mail with voice mail, fax, and telex services.

 **Tip:** Remember that X.400 is not a product but a specification. You cannot get X.400 for your mail system, but you can look for products that are compatible with it.

There are different versions of X.400 (1984, 1988, and more recent), as well as slightly different implementations of each. In other words, X.400 compatibility means more capability to communicate, but doesn't guarantee a smooth conversation. Fine-tuning will still be necessary in many cases. The 1988 version added formats for nontext binary messages.

The weakness of X.400 is that it doesn't have the infrastructure of SMTP or MHS—it doesn't have directory systems or lots of software, yet. One of the reasons these are slow in coming is that X.400 is large and complex, requiring lots of setup and configuration. When added to the fact that many X.400 implementations are of the 1984 standard, and so can move only text information, it isn't surprising that X.400 hasn't become as popular and widespread as some predicted. Several minicomputer makers, including DEC (with its MAILbus 400) and HP (with OpenMail), offer X.400 products that can act as backbones (central message transport paths) for E-mail systems.

## Directory services—proprietary, StreetTalk, X.500

The E-mail directory contains the usernames for a system and a means to find those names. The directory is easily as important as the messaging features, but is often neglected by those new to E-mail. A directory could list everyone by their username or could organize those names into departments, divisions, and so on. You should look into what levels of organization a directory permits and how that will affect billing divisions, bulletin-board access, mailing lists, forms use, and system administration.

The real problem in directories arises from large networks. On a small network the directory can list every user. Even when there are several post offices on a single network, those post offices can exchange messages about directory changes, to keep themselves synchronized.

However, if the network, LAN or WAN, has too many users and too many post offices, that scheme breaks down. Too much of the network traffic will become directory-change messages. In practice, this can reach 90 percent of all network traffic even with only 200 nodes on the net (hard to believe but true), hurting performance severely.

The answer must be to leave separate and different directories in post offices that are remote from one another. Then you need some way to search a distant directory for a username. Without that, a message could be sent on a quest for the right post office with the recipient, and never find its destination.

**Tip:** If you're trying to guess someone's username on a commercial-service E-mail system, try their first initial and last name like this: "probinson." Then try their first and middle initials with the last name. Many services use this scheme for the default username.

If your E-mail can read the setup files for your network operating system, you won't have to do as much work creating or maintaining a post office directory. The prime example of this is an E-mail program that can read the Novell NetWare Bindery. This is a file the NetWare operating system uses to identify its users. The bindery files contain information about each user and the basic information about that users' directories and other such network setup information. If it cannot read the bindery, your installation person or administrator must create a directory from scratch.

Some E-mail programs offer utilities to automatically propagate all directory changes to the various servers, post offices, and other directories on the network. Some don't have any such tools. Banyan's VINES network operating system has a naming feature called StreetTalk that is being picked up by some competitors as a tested solution for directory propagation. Lotus's LAN E-mail program cc:Mail is evolving to have its own propagation utilities. Then there is Soft*Switch, the choice when no other tools are available—it has programs that integrate directories from various systems, bringing in all directory listings, converting and translating them into a common format, and then propagating them back out.

Eventually all E-mail owners may have access to a coordinated, global directory. This would list everyone who wanted to be listed, could quickly search for an address and return it to the searcher, and would keep up-to-date with address changes without crippling E-mail systems with a host of address-change messages.

It is difficult to discover an E-mail address you don't know. On your local E-mail system you can quiz the directory and hope that it has been maintained properly. Outside the local site, however, you can only hope the person you're writing to has a subscription to some commercial-service such as CompuServe. If not, you're pretty much stuck with trying to identify his probable connection to a large WAN such as the Internet, and then addressing him through that. Finally, you can just call and ask for a recipient's address, hoping there is some combination of systems and gateways that connects your E-mail to their system.

The same CCITT committee that came up with the X.400 transport-services standard is promoting a new X.500 directory-services standard. This specification would help all the E-mail developers and managers come closer to a global directory. X.500 provides naming facilities for networks and improves addressing in large, distributed systems. The X.500 naming facility isn't just for E-mail but also for system messages, such as file and printer commands. The directory services of X.500 will fit into X.400, and the directories will be reachable by MTAs, UAs, or other services. In fact, they will be accessible to network users, and some are expecting large-scale X.500 implementations to make money as on-line yellow pages.

X.500 is only in an experimental phase with many organizations, however. It is a complex and expensive protocol to implement. The 1988 specification doesn't even cover synchronization of directories in a distributed system. This is in the 1992 specification; so far there are no products supporting the standard that are currently available, nor will there be any for the next few years. X.500 looks sure to grow in importance and real use, but for now is more potential than reality.

Even so, there is some concern about the effects of such a comprehensive directory. For example, a company may want its strategic partners to have full access to an internal employee directory without giving that same access to a competitor. This may be handled by treating the directories like internal phone directories.

The NADF (North American Directory Forum), a consortium of 17 of the largest E-mail network providers, has even published a User Bill of Rights about entries and listings in the X.500 Public Directory. The rights include:

- the right not to be listed
- the right to have you or your agent informed when your entry is created
- the right to examine your entry
- the right to correct inaccurate infomation in your entry
- the right to remote access of information from your entry
- the right to be assured that your listing in the Public Directory will comply with U.S. or Canadian law regulating privacy or access to information
- the right to expect timely fulfillment of these rights

### User agent (interface)

The user agent is the part of E-mail the user sees. It is the display of commands, menus, options, windows, and other elements on-screen as well as the features the user can reach through those interface elements.

All E-mail systems offer the basic features for writing, sending, and reading messages. Most offer a fair selection of the intermediate features as well, for automating the process of sending a message to multiple recipients and for saving received mail in a more organized fashion. As for advanced features, some have them and some don't. Typically, the advanced features can completely automate the reception/response/storage process as well as encrypt messages to protect them from the wrong readers.

The selection of features in any given E-mail system will vary, and just hunting for the longest feature list is a mistake. You may not even care if some features are missing from the E-mail you choose. Look for the features you know you'll want and those you may soon use. Don't scrimp on administrative features though, the kind that help you manage the E-mail system (explained in Chapters 4 and 5). You'll probably end up wanting more of these features than you initially think, and they are easily overlooked in the chase after user features.

What features are basic is pretty clear; what are intermediate or advanced depends on with whom you're talking, and is mainly determined by how many programs have such features.

### Basic Features

- *create*—an editor of some sort to write messages
- *send*—a command to send a written message
- *notification*—audible or visual alert of received messages
- *inbox*—a window to see a list of messages
- *read*—a window to view and scroll through a message
- *save*—the option to save messages on disk

### Intermediate Features

- *outbox*—a list of confirmed "sent" messages
- *forward*—to easily send a message on to others
- *carbon copies (CC)*—to send a copy of a message to another
- *blind carbon copies (BCC)*—to send a copy of a message without leaving visible record of that in the message
- *attachments*—to attach one or many files to a message
- *encryption*—to encode stored and transmitted messages for privacy
- *filing*—to save messages in topical folders
- *message priorities*—to assign urgency levels to messages
- *mailing lists*—to create lists of recipients who can all be sent a copy of a message just by putting the list name as the destination

### Advanced Features

- *viewing attached files*—to see graphics, fax, spreadsheet, and other attached files without opening the appropriate application program
- *searching messages by criteria*—to dig through saved messages looking for those of particular date, subject, sender, or other criteria
- *rules-based message management*—to organize and handle received or stored messages by logical rules

### Structure of a message

Messages can only move because the E-mail programs know what the message is and what the address is. This requires structure. A typical message has two parts: the header and the body (also known as the envelope). The header is the addressing information, the body the readable text.

The header is divided into these parts: to, from, cc, subject, time, date, and message number. Some information must be entered by the sender when addressing a message; some the system enters automatically.

| Section | Function | Entered by |
|---------|----------|-----------|
| To: | the recipient name | sender |
| From: | the sender's name | system |
| cc: | additional recipient names; their names will appear on the message. | sender |
| bcc: | (only on some systems) more recipients; their names won't be on the message | sender |
| Subject: | optional, message description | sender |
| Time: | time the message was created | system |
| Date: | date the message was created | system |
| Message #: | some unique identifier | system |

## Attachments

Most E-mail packages let you "attach" files to a message. When you do this, those attachments, or "enclosures," are like clippings dropped into an envelope: they travel along with the message to the recipient. This is so much easier than the traditional file-transmission muddle of setting up telecomm programs, choosing protocols (such as Xmodem and Kermit), and monitoring the results.

Some systems only permit attaching text files; others permit attaching any kind of file, including graphics, spreadsheet, and even "binary" (meaning programs). In the future, you'll be able to attach voice and video files (see the Multimedia section later in this chapter).

In the early days of E-mail, you were lucky to attach even a single file to a message. More recently, some systems allow an unlimited number of file attachments per message, although quite a few still impose some limit, either on the number of files or on the total size (in KB or MB) that can move with each message. These are sometimes the administrator's prerogative, allowing the administrator to set limits that will permit most people free use of the E-mail system without hampering performance too much. (Moving lots of huge files with messages can fill up the network's capacity, slowing down the movement of urgent information.)

## Mailing lists

Mailing lists are an essential tool in E-mail. A mailing list is a list of recipient names. By using the name of the list alone, you can send a message to everyone on it.

Some mailing lists are for the "group." These are put into the directory by the administrator so they can be used by anyone. Some mailing lists are registered only for some users and are limited group lists. Some mailing lists are private, only for the person who created them and anyone else given them. Some mailing lists are public, created solely by the user.

**Figure 1-5.**
**The inbox of**
**received mail and**
**the directory list of**
**possible recipients**
**are found in**
**separate windows**
**of Microsoft Mail**
**for AppleTalk**
**Networks. The**
**directory can**
**include single**
**names for mailing**
**lists, which can**
**then be displayed**
**in yet another**
**window.**

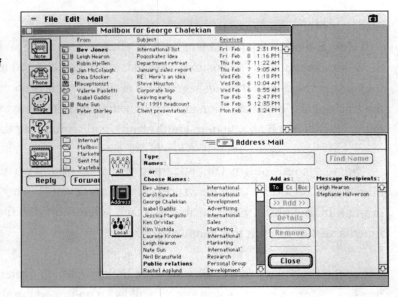

## Message management

As more people use E-mail, there is more E-mail to read. As the uses for E-mail multiply, there is again more E-mail to read. More E-mailers and more reasons to E-mail adds up to lots and lots of messages.

Some of those messages will be urgent and important, some urgent and unimportant—urgent to the sender but not to the recipient. Some will be just plain junk.

When the day comes that you sign on to E-mail and discover 100 or even 500 messages waiting, you'll know what today's E-mail gurus and fans know: E-mail is great only if properly managed. Message management will become a serious issue to you, too.

Most E-mail packages offer some simple tools for rudimentary message management. The E-mail program might let you flag a message as urgent—so it will be delivered immediately and show an asterisk or other symbol representing urgency on the recipient's screen. Your E-mail program may also let you sort received mail by date sent, by sender, or by other characteristics. That lets you tackle your inbox in an organized fashion.

More powerful software can do more than that. The premier example is Beyond's BeyondMail. This program, described in Chapter 5, offers a complete rule language for writing small message-management programs. (It sprang from work at MIT on an "Information lens," for filtering large quantities of mail.) The language lets you at least sort all incoming mail by any characteristic: date, subject, sender, and size, for example. The language can also set the computer to watch for messages with particular characteristics, then automatically forward, reply to, or archive them. BeyondMail can even cue the actions of other programs according to the information received in your E-mail inbox.

You could use BeyondMail's rules to automatically deal with a large percentage of your mail. You could tell it to reply to all nonurgent messages: "Thank you for your communication: I will give it consideration when I return to the office." Or, you could set aside an exception for incoming sales summary attachment files from headquarters: You could have these sent to a spreadsheet program (automatically started up) for analysis by your own equations, and then forwarded to someone else in the report chain. Finally, you could have any urgent messages dumped into an alternate's or a secretary's inbox for their immediate handling. Finansa's WinMail offers similar rule-based abilities to sort incoming mail.

Every E-mail system lets you store received messages. Sometimes this is referred to as "archiving." Many also keep copies of your sent messages in an "outbox." You can save those to disk as well. (If your E-mail doesn't have an outbox, and you want to keep copies, just make yourself a BCC recipient of every message.)

 **Tip:** To keep copies of a sent message, send yourself a BCC for that message.

The simplest way to store messages is often just to leave them in your inbox or outbox. Some systems get the same effect from a command that lets you save your messages on the server. Don't do it! Saving on the fileserver for a few messages is okay for a short while and only if absolutely neccessary. If everyone stores messages on the server, it will slow to a crawl and possibly quit working altogether.

 **Tip:** Remote E-mail packages often leave messages in the inbox even after they've been read. If you're working remotely, check into how your E-mail system treats your messages.

What you want is to store important messages locally, on your own hard disk. (Naturally, if you're at a diskless workstation, you're stuck storing to the server or printing your messages to save as hard copy.) Some E-mail systems only let you store to a single directory on your hard disk, often a directory the E-mail system set up for this purpose. That does retain the message, but will make it hard to find later among a welter of other stored messages.

Better E-mail systems let you create your own directories and subdirectories on disk, often calling them "folders." Some programs have their own folder system for this; others are less flexible because they make you use the DOS and NOS directories and subdirectories for filing. You save messages to the appropriate folder, organizing them by subject, date, sender, or other criteria.

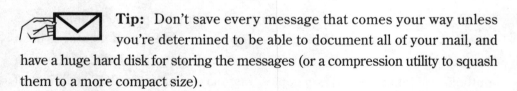 **Tip:** Don't save every message that comes your way unless you're determined to be able to document all of your mail, and have a huge hard disk for storing the messages (or a compression utility to squash them to a more compact size).

One rare feature in E-mail archiving is the ability to *thread* information about messages—that is, to have messages from an ongoing correspondence linked, even when stored. It's quite handy to be able to re-read a correspondence that lasted days, weeks, or months, without having to leaf through all the unrelated messages that came and went on the days in-between.

Filing messages in folders or directories is a nice first level of organizing your stored messages. Even better is searching through those messages by criteria: You request messages with a particular date, sender, subject, keyword, or other ingredient, and the E-mail program delivers them to you.

Few people delete all their read messages. Instead they archive them, storing them on disk for later reference. That soon leads to several other problems, however. First, the server disk can become crowded in a hurry when you and many others are storing old mail there. Chapter 4 covers solutions to this problem.

You could also have your own trouble with archived messages. Because E-mail turns everyone into an information producer, or at least a copier and forwarder, you'll have lots to store. Even with folder organization you'll be amazed at how quickly your received messages pile up. And because the messages are often free-format and not easily summarized into a standard database or spreadsheet, they won't be easy to search through later, not to mention the difficulty of storing and searching through any attached files.

A few programs to tame the huge archive problem have appeared. Folio's MailBag is a good example. The client program, described in more detail in Chapter 5, lets you tag any messages for archiving as you read them. The tagged messages are routed to a queue until the MailBag server program routes them to the appropriate "infobase." Messages appended to that infobase are fully indexed so they can be searched not just for their subjects or senders, but for any words, phrases, numbers, or combinations of those. The messages are also compressed to save disk space and can be retrieved quickly when pinpointed by their characteristics or contents. The infobase technology Folio uses is also at work in the HELP system for NetWare. It is a specialized database tailored to working with free-form information.

## Security

Security is essential to E-mail: People won't send messages if they fear those messages will be read by the wrong recipient. There are a number of ways E-mail systems provide security, from passwords to encryption and even dial-back schemes.

### Network security features

Most E-mail security starts with the network operating system. Networks typically have some security features built-in, such as administrator-controlled access rights to files and directories. However, each network operating system has different security features. Some offer many, others only a few.

Most NOSs have at least simple passwords for logging in to the network, to keep unauthorized people from using the net's resources at all. More sophisticated security requires specific passwords to reach particular directories or files. Typically, the network administrator can grant and restrict access rights for individuals, groups, or all.

### Passwords

Passwords are codes or words you keep secret, and that you must type in to enter E-mail, to use some command, or to read a message. Passwords are used in many places in E-mail. The lowest level might be to log-in or even enter the network itself. There could also be a separate password for receiving mail.

If you want an extra level of security for remote users, install a dial-back scheme, which asks the remote user to dial-in to the network. The network recognizes this dial-in, but does not grant access. Instead, it disconnects, then dials the stored phone number for that remote user, allowing access if the connection is made. This prevents unauthorized users from getting in just by knowing the authorized user's password; they would also need to call from the authorized user's number.

The next level of E-mail security might be user lockout. This limits the number of times users can enter their password at one sitting. User lockout prevents someone from experimenting with many possible passwords, hoping to find one that fits. Programs with lockout also log any lockout incidents, so the system administrator can later see when and where someone was denied entry to the program.

Incidentally, passwords are more often guessed than you might expect because people are often lackadaisical about them. One problem is that they are sometimes written down near the workstation or in a file called something like "password."

 **Tip:** Don't write your password down near your workstation and don't use a too-simple password, such as your name, your address, or an obvious word such as "password" or "sesame."

Some E-mail programs have password expiration, where the system administrator sets some time before passwords die into "nonvalid" status. This both encourages regular users to change their passwords from time to time and helps shut forgotten users or accounts out of the system. Otherwise, someone who has not had access to the system in a while may be able to slip back in when he is no longer authorized to do so. On large systems, the administrator may miss such a status change. Unfortunately, password expiration probably means more work for the administrator, handing out new passwords to all authorized users who forget to change their passwords.

Password echoing, or "shrouding," may seem an almost paranoid level of security. When echoing is on, you'll see your password appear on screen as you type it. That's how some systems operate. But when a system with password echoing has the echoing turned off, you won't see the password appear on screen as you type it. Instead you'll see only asterisks or some other such character appear—as many asterisks as there are characters in your typed password. This prevents someone from looking over your shoulder as you type. In a busy office, you may indeed want this feature.

Some E-mail programs let you grant "guest privileges" so that someone else can read your mail. Usually this is used when a regular E-mail user is away from the network, and wants an assistant or coworker to check on his mail for urgent messages. Sometimes a "guest privilege" feature prevents the guest from seeing the content of the message, permitting him only to view the header, which would tell the sender's name, the time, and the date.

### Encryption

True message security, where the contents are not available to others, depends on encryption, encoding or scrambling of the message text. Many E-mail programs let you encrypt your stored messages. This prevents both casual readers from perusing your mail and, in some cases, can even prevent the system administrator from reading your mail. Only someone with knowledge of your encryption password would be able to read an encrypted message. (However, because most E-mail systems let the administrator set and change passwords, there is often nothing to prevent the administrator from assigning your account a new password, and then use it to get at your encrypted mail.)

If someone asks about the cc:Mail "code break," explain that in early 1990 someone found a way to decode cc:Mail's encryption, allowing him to read stored cc:Mail messages. The cc:Mail company learned of this and changed the encryption so that each post office has a unique key, there are several levels of encryption, and the key to the encryption can be changed. This ended that threat to cc:Mail security.

Encrypting your stored messages may not be enough. What about protecting them while they are winging to the recipient? For this you need encryption of transmitted messages, something you won't always get from an E-mail system that offers encryption of stored messages. Such encryption foils even attempted cable-tapping on your network, in which someone other than the recipient monitors traffic and captures a copy of a message. A few systems even let senders encrypt their own name so only the recipient will know who is writing.

**Tip:** Remember that with encrypted message transmission, you'll need a secure way to give the encryption password to the recipient. A phone call is the general practice.

### Implementation and training

Security features are only useful if they are used. Sometimes you may want to disable or turn off security features so that your E-mail is easier to use—no need to remember passwords and worry about what to encrypt. In general, however, it is good to have security features available. Their availability and use will encourage people to use E-mail for all sorts of memos and information. Security features should be part of any E-mail user training, and enabling them ought to be high on an administrator's list of duties.

### Authentication—signatures

The latest advance in security is authentication: E-mail schemes for ensuring that the message you receive is actually from the sender you think it is from. This is vital when messages are secret, and for EDI and EFT (document and financial) exchanges. Authentication uses a mathematical password and code. If the stored code matches the one from the sender, then they represent one and the same person. This is, in essence, an electronic "signature." Authentication is rare in LAN E-mail now, with the technology just appearing. Apple Computer's new OCE standard (covered later) is built to accommodate new authentication services. See that description for more details on one way to implement authentication. Bellcore has even created a tamper-detection scheme that puts a digital time stamp on a document for data integrity. The recipient could check the document to see if it had been read or altered on the way.

## Electronic Forms

Business uses lots of forms, pages with specified places to enter particular information. They are printed, stored, pulled-out, filled-in, collected, summarized, copied, and filed.

Forms are:

- "while you were away" telephone messages
- check requests
- purchase orders
- copy-machine repair requests
- inventory updates
- engineering changes
- sales-call reports
- insurance estimates

and many, many other things.

Computers can handle forms too, in many ways. The simplest approach is to draw and label blank forms on the computer screen, store them on disk, and then print them when needed. This saves on keeping a forms inventory and lets you keep the forms up-to-date.

The next advance in computerizing forms is to have software that lets you call up the stored blank form, fill it in on the computer screen, and print the result. This makes for neatly printed forms because it is much easier to precisely position information in the appropriate blanks and boxes than it would be on a typewriter. It also lets your computer hang on to information in a database, instead of forcing some person to "key it in."

As soon as such form fill-in programs appeared, another advance was added: calculations and database lookups. Because the computer can handle arithmetic and look up addresses or other data in a stored database file, you can employ these abilities while filling in forms on-screen. For example, you might enter the amounts in a column of check values, and the computer would automatically calculate the sum and print that in the "total" box. Or you might type the name of some person in one blank and then see that person's address appear automatically in the "street," "city," and "state" blanks.

 **Tip:** You can think of E-mail forms as a natural way of presenting, viewing, and editing information in a database.

But wait—that's not all. What happens to most forms? They are circulated to appropriate people in an organization, summarized with other similar forms, and finally filed away.

Computers can take part in that circulation and summarization process. A program could automatically take all the information from a series of filled-in forms, perform calculations on the collected results if necessary, store the information as mentioned before, then produce yet another form representing the gathered information.

That's where E-mail comes in: "Circulating" and "collecting" are natural verbs for E-mail. With E-mail software that permits and encourages, you may create forms for everything from taking phone messages to counting sales results or even ordering pizzas. E-mail can then move these forms to the people who need them.

 **Tip:** Sending forms through E-mail is an efficient way to move information because in most cases only the data needs to be sent. The form itself, with its labels and graphics, can be held in a central file server.

The most advanced E-mail forms software can even manage the movement of the forms from one person to the next, so you don't have to. This is sometimes called "work-flow" software, and is described in more detail in the section labelled "Groupware."

### Forms in standard E-mail

Some of the most popular LAN E-mail programs have forms capabilities. These may be built-in or added as options. Some options come from the same company that makes the main E-mail program; some come from third-party companies.

**Figure 1-6.
Notework offers
a pop-up phone
message form, a
typical first use of
forms in E-mail.**

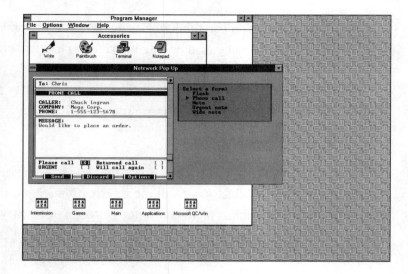

For example, of Macintosh-based LAN E-mail programs, Microsoft Mail, QuickMail, and WordPerfect Office have forms options. QuickMail has a utility called QuickMail Form. WordPerfect Office's Forms Maker can make forms for the Mail, Calendar, and Notebook utilities of that program.

Microsoft Mail offers Form Designer and Form Mover utilities that work from HyperCard. (HyperCard is a Macintosh program that's particularly easy to use and is bundled with all Macs. It combines a simple database structure for finding information with a simple language for automating Mac tasks and linking objects on "cards," displays on-screen that look very much like forms.) Hyper-Card utilities let an administrator create or modify forms for use with both Microsoft Mail and its related Schedule+ program. Note and Phone messages, and some others, are included as examples.

Forms can be quite complex, and can be installed on the server for use by everyone on the E-mail system. The administrator may choose whether a form can be sent and read or only used to read received messages. Some forms might be best for particular workgroups or departments, while others would benefit everyone on the system. Because the members of one workgroup or department are typically installed on one server, the administrator can install some forms on

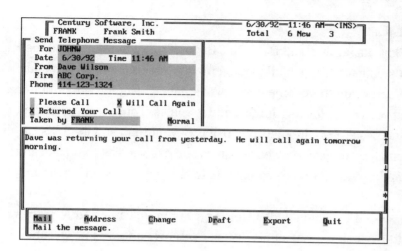

```
┌─ Century Software, Inc. ══════════╤══6/30/92══11:46 AM══<INS>─┐
║  FRANK      Frank Smith           │ Total    6 New    3         │
┌─Send Telephone Message ──────────────
  For  JOHNW
  Date  6/30/92   Time 11:46 AM
  From Dave Wilson
  Firm ABC Corp.
  Phone 414-123-1324
  ─────────────────────────────────────
   Please Call       X Will Call Again
  X Returned Your Call
  Taken by FRANK                   Normal
├─────────────────────────────────────────────────────────────
│Dave was returning your call from yesterday.  He will call again tomorrow │
│morning.                                                                  │
│                                                                          │
│                                                                          │
│                                                                          │
│                                                                          │
│                                                                          │*
├─────────────────────────────────────────────────────────────
│ Mail       Address      Change     Draft      Export      Quit │
│ Mail the message.                                              │
└─────────────────────────────────────────────────────────────┘
```

Figure 1-7. OfficeMinder also offers a phone message form, so received phone messages can be captured, forwarded to the appropriate recipient, and perhaps even answered, while the caller is still on the line.

only that server, and so make them available only to people in that group. Other forms could be installed across the network in many servers.

PC LAN E-mail programs have similar forms abilities. Notework, for example, comes with a "receptionist" form, the same phone-answering form found in many E-mail packages. This form can be sent instantly to anyone else on the E-mail system, so they can see a flashing message that a call has come in. The recipient of the message can choose to pick up the call or reply to the receptionist about how to handle it.

Shana Corporation's Informed Manager and Informed Designer programs try to fulfill the "paperless-office" goal. They do this largely through electronic forms. Informed Designer is, naturally, for creating forms. Informed Manager lets you obtain, fill-in, transmit, and process forms electronically, using Informed Manager or Microsoft Mail. The Manager's work includes calculations, error checking, and formatting. The routing lets different people fill-out the appropriate parts of a form.

Other forms software for LANs may come in mail enabling of applications or groupware. Minicomputer and mainframe computer E-mail systems also have forms features, as do some of the public-service E-mail networks.

### Forms-oriented E-mail

Some E-mail packages are built for forms. Beyond's BeyondMail, described previously in this chapter for its mail-management abilities, can use Beyond's Forms Designer program to become very form-smart. Designer works under Windows, letting you create forms with text and graphics. Those forms can then be distributed and processed automatically using BeyondMail and its rules language. The information for forms can be imported and exported as comma-delimited files, the standard way for microcomputers to share database information.

Other forms-based E-mail includes Delrina's Communicator and Jetform's Jetform E-mail (described in Chapter 5). Because JetForm offers some workflow abilities, it is also described in the next section.

Forms abilities are built into some groupware programs. This is a natural step because one of the major functions of groupware is to share information among users, and forms help structure that information.

JetForm E-mail, for instance, is built on forms. It is also built on "workflow management," automating some of the work of distributing forms and collecting information from them.

Jetform lets you send messages in any of three formats. Data-only format is for standard forms, the sort of forms that all recipients already have. (Only the entered data will be circulating.) Data-and-form format is for senders who aren't sure all recipients have a copy of the form required to read the message. Data-and-form-as-text message format is for sending a text message that can be read by any E-mail user, not just those with JetForm.

You'll be notified which format a received message is in, then when working on it, JetForm supports database lookups, calculated fields, and data validation. It prompts you for the fields you must fill in to send a form and lets you print a copy of the blank form or a copy with the data. The first release of Jetform worked with Da Vinci eMail for Windows, but versions for other E-mail packages were planned.

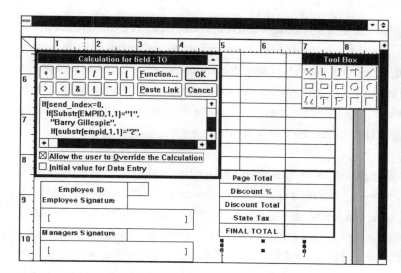

Figure 1-8.
When designing forms with a sophisticated program such as Jet-Form Designer, you can place graphics and text on the form, as well as add such features as calculated field rules. These can collect information from the form and create calculated results from it.

## Mail-enabling Programs

E-mail began as an independent program. You would leave your word processor or spreadsheet to attend to E-mail, send and receive a few messages, then move back to your other applications. Soon, most E-mail packages included a utility that could run alongside your other programs, either as a memory-resident TSR (Terminate and Stay Resident) on DOS PCs or as a desk accessory (DA) on Macintoshes. That let you switch back and forth between E-mail and other applications quickly and smoothly. These systems often had a notification utility that would pop up over your other applications whenever new mail had arrived in your mailbox.

But people asked for E-mail that wasn't so separate, E-mail that you could use directly from whatever other program you were using. If you were in a word processor, you might want to directly and immediately send your word-processor document to someone else on the network. Why use the intermediate stages of changing to E-mail, checking your inbox, reading your message, saving the message's attached word processor file to disk, returning to your word processor, or opening the received word-processor file? Instead, why not have the document appear directly in your word processor? Or in a spreadsheet, you might want to mark some section of the values in the current worksheet to zip off to someone else for checking.

To make this possible, a few E-mail software developers began adding applications programming interfaces (APIs) to their E-mail software. (API is a common term in computing that refers to a structure of documented connection points to a program that other programs can use to share information or commands with the first program.) Microsoft and CE Software, for example, did this to Microsoft Mail and QuickMail on the Macintosh.

That meant application programs could be written to look for and recognize Microsoft Mail or QuickMail on a computer, a process called "mail enabling." If mail-enabled applications found an E-mail program for which they knew the APIs, some basic E-mail commands would appear in the application's menus. Microsoft's Excel, for example, would look for Microsoft Mail, and if it found it, would include send and receive commands in its File menu. It could move worksheets, charts, or macros. You could even use Excel's macros to automate this process. Similarly, Microsoft's Word could move word processor documents, complete with their formatting and styling.

Aldus's PageMaker program could show E-mail commands. From version 4.0, PageMaker had direct access to Microsoft Mail (on the Macintosh). Three new commands would appear in PageMaker's File menu: Open Mail, Send Mail, and Place Mail. Open Mail displays a list of mail messages that contain Page-Maker files. You can then open these files directly, without first saving them to disk. Send Mail lets you send an open PageMaker publication to other Microsoft Mail users. If recipients have PageMaker, they can then open the document directly. If not, they can save it to disk to open later. Place Mail can import Word files and text from any PageMaker documents attached to mail messages.

Bravo Technologies shows an example of a lesser-known mail-enabled application. MacGraphX is a graphics, charting, and presentation tool for the Macintosh. When used with Microsoft Mail, it can distribute charts and graphs to anyone connected to the Mail system. A Send Mail command in the File menu can send graphics as MacGraphX, PICT, or Data Export files.

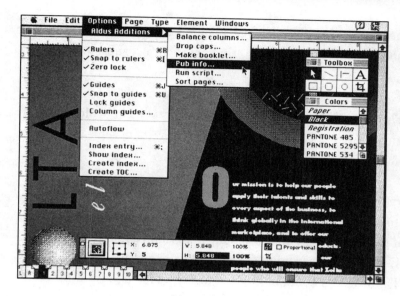

**Figure 1-9.**
**Aldus PageMaker can use Apple's Publish-and-Subscribe feature in the Macintosh System 7 software to send and receive messages with other programs.**

This hodge-podge approach to mail enabling scared most software producers, however. Application developers did not want to have to incorporate understanding of a dozen different APIs into their programs. E-mail developers wanted as many applications as possible to use their E-mail's services, such as message-transfer and directory services. (New services were appearing and becoming important also, such as authentication.) Also, operating-system software developers wanted to capture more of the value of E-mail and messaging by incorporating some of the basic services into their operating system software.

After all, mail enabling was already complicated when just two programs were involved: an application and an E-mail program. When projected into the future, mail enabling could clearly help computer users if it linked more programs. One application might send something to another, which would send it to yet another, grabbing information from yet another, and so on, to process and distribute information in complex processes and webs. At that point, mail enabling clearly needed some standardization.

In the end, the most important mail-enabled applications will be those your organization creates for itself, the programs that give your organization a strategic advantage in its pursuits.

 **Tip:**  Use APIs to create strategically important applications to improve service, cut design time, improve decisions, and so on.

### Application Programming Interface (API)

The answer to standard mail enabling was some sort of standard API that would be a set of programming rules which all programs could follow to link into a system's E-mail and messaging services. For example, by supporting a messaging API, a program could be written to recognize and produce standard signals for such events as alerting users of an incoming message, asking for the address of a package of data, and looking up a username in a system directory.

Without APIs, programmers would have to come up with their own messages and understand and incorporate all the messages of all other programs as well. That is too much work, so programs don't learn to understand each other.

However, developers didn't create a single "standard" API, although they knew that whoever controlled the standard would have great power in the software market. The standard bearer could dictate the direction of computing and could always ensure its own products got there first. Most people could see, too, how the back-end services of messaging were separating from the front-end interface portion of E-mail. (This is discussed earlier in this chapter.) The back end could easily contain the APIs.

With those forces and fears at work, it was natural for several possible standard APIs to emerge: MHS, OMI (which evolved into VIM), MAPI, and OCE, all of which have been defined in the following section. Each API creator thinks a single standard would be best and that his is the one. The practical result is that a messaging service should support as many of the big name standards as possible—they are not mutually exclusive.

Don't entirely believe the press about such standards. Announcements are not shipments, and shipments aren't necessarily complete. For example, in early '92 after lots of talk about MAPI and VIM, only MHS was actually available to developers. And as VIM was scheduled for release in early '92, actually only the transport services were to be included. Directory and other services were going to be held back for a second release.

### Message Handling Services (MHS)

I described MHS earlier in this chapter. Message Handling Services started as a part of Action Technologies' E-mail software, then became part of Novell's NetWare network operating system. Clearly in competition now with Microsoft's DOS and Windows operating systems for individual PCs, Novell is trying to become the provider of back-end messaging services on networks. MHS is therefore being improved and enhanced.

MHS has already been used as the foundation for mail enabling such applications as MultiMate, Framework, and 1-2-3 (using the @Mail add-in mentioned in Chapter 5). Software Publishing's Professional Write Plus for Windows offered built-in E-mail that depended on MHS E-mail. Even such workflow managers as BeyondMail and MailMan (both mentioned in Chapter 5) are built on MHS.

### Vendor Independent Messaging (VIM)

Lotus Development had two reasons to want a hand in making the standard API: Notes and cc:Mail. Both of these programs offered E-mail that could suffer in the market if Lotus wasn't involved in the API process, so Lotus convinced some major partners, including Apple, IBM, and Borland, to join it in announcing the Open Messaging Interface (OMI) API. Soon, Lotus applications such as the word processor Ami Professional were mail-enabled, using

OMI. Lotus also promised mail-ready versions of 1-2-3 and Freelance Plus, and of all its applications.

Later, Lotus and its partners improved OMI and extended its services. They renamed it Vendor Independent Messaging (VIM) interface. VIM is a set of function calls that programs can use, not a file-based format such as the MHS SMF specification. VIM helps programs communicate with each other and with users, across and between networks. A second-generation VIM may include routing and scheduling services.

### Mail Applications Programming Interface (MAPI)

The direct competitor to VIM is Microsoft's MAPI, an acronym for Messaging Application Programming Interface (sometimes called Mail Applications Programming Interface). Microsoft too wants to play a major role in the API debates, hoping to extend its dominance of the operating system market (with DOS and Windows) to network operating systems (with LAN Manager) and E-mail (Microsoft Mail). Along with MAPI will be the Open Database Connectivity (ODBC) specification, which will give API services for SQL databases. MAPI has APIs for both front-end user agents and back-end servers. It will be part of Windows NT. Microsoft is also working on directory services for Windows NT that will include global naming. Finally, part of this plan is to release scheduling, document management, and even workflow automation applications, all adhering to these specifications under Windows. This effort is called WOSA (Windows Open Services Architecture).

### Open Collaboration Environment (OCE)

Open Collaboration Environment (OCE) is Apple's contribution to the mail-enabling confusion, but it is not simply a competitor to VIM and MAPI. Instead, OCE also offers several services aimed at the future of shared information and tuned for the Apple Macintosh operating system. In fact, OCE will support VIM.

OCE provides E-mail and messaging through an open architecture. Developers will be able to plug alternative software services, such as directory handling, data encryption, and messaging, into the OCE structure. In turn, OCE services will be available to any third-party developer who wants to use them.

There have already been APIs for the Macintosh, from companies such as Microsoft (Microsoft Mail) and CE Software (QuickMail). These allow popular Macintosh programs such as Excel, Word, and PageMaker to directly send and receive mail from their own menus. For instance, this mail enabling would let you send a spreadsheet directly from one spreadsheet program to another. These APIs depend on Apple's Interapplications Communications (IAC) and AppleEvents Interapplication Messaging (AEIAM) of System 7 (the latest version of the Macintosh fundamental operating system software). AEIAM lets programs exchange data, messages, and common commands with other programs on the same computer, as long as those other programs support AppleEvents. On a network, AEIAM lets programs on different Macintoshes share information and commands.

AEIAM, however, does not allow use of a directory or a store-and-forward architecture, which are crucial parts of most E-mail systems. Information sharing must be immediate and manually routed. The proprietary APIs from Microsoft and CE had proprietary ways around this, but that meant differences in quality, reliability, and speed.

OCE will standardize such work and offer common directory and store-and-forward services, as well as encryption and authentication. OCE will be the middle manager for all mail handling, for all programs that pass messages through APIs such as VIM or MAPI. In fact, VIM support will be part of it, according to Apple plans in mid 1992. As with other API and structure standards, OCE will be invisible to most users.

OCE's Messenger Service specification will allow System 7, the Macintosh operating system, to have a module for store-and-forward messaging, for messages to users and to programs. Its directory services will provide a common means for naming and identifying users, no matter what mail system they're using. OCE's directory won't just keep the list of usernames and network addresses that today's typical E-mail server keeps, but will allow a directory of any arbitrary collection of data, phone numbers, and so on. Any application programmed for the API will be able to get at such information.

Authentication services in OCE will provide a dual-key encryption system for digital signatures to messages. All users will have two unique numbers or keys from a numerical sequence: the private key, to which no one else will have access, and a public key, which they will give to people they'll send authenticated messages. OCE will generate a unique fingerprint for any authenticated document, based on the contents of that document. This fingerprint will be encrypted with the private key and attached to the message. The recipient then uses OCE to generate a second fingerprint from the document, and then uses the sender's public key to decrypt the original fingerprint. When compared, the fingerprints should match, proving the document came from the person with the private key. If they don't match, the purported sender isn't the real person. This authentication can also extend to program-to-program communications.

IBM has announced that it will add AppleTalk's network protocols to the OS/2 protocol stack. That will let the Macintosh share files through an OS/2 server. IBM is also developing a multiprotocol bridge/router that will include AppleTalk. With these developments, OCE may not remain solely a Mac artifact.

### XAPIA association

XAPIA is not an API but an association. The X.400 API Association (XAPIA) is dedicated to developing APIs for the X.400 standard. It works with transport services only and does not specify directory services or message-store services.

## EDI and EFT Standards

Large corporations are looking at steps beyond simply moving form information on E-mail. They are looking to Electronic Data Interchange (EDI) and Electronic Funds Transfer (EFT) to decrease paperwork and paper shuffling; time spent collecting information, processing orders, routing, and approving reports; and miscommunications with suppliers and customers.

EDI seems tailor-made for a business era hot for just-in-time production, tight links between suppliers and users, and cooperative design and marketing. With EDI a company can electronically exchange data with suppliers, customers, or any other entity. The information does not have to be printed on paper, mailed, opened, read, and filed. In some cases, a person may not be able to view the information until some computer program has manipulated and summarized it. With EFT, users can immediately have payments sent from debtor to creditor without the time and expense of paper purchase orders, bills, receipts, and the like.

Naturally, such huge changes in traditional business processes require similarly enormous changes in staff attitudes and behavior. Implementing EDI and EFT is not as simple as hooking up E-mail systems and attaching a payment or inventory table file to your next message. It demands careful analysis of information flow, attention to security, cooperation with recipients, and training of staff.

### EDI and EFT examples

EDI and EFT have been popular topics at electronic-messaging conferences and are particularly popular in Europe. However, significant examples are blossoming in the U.S.

Pizza Hut began EDI when the company consolidated regional accounting offices in 1988. Vendors were sending bills that Pizza Hut staff would open, code (put three pieces of information on each), and then type into their McCormack & Dodge accounting software. To reduce the number of steps in this process, Pizza Hut started pushing its largest suppliers toward EDI. Now 75,000 of Pizza

Hut's 175,000 monthly invoices flow via EDI and FileNet WorkFlo software, and that's with only a few of the 90,000 firms suppliers set up for EDI. The WorkFlo software automates the movement of graphics and forms among staff and applications on the network. (See the discussions of groupware and workflow software later in this chapter.) To continue expanding EDI, Pizza Hut may install document imaging systems: hardware and software that could scan paper forms into graphic files on the computer and then move those electronic forms instead of paper. The firm reportedly expects a 25 percent productivity improvement, a three-year payback for the imaging systems, and a 40 percent reduction in the volume of paper shuffled and filed. Pizza Hut is looking forward to using EFT for making electronic payments to some of these EDI partners.

Nordstrom, a major retailer, created a Vendor Information Partnership Express (VIP) program in conjunction with MCI Mail (see Chapter 8 for details on the MCI Mail public messaging service). This electronic messaging service involves E-mail and EDI. Around 27,000 vendors and thousands of Nordstrom employees are linked by their internal computer networks and MCI Mail as a bridge. There are more than 3000 active mailboxes on the system, and 3.5 million messages move on it each year. Using a custom version of Lotus Express—a PC program for accessing MCI Mail—vendors can reach into Nordstrom's mainframe computer to check the status of purchase orders, shipping dates, and invoice payments. They fill out a preformatted inquiry form, send it via MCI Mail to the Nordstrom gateway, and route it over Nordstrom's internal E-mail to a database. A CICS transaction (a mainframe database) locates the needed data, sends it back to the gateway, reformats it, and moves it over MCI Mail to the supplier again, all in about 10 minutes. Previously, performing telephone inquiries took hours or even days. Nordstrom even offers discounted long-distance calling rates for vendors that use the system.

This strategic arrangement helps assure on-time delivery of merchandise. Nordstrom's sets a window of delivery for suppliers and requires them to take back orders if they are late. The company estimates the system has decreased late orders from 60 to 80 percent, saving return freight costs as well.

The Harper Group is an international freight forwarder that uses EDI to move Honda cars from Japan to the U.S. Honda sends an EDI invoice to American Honda in Los Angeles. The details of the invoice—quantity, part numbers, tariff numbers, and values—move on to Harper's computers in San Francisco. Those systems add more information, such as textile visas and antidumping information, and pass the augmented record to U.S. Customs. Then, Customs uses EFT from its ACS (Automated Commercial System) to move Honda's duty payment directly from Harper's computers, which then bill Honda. These transactions move through public networks, such as Tymnet and Sprintnet. The results are that customs documentation that takes weeks to process with lots of labor is handled in minutes with a minimum of labor by EDI.

### EDI tools and standards

Several standards have appeared for EDI software, including the American National Standards Institute's (ANSI) X.12 and the European EDIFACT (EDI for Administration, Commerce, and Transport). The standards set guidelines for the exchange and translation of information in EDI processes. Another standard is the X.435 from CCITT.

A number of companies offer software for EDI including Western Union, DEC, IBM, GE Information Services, and the API Group. DEC is focusing on EDI systems, EDI document translation software, and integration of its EDI products into popular business applications. It will support EDIFACT and X.12. Texas Instruments (TI), a major EDI user, is now selling EDI software commercially. TI developed most of the software for internal use during the 1980s to support its EDI program with more than 1700 partners in 20 countries processing 11,000 EDI documents each month. Products from TI's Information Technology Group include a communications gateway, translation software, an EDI management system, a mapping program, a test facility, and a version of TI's electronic procurement system. The software runs on an IBM MVS mainframe.

The translator takes incoming messages and converts them into the proper EDI format for transmission to the particular trading partner. The gateway uses artificial intelligence (AI) to spot errors in any outgoing transmission and will automatically correct the error and resend the message. Unlike some software that will abort the entire transmission, TI's just re-sends the faulty part. The mapping software works under Windows, letting EDI personnel record how EDI data is to be mapped into a particular application program. It also lets the two partners in an EDI exchange dictate how they will use a specific EDI document. The management system runs on the mainframe and records information on trading partners, such as what EDI document version they use, what communications protocols they prefer, which network can be used to reach them, and how they can be billed. The test facility lets partners test transmissions.

TI's software supports X.12 and EDIFACT. Such software is expensive: The gateway alone costs $100,000. The translation, test, and management programs together cost another $100,000. However, those prices must be measured against the productivity and quality improvements possible with EDI's speed and simplification of the paper mountains used today.

More information on EDI and EFT standards can be obtained from the Data Interchange Standards Association (703-548-7005) or the Electonic Data Interchange Association (703-838-8042).

## Groupware

Electronic mail communicates textual, graphic, or even voice ideas, but linked computers can do even more. With the right software—called "groupware"— they can tie workers together in other ways. (Most such programs depend on a local area network to link individual computer users, but some can also act at a distance through remote links, just as E-mail can.)

For example, a groupware program might schedule the activities for an entire department or organization. Such a scheduler would keep a central calendar, listing everyone's availabilities and offer each individual the ability to inspect and modify that calendar. This allows individuals to pinpoint when others are free and to set up meetings with several colleagues at a time.

Another groupware example could be an editing program that allows several people to critique a document concurrently. The program could collect comments for final action by a central coordinator. A related type of program could allow all the participants at a meeting to contribute to and view the meeting notes as they are created. Each participant could have a terminal of some sort in front of him to which he could type or draw comments and his understandings. This eliminates the need for someone to keep minutes and publish them after the meeting, and would hopefully bring the participants' understanding closer to what appears in the minutes.

When groupware automates the flow of information, such as of imaging files, it is sometimes called "workflow automation" software. AT&T and NCR have developed the Rhapsody workflow program in this vein. Lotus Notes can perform similar work, although it is set up more to share information than to move it along a certain sequence of users.

**Figure 1-10. Notes can store documents with both text and graphics in its database.**

Figure 1-11. The ability of Notes to display a database in different "views" permits each user to customize his or her approach to information, while keeping that information the same for all.

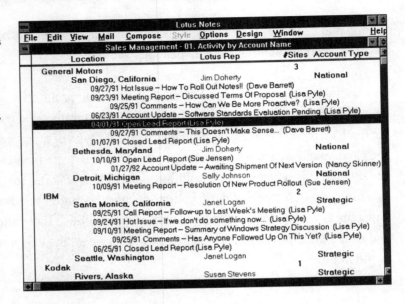

Even video teleconferencing can be considered a form of groupware when it uses the computer as a controller or the computer screen as the television. Teleconferencing lets people in different locations see and talk to each other, saving travel costs and time. (See the following teleconferencing discussion in the Multimedia section next.)

Certainly the best-known groupware program is Lotus Notes, which is essentially a central database for workers on a network. Everyone on the network can contribute to the database, though with varying access rights, and can see what others do to it. The database does not just hold numbers and codes as some simple databases do, but full documents. Notes also has its own E-mail, although this is converging with Lotus cc:Mail. Notes is a powerful group tool for brainstorming, passing documents through a group, handling forms, collecting comments, incorporating changes to those documents, and so on. It is not cheap. Unless you buy it from a special VAR, you need to buy a license from Lotus for a minimum of 200 users, at nearly $63,000. You'll also need an OS/2 server to run it.

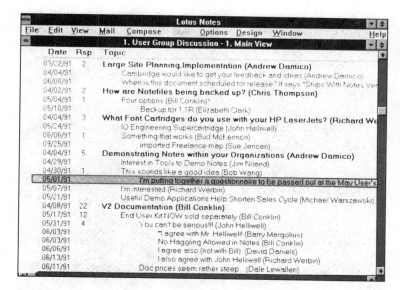

**Figure 1-12.**
**Lotus Notes can be used as a conferencing program, for capturing and organizing the comments of a workgroup.**

## Portable, Wireless E-mail

If you want to access your E-mail while traveling, you have a variety of choices. You can use a modem to dial-in to the network and connect via modem software or a real E-mail remote package. You can use one of the new AT&T Public Phone 2000s with color monitor and keyboard; you can jump further into the future by picking up some wireless E-mail technology.

Cellular phones have been phenomenally popular because they provide portable phone service. Many people expect portable E-mail service to become quite popular too. There are a number of schemes to implement this portability. Some only broadcast E-mail to wireless, remote computers. These typically use pager technology, which depends on broadcast radio to send the messages to computers. Others also provide a way for the remote computer to return mail to the main network. Eventually, the adoption of personal telephone numbers (PTNs) would allow messages to find the recipient wherever that person is—at the main office, home phone, or on the road.

Wireless E-mail can be useful for those who have traditionally used pagers; where a pager can at best provide a notice to call a particular phone number for

**Figure 1-13. HP's 95LX palm-top computer can be connected to a Mobidem wireless modem to receive E-mail anywhere, without telephone line connections.**

a message, E-mail can provide the entire message. E-mail can store the message and you can check it at any time. For example, HP is planning a wide range of communications services for its "palmtop" PC, the 95LX.

Anterior RadioMail connects public and private E-mail services, including numeric and alphanumeric pagers. It even works as two-way communication with portable or pocket PCs that have radio modems. Oracle Corporation users can depend on RadioMail to forward messages to their pagers, which can store the first several hundred characters of the 20 most recent messages. These messages can come from AT&TMail, CompuServe, Internet, UUCP/USENET, and from nationwide packet data-radio networks such as Ardis and RAM Mobile Data. Oracle has its own PostCard program to link its inside E-mail to Macintosh computers.

Motorola is building a radio-based E-mail system that will link hand-held computers to the EMBARC network (Electronic Mail Broadcast to a Roaming Computer). The hand-held system would need only the DataStream receiving unit to receive up to 56 messages via a 1200bps radio signal sent by one of 70 transmitters on satellites. Motorola and other developers are adding interfaces to existing E-mail software to support the DataStream unit. ExMachina is making a Macintosh program called Notify! that will let portable Macs use this receiver technology. BT North America has announced wireless access of the Tymnet data network through Motorola's Ardis wireless network. (Ardis is a joint venture with IBM.)

AT&T has agreed with SkyTel to create a new E-mail–through-pager technology service for users of the AT&T Safari notebook computer. This would equip the Safari with a wireless mailbox, a pocket-sized pager adapter, and special Windows software. Subscribers to the service using the pager could capture up to 20 messages from the EasyLink commercial-service E-mail system and read them on screen. (SkyTel's research shows that 60 percent of its current pager owners carry laptop computers.) The next stage in this plan would allow Safari users to send messages via a cellular phone link.

## Multimedia Systems

Why should E-mail only transmit text? The most sophisticated systems already permit the use of fancy fonts and even graphics in messages. Most systems allow you to attach graphics files to messages. A few even let you attach sound files.

In the future, with the cabling to handle larger messages and files, and the software to understand the process, E-mail may even carry other media such as video. The first step would probably be to send video clips as attached files. With adequate compression—using software to squeeze the files even smaller by eliminating redundant information—these could be sent along networks or even over very fast modems. The recipient could then decompress a video—perhaps automatically through software—and watch it.

## Multimedia products

Lotus has already announced that it will add sound, animation, video, and other multimedia elements to Notes and cc:Mail, its two leading E-mail programs for PCs. Notes has demonstrated moving video E-mail using RTV (Real-time Video) capture.

Price Waterhouse, Deloite Touche, and Chase Manhattan use E-mail that includes voice synthesis. Innosoft International makes multimedia E-mail for VMS-based minis and mainframes. BBN Software Products' Slate is a UNIX multimedia document management system that can be used for real-time blackboard conferencing and E-mail. Students at RPI (Rensselaer Polytechnic Institute of Troy, N.Y.) run Slate on Sun and IBM workstations, attaching computer programs to their sent assignments and receiving comments that include voice.

Interactive, Inc. is developing M-Mail, an E-mail package that supports text, voice, pictures, video, and audio. This Windows-based program lets users incorporate sound and video images in E-mail messages. It works with most sound boards and standard Windows applications to create, send, and receive messages with visual, spoken, and written components. The current version works only on NetBIOS-compatible LANs with a single fileserver.

## Multimedia E-mail standards

There are no accepted standards yet for multimedia E-mail, but the subject is actively discussed at E-mail conferences. Standards will be necessary to let different E-mail systems exchange various media. X.400 specifies how to add binary and data files to electronic messages. The Internet Engineering Task Force proposed Multipurpose Internet Mail Extensions (MIME), to handle encoding and decoding of nontext messages. It defines how to extract PostScript, voice, binary, video, and other media from an E-mail message.

## Voice Capability

Pick up the phone, dial (or press) a number, connect to someone else, and leave a message on a machine: That's electronic messaging too, isn't it? Sure, but so far it remains separate from E-mail. Still, Voice communications, and more specifically, voice mail, is another messaging method you should consider when building your E-mail plans.

Voice mail started in the late 1950s when the first tape recorders were attached to telephones. These primitive answering machines evolved into the advanced models of today, which let you retrieve your messages remotely (with another phone call). The most sophisticated machines don't even use tapes to record messages anymore. They use chips, just as computers do, and so make it easier for you to delete messages you don't want and hang on to the ones you do.

Even more advanced is the true voice-mail system, which is entirely dependent on a computer. Voice mail can accept, store, play, forward, and otherwise manipulate voice messages pretty much the way E-mail can manipulate text messages. AT&T had the first such system, but was not legally allowed to sell it freely. Smaller companies broke that ice in the mid 1970s to early 1980s. Then larger companies such as IBM, Rolm, and Wang got involved. (Rolm was a famous maker of telephone PBX exchange switches by then.) In the past few years laws changed and the split parts of AT&T, such as some of the local Bell operating companies, have begun offering voice mail.

Because of those roots, most voice mail entered companies through telecommunications channels, not through computer channels. Most voice mail was integrated with a company's phone PBX. And most voice mail installations meant significant capital expenditures, unlike E-mail, which typically involved smaller, incremental expenditures.

Voice mail works a lot like E-mail. Each user has a "box" that catches messages whenever he or she is away or on another phone call. An "outgoing" message announces that voice mail is ready and offers to take a message for the caller, to connect the caller to some other department or individual, or to connect the caller to the receptionist. Some systems have a directory where you can find an individual's extension by typing the letters of his name on the phone's keypad. Additional features include the possibility of notifying a pager whenever voice mail is received.

When a message is captured, it is often given a time and date stamp. Then, a voice-mail user can call at any time to retrieve the messages, hearing them in sequence and deleting or saving them as desired. (There will be some limit on how many messages can be saved for how long.) Some systems also offer an option to forward messages, and a few even have address lists (you leave a message, then send it to everyone on the list). Some systems let you edit messages, inserting or deleting parts. Other systems let you have passcodes for security.

Typically, voice mail is brought in to lower the cost of answering phones. It also permits lengthier, more-meaningful messages. Instead of having enough receptionist or secretary power to field every incoming call, voice mail is installed to spread those calls out for the actual recipient to take, either directly or when there is an opportunity. Also, voice-mail messages permit the caller to leave such details as address, reason for calling, and so on, more reliably than a secretary may have time or inclination to detail on a message pad.

Voice mail tends to show up first in places where "phone tag" is most important, such as in sales positions. System costs have dropped considerably in the past few years as volume service helps with economies and as improved electronics cuts the cost of digitizing the voice signal into digital information that computers can store. The dropping costs of computer storage and improvements in storage compression have helped too. After all, voice mail can demand lots of disk space. Caswell notes that 1.5 minutes of spoken information takes up 300K when stored as voice sound, but only 1.6K when stored as ASCII text.

As with E-mail, voice mail faces misunderstanding, dislike, and resentment. Many people don't like leaving messages on answering machines or voice-mail systems, feeling them cold, inhuman, even insulting. ("I'm not important enough to merit a human reception?") Such attitudes typically diminish with experience and as voice mail becomes more common throughout society.

Voice mail has some serious limits. For example, voice can get a lot across face-to-face, and voice isn't a good medium for store-and-forward systems (the style of E-mail). You can't scan a saved voice-mail message and search for it by key words the way you can text E-mail. You can cut out a piece and forward it with another message, as you could easily with E-mail. Only short messages are typically effective with voice mail. Even then, they can't yet integrate with most computer systems because the technology of voice recognition, to turn voice messages into text files, just isn't practical yet. There are a few examples of it, but they are expensive, slow, and often require training to a particular person's voice.

For those reasons, voice mail will almost certainly remain a separate, parallel message system for some years. It will run beside E-mail but won't integrate with it.

### PC voice mail

There are boards you can plug into a PC to give it voice mail capabilities. Such boards don't just make a PC an answering machine but let it offer the caller options. You may leave different messages for different callers, which they reach through passcodes. Using one of these boards and the associated software can take your PC out of service for other uses, but simple PCs are inexpensive enough that you may just buy a separate PC for voice mail.

### Voices on LANs

A few LAN E-mail programs can carry voice messages across the LAN and let you send and receive voice mail. Old-fashioned voice mail did not use LANs, but instead appeared in systems that interface with PBXs (Phone Exchanges) or as optional items in telephone systems as described before. LAN voice mail is easier at times than typing electronic messages but is limited when compared to the most advanced phone voice mail. It usually involves using a special phone handset attached to a computer workstation, although sometimes it only requires a microphone. You can send solitary voice messages or attach voice messages as annotations to files. Voice can have quite a different effect from written messages, even when the words are the same. See the Etiquette and Ethics sections in Chapter 3 for more on this.

Both Artisoft's LANtastic network operating system, with its built-in E-mail, and Futurus's E-mail system for Novell and NetBIOS-compatible networks, can handle voice messages. Both use the Artisoft Sounding Board voice adapter card, which plugs into a PC. This changes voice messages into digital information when recording and digital information into voice when playing it back. The Sounding Board has its own telephone handset you pick up and speak into to create voice messages or annotate files with voice.

LANtastic can both send and store voice messages and even carry voice in "real time" as a chat feature. This lets you make a call across the network just as if you were making a phone call. This ability is a background process, so you can still do other things with the PC while using LANtastic voice communication. There is a programmer interface for adding other sound to programs.

**Figure 1-14.
Artisoft's LANtastic
Network offers
voice-messaging
along with its
E-mail.**

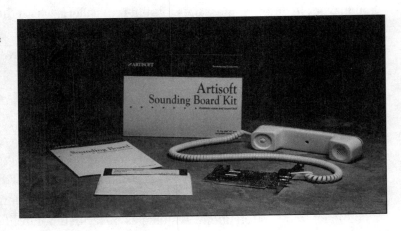

Futurus uses the Sounding Board as part of regular E-mail, for adding voice to E-mail messages. You create a message with a recipient and subject, as you would for a text message, then record your message through the board, and send it as you would any other message. Playing back a voice message is just as easy: It comes in, and you press the appropriate keys to play the message through the headphones.

The NeXT workstation can attach voice notes to files or send voice messages alone through the system's E-mail. NeXT is based on UNIX but has added special sound hardware and software that is not found on typical UNIX workstations.

## Video Conferencing

Real-time video conferencing is related to E-mail—it also moves communications across LAN and WAN lines. Unlike E-mail, though, it is not a store-and-forward scheme. Instead, it shows both or many communicators an immediate video and audio signal from the other communicator. It isn't cheap, requiring a fast network, a powerful PC with graphics hardware additions, a video camera at each end of the line, and the right software. That can add up to many thousands of dollars for each computer involved.

The savings, however, can be significant too. The time and expense of travel could be cut for many events (not for all certainly: Hands-on, personal attention will always be necessary in human relations, both business and personal). For example, the U.S. Congress is using video teleconferencing in hearings on the future of DoE (Department of Energy) labs in New Mexico and California. The idea is to save money on quick hearings and avoid the travel expenses of moving witnesses.

AT&T and Compression Labs have developed the Cameo Personal Video System Model 2001, a $2095 version of the technology in AT&T's VideoPhone that works with the Apple Macintosh. The package includes Macintosh software, a Video Processor module (to compress the video information) that plugs into the

Macintosh serial port, and an auto-focusing Camera Module from Sony. It runs on the higher-powered Macintosh models such as the IIci, IIfx, or Quadra and requires a video digitizer card, QuickTime software (Apple's digital video software) in the Mac, and an ISDN card. Cameo uses one channel of the ISDN for video, the other for voice. Even then it shows only 15 frames/second of video, one half the speed of normal television. That means the images will be more jerky and crude than normal television would display, and even slower when files are transferred over the system or some other program is sapping part of the its power.

**Tip:** The quoted price of a video conferencing system may be unrealistically low because requirements such as ISDN, video digitizing, video camera, and other such hardware are left out of the tally.

There are some other notable teleconferencing products. DECspin is a tele-conferencing system from DEC that runs on up to six RISC-based DEC work-stations running Ultrix (a form of UNIX). It lets users hold live teleconferencing and record the conference for later viewing. Northern Telecom, with Workstation Technologies, Inc. of Irvine, Calif., is developing technology for compressing and displaying video images through ISDN. PictureTel of Peabody, Mass., has a video conferencing system that works on a dual twisted-pair LAN—an inexpensive LAN cabling system that also needs an ISDN link. IBM's Person-to-Person/2 lets you conference in real time over a network, viewing the other person as though on a picture phone.

## Summary

E-mail is based on interconnected computers, from terminals hooked up to mainframes to PCs linked in a network. Even the networks can and are connected into larger WANs using gateways. Inside this arena, E-mail software is divided into various components: user agent (the interface of commands for the user), directory services (for keeping a list of addresses), and transport agent (for moving messages from sender to recipient). There are de facto standards such as MHS for exchanging messages from one E-mail system to another, and official standards such as X.400 for addressing and X.500 for directories. MHS is very popular and X.400 less so. X.500 is only beginning to enter the real market.

E-mail messages can be simple text letters, but technology is heading for exchange of sound and video messages, for transmission of funds and documents (EFT and EDI), for on-line conferencing, and even for complex work automation and collaboration (groupware) programs.

# CHAPTER TWO

# Choosing E-mail

There are many forms of E-mail, and many ways to interconnect them. Which form will be best for you depends on your situation. What you have used, where you will use it, what you will send, and many other factors are critical to choosing the right E-mail. This chapter tells you which questions to ask and what answers to look for.

As you choose, you will be considering all the various factors:

| | |
|---|---|
| messaging | gateways |
| archiving | administrator security |
| word processing | documentation |
| user security | cost |
| speed | ease of use |
| installation | ease of learning |
| administration | expandability |
| server maintenance | technical support |

and more. Ultimately, they boil down to four major issues for users and two for administrators. Users want easy, quick, safe, and certain delivery of the mail. Administrators want easy and reliable system maintenance.

 **Tip:** Most E-mail systems will advertise that they "can" do most any messaging function. The question is, How easily do they do it? For software developers, E-mail is easy to do, but hard to do well.

 **Tip:** Keep your sense of humor and your notes. The first you'll need because of all the pitfalls and moving targets of choosing and managing E-mail. The second you'll need to defend your choices against all those who haven't studied the details, but have only read some brief article touting this or that system.

Once you have a feel for what you want, what you've got, and what you can afford, you need to concentrate on four aspects of E-mail:

Company concerns ...............strategies, goals, culture and history.
System basics..........................system planning for now and the future
User features...........................specific options for users
Administrator features...........specific tools for administrators

User features, naturally, are all the things your users will notice: how easy it is to send a message, to reply, to make mailing lists, to store messages, how quickly do messages move, and so on. These are mentioned in more detail in "User Features" later in this chapter.

Administrator features are all the things your administrators will notice, the utilities and commands they'll use to install, manage, optimize, and safeguard the E-mail system. These are described in the "Administrative questions" section.

The Big Questions are the philosophical questions that don't directly affect the daily work of users or administrators.

## Company Concerns

The overall direction and strategy of you company will have an affect on you E-mail decisions and may determince what products you research and how to structure you questions and evaluations.

### Your strategy

Before you think tactically, think strategically. Think of functions before you think of features. You must know what those needs are before you know if a particular E-mail system will meet your needs. Think over the following questions and write your answers down:

■ What do you want out of E-mail?
■ What E-mail and messaging technologies are you using?
■ What can you spend?

Your partial or complete answers about your goals, history, and budget, will help you plan and aid any potential suppliers that will craft intelligent systems and solutions for you.

### Your goals

To figure out how to get somewhere, you need to know where you're going. You need a goal. That goal may change as you watch how your organization's people actually use E-mail, but it's important to start with at least some destination in mind.

Start thinking strategically by analyzing what you want from E-mail. Major possibilities include:

■ messaging quickly and easily among organization members
■ transferring files among organization members
■ providing a foundation for group applications, for work-flow programs
■ moving messages and files to and from people outside the organization
■ automating electronic data and financial information within the organization and to external organizations

You may want some or all of these things, and you may want some now and the freedom to add others later.

**Tip:** When deciding what you want from E-mail, ask all potential users for suggestions. When asking, provide them with a list of typical uses in other organizations as a starting point for their ruminations. For example, are you looking for specific changes in your organization? Some possibilities may include:

- 15 percent increased productivity in white-collar workers
- 20 percent decrease in telephone call costs
- improved decision-making through better-informed workers
- tighter teamwork through improved communications
- decreased turnaround time on time-critical projects

If so, you need to not only translate these ideas into E-mail functions and features, but also set up some sort of measurement and monitoring process.

### Your history

To figure out how to get to your E-mail destination you also need to know where you're starting from. Your organization's physical and cultural structure are important factors, as is its experience and investments in messaging systems. E-mail does not operate in a vacuum.; neither is it simply another way to send a memo from here to there. It affects who, when, and how communications take place. That means it affects more than just wires and screens—it affects the people and their habits.

### Physical geography

The physical location of you and your coworkers is another very important consideration. You want to know and consider these questions.

- How are the people in your company distributed?
- How many people will use the E-mail?
- Are they all in one building, in several buildings at one site, or in buildings around the country or the world?
- Are some potential users remote, permanently at sites distant from most others in your organization?
- Are some potential users sometimes remote because they are mobile?

Your answers will determine the most cost-effective E-mail "architecture" for your organization.

## Organizational culture

Beside the actual physical locations of your organization's members, you must consider the social or cultural hierarchy of those members. You must realize that E-mail can challenge today's culture by offering easy and direct interaction between almost any two people in the organization. If you don't want this to threaten or disrupt today's culture, you must bend your E-mail plans toward protecting that culture. Some of the benefits of E-mail may come from that very change in structures, however, so consider such the likely scenarios very carefully.

For example, the message-writing style, use of E-mail for personal subjects, topics and members chosen for bulletin-board conversations, and presence in directories of important or senior members of the organization can all be structured to provide anything from a messaging free-for-all to a more rigid, traditional communication scheme. Think about what you and your organization want.

## Current messaging systems

The people in your organization already communicate. They may be using:

| | |
|---|---|
| memos | paper messages routed through interoffice mail |
| fax | paper messages "telecopied" through the phone |
| telex | paper messages sent from one telex machine to another |
| letters | paper messages sent slowly through the postal system |
| telephone calls | voice messages sent immediately through phone lines |
| voice mail | voice messages recorded for listening later, sent through phone lines |
| E-mail | text messages sent from one computer to another |

The E-mail systems you choose can replace (this is unlikely), augment (this is probable), or integrate (this is desirable, but only sometimes possible) whatever communications schemes already in use.

E-mail could replace memos entirely, though that may take some time. More likely, it will add a new channel for fast, simple memos, while longer, more-durable memos will still move on paper.

It will not replace fax messages for a while, because as explained in Chapter 1, E-mail systems can easily send faxes, but are not yet adept at receiving and routing them to the right person. Even integrating your outgoing faxes can be difficult because few E-mail or computer systems provide a simple means to "sign" documents and then fax them from the computer.

E-mail can entirely replace sending of telexes, which few people truly need to do. (Telex is now largely used in the U.S. to send international messages to locations that don't have a fax machine.)

Some letters will be replaced by E-mail for shorter, quicker messages. Longer letters will still be sent as paper because some people don't have the means to receive E-mail (though the hard-copy postal option of some E-mail systems may beat this problem). Also, electronic messages cannot carry enclosures or the personal touch that traditional letters can.

E-mail could partially replace telephone calls and voicemail because you could send some messages more thoroughly by E-mail than by quick phone calls. However, like letters, telephone calls can offer a more personal touch than can E-mail.

Phone calls can also be made to many more places than E-mail can reach, because more people have phones than computers. Finally, telephone calls are interactive, and therefore are more like conferencing than like straight E-mail; voice-mail more resembles E-mail.

## Current E-mail systems

An "E-mail inventory" is what you need to get started. Find out what systems are in place and what applications people are using.

Then you can use this analysis to understand what can be saved, what can be extended, and what must be deleted from the existing systems.

Determine if you have a mainframe E-mail system that should remain in operation? Perhaps it could be extended by connections to LAN E-mail systems, working as their backbone and backup server.

Do you have several LAN E-mail systems throughout the organization. You could interconnect these with gateways, or via gateways, to a backbone. You could also try to persuade the users to switch to one LAN E-mail package. (That would buy consistency, but might alienate some users. People tend to fall in love with the E-mail they use, and different groups are attracted to different features in E-mail, and so to different E-mail programs.)

 **Tip:** Remember that whatever you put together today will almost certainly grow later: Don't put limits on that.

### Your budget

Naturally, whatever you choose must fall within some cost restrictions. How it will fit your budget  is a slippery question, involving both hard and soft costs and benefits.

## The Big Questions

The answers you give to the following Big Questions will direct your E-mail choices. Those answers should be themes to keep in mind when making any of the more specific choices of features and tools. In the end they are more important than the presence or lack of any specific option for users or administrators.

### System architecture

The first big question is system architecture. What underlying structure should your E-mail have? For most organizations, the architecture should be open, modular, scalable, and ready for the future. These attributes often overlap and need some explanation.

### Open systems

"Open" is a popular word in computing, but one that is often confused by computer makers. It generally refers to systems that let you choose the computer platform, operating system, and network operating system you like. This makes the computing system less expensive so you can buy on performance and price. It also makes the system more flexible—you can add pieces from almost any vendor and they'll "plug-and-play" without trouble. Finally, it makes the system easier to maintain—they'll be understandable to technicians without a lifetime of study of that one particular system.

Open systems get these advantages by being built to work from or with commonly-accepted standards, whether those are de facto or official. Particular questions and answers that you want to know are:

- Does the E-mail follow or support X.400, X.500, MHS, and other standards?
- Which versions of the standards are supported?
- Does the vendor promise to continue to follow standards?
- Does the vendor work with strategic partners and developers who follow standards?

E-mail that follows standards should also work with as many of the other traditional applications, mail-enabled applications, and groupware applications as possible.

### Modular system

An open architecture saves you from being enslaved to any one supplier. If your system adheres to standards, you should be able to mix and match the pieces. For example, you can take a message transport from here, a user interface from there, and a directory services module from somewhere else and create one system.

Modularity is the natural next step after adhering to open standards. Although E-mail systems did not afford this five years ago, more and more are moving that direction now. They are separating the basic functions into a "third generation" of E-mail so that you'll be able to choose the user agent, message transport, directory services, and mail engine that make the most sense to you.

A major pressure for this modularity is coming from the network operating systems suppliers, such as Microsoft Corp. and Novell Corp. Both are discussing plans to add "back-end" services such as message transport, directory services, and a mail engine into their operating system software. This would force most E-mail providers into emphasizing the user agent. However, some of the operating systems plans include modularity so the built-in services could be replaced with others. This would create a market for those services, sold separately as modules either from third-party software developers or from the main E-mail companies.

**Scalable**

Almost any LAN system will grow, to reach more people in the organization, to grow as the organization grows, and to reach out to more people outside the organization. Knowing this, you should ask any vendor how easily its E-mail package can be scaled to a larger organization. The following questions are also very valueable for you to ask in your intial discussions.

- Are there limits on the directory size?
- Are there limits on the number of servers allowed?
- Are there message-number limits?
- How difficult is it to add users and post offices?
- Will performance fall dramatically at some point?
- Does the vendor have experience growing other installations?
- Does the vendor have experience with client/server computing?

Most new E-mail installations are based on personal computer (PC) networks or LANs. Most LAN applications, including E-mail, are becoming "client/server" systems, where a server is a central computer handling most processing tasks, and clients are individual workstations connected to the server. Clients handle the interface tasks and limited processing.

Client/server systems are pretty easily scaled by adding a lot more clients and a few more servers. Even in client/server computing, however, you need to watch out for limits imposed by the software, the storage capacity, or the network traffic.

### Backbone

Many large E-mail installations depend on a "backbone" architecture. This places a large computer and communications system as the heart of the E-mail. The backbone computer acts as a hub (see the routing information in Chapter 4) or translator to move messages between more local or regional networks and remote sites. Sticking to the X.400 standard will help each local E-mail site communicate with others over the backbone, even if the sites use different E-mail systems.

Often the backbone can be a mainframe computer that is not being used to full capacity within an organization. Another possible backbone can be a commercial-service E-mail system or a large network such as the Internet.

**Tip:** Choosing a backbone architecture decentralizes control. The backbone does not impose directory and other standards, it just helps the local E-mail systems communicate. This choice should be made while considering the organization's culture; Is centralized control a key part to the existing procedures, or can control be relaxed to gain the local benefits of decentralization? Remember that communications costs may increase when control is relaxed.

### Consider future plans

Your E-mail's architecture should provide the basics for, or at the least not prevent, participation in future technology. E-mail is becoming the foundation for all sorts of communications technologies. You'll want:

■ support of major APIs for application enabling, such as MAPI, VIM, and OCE

■ object-oriented programming support for developing mail-enabled applications (including development tools)

■ support for important groupware products

■ support for sending, receiving, and viewing multimedia file attachments and future conferencing

■ full support for fax routing as it becomes available

### LAN, host, or commercial-service?

The debate among host-based, LAN-based, and commercial-service E-mail is becoming moot. All of the leading development work is happening on LAN E-mail. Unless you're an individual or a small, widespread organization, you'll almost certainly choose LAN-based E-mail. The questions you'll ask will most likely be:

■ Which LAN-based E-mail do I choose?

■ How do I connect various LAN E-mail systems together?

■ How do I take advantage of the mainframe or minicomputer mail I already have?

■ How do I take advantage of commercial-service E-mail features?

### Host-based E-mail

Host mail can be a good choice if you already have a mini or mainframe system and want to enhance it, and if you can gain the benefits of LAN E-mail by integrating LANs with the host. Though there are major and useful E-mail systems set up on a mini or mainframe, few new host systems are being installed. Host hardware is expensive, especially in the initial capital investment. What's more, all the other applications to which E-mail will eventually be tied; accounting, personnel records, and so on, are largely moving from the host to LANs and client/server systems. This "downsizing" is much less expensive than buying and maintaining new, larger host systems. For more information see Chapter 7.

### Commercial-service E-mail

Commercial-service E-mail can be the perfect answer for individuals or for small organizations where each member is remote from others. It offers direct connection to outsiders, provides service from anywhere in the world, affords high reliability, and low maintenance. As well as, access to databases, fax transmission, and even hard-copy delivery. However, it will cost more per user than E-mail in a large LAN system, and won't offer the internal security and control of a LAN-based system.

Although most commercial-service systems could provide mailboxes for all the people in an organization, and those people could all dial in through their own modems. There are many disadvantages such as more expensesive (sending mail on LANs would probably be cheaper) and less flexible (many systems wouldn't carry certain types of file attachments).

A commercial-service E-mail system could, however, provide a key gateway or link to other E-mail systems even if you have host or LAN E-mail in-house. You could include a gateway to a popular commercial-service system such as MCI Mail or EasyLink to reach customers and suppliers.

**Tip:** Using a commercial-service system as a route to people and services outside the organization can help preserve the security of your internal directories and other software assets. It can also save you money because you don't have to handle maintenance of that external part of the system, or pay for any received mail.

### LAN-based E-mail

LAN-based E-mail is the answer for just about everyone (excepting those mentioned previously). It offers the most realistic costs, and control, while offering access to technological advances.

**Tip:** Cost may be today's best reason to use LAN E-mail, but integration of technologies will be tomorrow's: You'll need LAN systems to link to mail-enabled applications, groupware, and other advanced computing and productivity tools.

However, determining the right LAN system you need is just the beginning. You still need to consider the total system architecture that will link the LANs. This could very well include mainframes (such as for backbone or backup work) and commercial-services (for backbone or gateway work).

### Performance, reliability, and security considerations

Users must know their messages will be delivered soon and safely (without being intercepted and read). That means ensuring performance, reliability, and security. Questions that you may want to ask a vendor or supplier are:

- How many users can the E-mail system handle at once?
- At what point does performance degrade?
- How quickly does the directory respond?
- How will file attachments, especially large ones, affect performance?
- How will gateways affect performance?
- Can messages be restricted by passwords and hidden by encryption?
- Are passwords, stored messages, and transmitted messages encrypted?
- Is Multi-LAN support available?

E-mail needs to connect everyone and needs to work with current systems. Both motivations suggest that the more platforms and LANs an E-mail system supports, the better.

Running with DOS is not enough. Your E-mail program must also coexist with a LAN operating system, the software that makes the network run. This software is typically divided into parts that run on each workstation on the network (the network drivers that load into RAM, as previously mentioned) and parts that run on the network server.

Novell's NetWare is by far the most common operating system. Microsoft's LAN Manager is in second place, far behind, and Banyan's VINES is also in the race. Whatever network operating system you have, check to see that the E-mail you're interested in will run with that NOS (Network Operating System). You don't have a NOS yet? You haven't yet set up a LAN? Then you'll need more than this book. E-mail could be the only reason you need to network, but you need to learn about networks in general to make a wise networking choice.

Ideally E-mail would support these networks:

- Novell NetWare
- IBM Token Ring
- Microsoft LAN Manager
- Banyan's VINES
- PC LAN
- 3Com
- NetBIOS
- LANtastic
- 10Net
- DEC PCSA
- Tops
- AppleTalk

Realistically, an E-mail package may be acceptable if it only supports Novell's NetWare.

### Multi-platform support

E-mail is easier to use if it runs on all the various computers in an organization. The client versions should ideally follow the standards of each platform, and yet be similar enough to the versions for other platforms that no retraining is necessary. A user should be able to move from one system to the next quite easily.

The most likely platforms that E-mail would ideally have client versions and administrator tools together are PCs running DOS, Windows, OS/2, Macintoshes, and UNIX workstations.

### DOS platform

Programs written to run on a PC or compatible system are typically written to work with the DOS operating system. They could be written instead to run under some other operating system, but DOS has been popular enough to drive most competitors out of the market. In fact, the most common PC operating system alternatives are "DOS-compatible," and should be able to run programs written for DOS. There are only three exceptions to this rule: Windows, OS/2, and UNIX.

The PC-compatible system is clearly the most popular in the world. Expert estimates in 1992 put the number of PC and compatibles in the world at 60 to 70 million. They make up 85 percent of the business desktop computers sold in the U.S. A similar, though somewhat smaller, dominant fraction is estimated in Europe, South America, and the rest of the world. Japan's computer market is, however, dominated by machines made by NEC, and is more factious than the U.S. market. The NEC machines are not PC-compatible.

 **Tip:** A requirement for a certain version of DOS to run your E-mail program means you need that version of DOS or a later one.

RAM (random access memory) is the chip memory that computers use to hold programs and data on which they're working. The PC running DOS has a smaller ability to use RAM than does a PC running Windows or a Macintosh. Its "memory management" is more restricted. In most cases a PC running DOS must be able to manage all active software in the first 640K of RAM, even if more RAM chips are plugged into the computer. This means that routines or pieces of DOS must stay in memory along with other utility programs such as print driverssoftware. Peripheral drivers allow your printer, CD-ROM drive, or other peripherals to run in conjunction with your system. Network drivers connect DOS to the network operating system. If you want to run the application program and have your E-mail's "notification utility" (the little program that tells you when new mail has arrived) running concurrently, your PC's RAM may be cramped indeed. Programs that runs and coexist together are called "RAM-resident" because they  stay or reside in memory while you start an application program. Another term for this is TSR (Terminate and Stay Resident)

because such programs remain in memory even after they terminate or stop working. A normal program unloads from memory after it stops running. Notification utilities reside in RAM and alert you to incoming mail. Some also offer bare-bones abilities to create or reply to a message. The smaller this notification utility is—the fewer K of RAM it uses and the better.

### Windows platform

Microsoft Windows is the software "environment" or "graphical user interface" (GUI) that sits on top of DOS. That is, it is the extra piece of software that gives the typical PC a screen of pull-down menus, icons, and other such "easy-to-learn-and-use" images. Apple Computer popularized the idea of a GUI with the Macintosh system, convincing many people that it reduced the learning curve and made it easier to use new programs. A standard GUI across applications helps the user get to the important features of new programs. Programs written for DOS will run on a PC that has both DOS and Windows, but they won't use these new features of Windows. To take advantage of this user interaface, you need a program written for Windows. These programs collect their commands into the same general menus, so learning one program means you've halfway learned the next. By contrast, DOS programs arrange their menus in any which way: Learning one program rarely helps you learn the next. For this reason, many people feel Windows programs are easier to use than DOS applications. However, Windows programs also demand more hardware power and expense than typical DOS programs. Windows also complicates running on a network, though these problems can be solved and are diminishing as more people gain experience using and debugging networked Windows.

In other words, it is best to use a Windows E-mail program if you're going to run Windows on your PC. Some of the Windows E-mail programs are "ported" (rewritten to run in Windows) versions of well-known DOS E-mail programs. Others are available only for Windows.

 **Tip:** Only use Windows E-mail if you have the hardware to run Windows practically: at least a 386 processor, 2 to 4MB of memory, a 40MB hard disk, and an EGA or VGA display.

**Tip:** Ask suppliers if a Windows E-mail program supports the latest Windows features, including true multitasking, DDE (Dynamic Data Exchange) for moving data automatically from one Windows program to another, and OLE (Object Linking and Embedding) to automatically call necessary linked applications to handle documents with more than one type of data.

### Macintosh platform

You can find another popular operating system on the Apple Macintosh. This operating system does not run on non-Macintosh PCs. E-mail programs written for DOS or for Windows won't run on the Macintosh, nor will a program written for the Macintosh run on PCs. Some companies, however, offer versions of their programs for both the Macintosh and PC-compatibles. And there are some popular Macintosh E-mail programs that aren't available on PCs. With Macintosh E-mail you need to know if it will support Appleshare, System 7, and VIM and OCE. See Chapter 1.

### UNIX platform

UNIX is commonly thought of as an operating system for workstations, minicomputers, and mainframes. In fact, it is also available on most PCs. UNIX has built-in basic E-mail, as explained in Chapter 6, but you can also find versions of more sophisticated E-mail programs to work with it. They will sometimes depend on a simple command-line interface, but can also support graphical UNIX interfaces such as Motif and Open Look. UNIX E-mail should support such UNIX communications standards as UUCP and SMTP.

### Gateways and connectivity options

As explained in Chapter 1, E-mail is most useful if it can connect to other E-mail. Who would want a postal system that could send letters within town, but couldn't send or receive information to other cities, states, or countiries? Connecting networks and E-mail, in this way is known as connectivity. Gateways are an integral part of connectivity. Gateways open an E-mail system to other E-mail systems; shuttling messages from LAN to Host to Commercial service to another

LAN. The more connectivity options there are, the happier you'll be. This is true for transport services, gateways, and remote access.

### Transport Flexibility

Ideally, your E-mail will work with whatever communication lines you already have set up. As mentioned previously, the more networks and platforms it works on the better. Also, it will save you time and money if it runs across asynchronous communications, X.25, SNA backbones, ISDN, and PDNs (Public Data Networks). See Chapter 1. For more detailed information on these topics read books specifically dedicated to networking and internetworking.

### Gateways

At the least you'll want gateways to allow fax transimission, access to remote locations, and support for MHS and X.400 protocols (in pretty much that order). By ensuring that your system supports these options, You'll face fewer "What, we can't do that? Who chose this system?" questions. The next set of important options to consider are gateways to PROFS, All-In-One, MCI Mail, EasyLink, and other minicomputer and mainframe E-mail systems.

Also, the easier the gateways are to use (transparent to users) and to administer, the better off you'll be.

 **Tip:** It's a good sign if E-mail is supported by major gateway makers such as Soft*Switch, Retix, and Touch Communications.

### Remote access

You may have remote users and will want connections to them (this is also explained in the User Features section). To support them, your E-mail will need to give them access to the directory, message storing, and mailbox management. More flexibility is better in deciding how they'll access the system, such as allowing full access to the LAN or limited access to a mailbox.

## Cost

Of course, cost matters. You can get cost estimates for hardware, software, training, maintenance, and telecommunications from whatever vendors you choose to investigate.

Unfortunately, these costs won't be as concrete as you might like. Although hardware cost estimates may be quite stable, and software costs may be less so, training and maintenance costs will probably exceed conservative estimates for most vendors. Maintenance could be several times greater than the estimates.

**Tip:** Some estimates put 80 percent of the costs in the first year for training and administration. A big part of administration costs will be directory maintenance: the more that can be automated the better.

Telecommunications costs could be the worst offender, and are very hard to pin down until the system has been operating for awhile. It will be very difficult to project which gateways will be busiest, how many files are moving at the same time, how large the average files in transit are, and which remote sites will be calling most often. People will come up with new uses for a messaging system that the plans didn't include, and these could easily balloon telecomm costs in one area or another.

Return on investment is also difficult to calculate. It will be easier to calculate if you're comparing the costs of replacing a system, such as moving from host-based mail to LAN-based mail. However, it will be quite a chore if you're looking to balance productivity, work quality, and customer satisfaction against the costs of a new or greatly expanded E-mail system. The costs are often hard and precise; the returns are often soft and difficult to measure.

That does not mean E-mail doesn't provide a return on your investment. Think of the costs and benefits of your organization's telephone use as an analogy. You wouldn't imagine running an organization without telephones, but just exactly how do you figure the soft benefits of telephones? For example, you can easily recognize benefits such as:

- more immediate communication
- direct contact with customers and suppliers
- improved channel for information flow among workers
- managers spending more time on their primary work instead of supervising clerical tasks

In the long run E-mail could do more to improve the quality of our work than the quantity. That makes productivity measurements a real exercise.

 **Tip:** Remember to prepare for such costs as system down-time, corporate-information resource sharing (time on the mainframe, telephone line use, and so on), and exploring/planning for system enhancements.

 **Tip:** Whatever training and administration costs you estimate, increase them by 25 to 50 percent for a more realistic budget estimate.

Most E-mail systems will cost less per user the more users you have on the system. There will, however, be spikes in this declining costs curve as you add or change options and the number of users.

Costs will increase when you add user licenses, server licenses, file servers, hardware connections, and gateways. Also, E-mail tends to cost less each year as hardware and software prices decline, and old-fashioned communications prices tend to climb each year as secretarial time for typing memos rises.

 **Tip:** Some E-mail systems that are competitively less expensive for a small number of users may become more expensive for a large number of users.

 **Tip:** One of the advantages of using LAN E-mail over host E-mail is the smaller capital costs. Host mail means immediate large investments in hardware and software. LAN E-mail investments can be more incremental.

Most LAN E-mail systems require you to buy two packages of software. The first package is a "platform pack" with the basic server software and system-administrator utilities. Then you'll need user packages which include the software for individual E-mail users. These you typically buy for 5, 8, 10, 20, 100, or even an unlimited number of users. The administration utilities commonly include a program that will help you track how many people are using E-mail on the network. This will help to identify who is authorized and who is borrowing and installing disks from other users. Sometimes a single package includes server, user, and administrator software. All of these need to be included when calculating costs.

### Relationships

Soft costs can depend on your relationships with vendors. You'll often be better off spending more for E-mail products from a vendor that:

- offers great technical support
- helps with installation
- helps with training
- offers guidance in planning the system
- sticks to open architecture and standards
- keeps you informed of updates
- tells you the direction of its E-mail package
- regularly updates and improves their E-mail software

than buying from a vendor with a lower price and a less defined, less committed attitude.

There are some advantages to choosing a program that has already been accepted by many others. Not that the best-sellers are always the best performers. That's not true in any area of software (nor, perhaps, in anything else). However, if you choose one of the market leaders, you're more likely to find a wider variety of add-on products and training programs for your system. A market leader is also better insurance of a clear future—of regular upgrades and quick adoption of new technologies and standards. When you choose a less well-known package, which may have superior features now, or choose a program from a smaller company, there is an increased chance that the program will disappear or languish. Then you'll face the expensive proposition of changing your E-mail foundation with the new software and new training that it requires.

In PC-based LAN E-mail, cc:Mail is clearly the best-selling product as of early 1992. Second place is taken by Microsoft Mail. On the Macintosh, QuickMail and Microsoft Mail for AppleTalk Networks are the leaders. These positions may change as the leaders move to a new generation of E-mail, splitting their products into the various services for modularity. Also, Microsoft's development of a new E-mail engine, code-named Spitfire, and its suggestion that basic E-mail services will become part of a DOS/Windows operating system will revolutionize PC LAN E-mail. Novell is also moving toward putting E-mail services into NetWare, with similar possible consequences for the market. The most popular Commercial-service E-mail is AT&T's EasyLink.

 **Tip:** If you're interested in PC-based LAN E-mail, keep your eyes on what Microsoft and Novell do by incorporating E-mail services into their operating systems.

 **Tip:** Getting support and maintaining a system is easier if most or all of the parts are from a single vendor.

This does not necessarily mean working exclusively with large vendors. Small vendors are often a better choice if:

- they are more committed to service
- they are close to your location and can provide hands-on help quickly
- you receive more personal service

With all vendors size is not as important as asking and verifying these following questions.

- Do they have a history to show—with references and examples of others using their products (including organizations like yours)?

- Are third party developers developing utilities and other additions for their products?
- Do they have strategic relationships with software and hardware developers?
- Are they financially stable?
- Do they have a long range business plan and commitment to customer service?

These decisions will also affect what channel you use when buying E-mail. For very small sites you can get by with commercial-service or LAN E-mail purchased over the counter from a software outlet. However, for any significant planning or installation you should look to purchasing support and installation from VARs (value-added resellers), systems integrators, and E-mail consultants. These experts will have experience with all the various trials and tribulations of planning, installation, and maintenance. This is the same advice you'd receive for most network applications: Networks are harder to install and setup than stand-alone applications.

**Tip:** Remember that E-mail for anything more than a small site is a much more complicated system-oriented task than other typical computer applications such as word processors and spreadsheets. Consider employing a systems integrator or consultant when planning and installing E-mail.

### User and administrator features

Does the E-mail system you are considering give your users the commands and options they need? Does it provide your administrators the tools and reports they'll need? The rest of this chapter slices those questions up and looks at their details.

## User Features to Consider

You'll want a lot of features for the individual E-mail users such as, commands and options to let them send and receive messages in a variety of ways. Keep the following two things in mind when lining up features for comparison: keep it easy to use and consider the most inportant features. Don't just count features—if you won't use them, they may just get in the way.

 **Tip:** More features can make a program more difficult to use. Don't base your buying decision on who has the longest list of features.

Most of today's E-mail systems offer many more features than those of a few years ago, from word processing to archiving and mailing lists. Most are also blessed with easier-to-learn and easier-to-use interfaces than those of the past.

**Tip:** No book can adequately list the latest features of individual programs—they change too quickly. Look to magazine comparison reviews in PC, PC World, InfoWorld, MacWorld, MacUser, Unix World, and so on.

### Is it easy to use?

This is the single most important user aspect of E-mail. That ease of use will differ from one user to the next—different people may prefer different approaches. Generally, the ease comes from the interface, the documentation and support, and the performance.

### What interface does it offer?

There are objective and subjective elements to the "interface" of an E-mail system, to the screen display, and to the keyboard options given the user. The subjective elements concern the "feel" of the display and input options. The reaction to this feel will vary from one user to the next. The objective elements are more easily described. Basically there are three kinds of interfaces: command-line, character-screen, and graphic.

Command-line interfaces are the hardest to use. These simply give the user some prompt (such as a "$" sign) and expect the user to then type letter and number codes for commands. This is the way traditional UNIX and host-mail systems work, and the way the bare-bones E-mail for some LAN operating systems work. Avoid it if at all possible.

Character-screen interfaces are the kind you'll find in most DOS PC-based LAN E-mail programs. Here there will be menus, lists, command-key options, and other ways of showing you what you can do and when messages are ready for reading or sending. These are better than command-line interfaces for just about everyone. Many people consider the character-screen interface to not be as easy to learn and use as a graphical interface, but some do prefer the screen-oriented approach. They like the quickest responses possible from memorized menu choices and typed commands. and are often called "power users".

 **Tip:** Character-screen interfaces can be easy to use if they have well-organized menus and "macros" for storing and replaying frequent command sequences.

Graphical interfaces, sometimes called "Graphic User Interfaces" or "GUIs" (pronounced "gooeys"), were popularized by programs on the Apple Macintosh and have since spread to other platforms such as PCs running Microsoft's Windows and to UNIX systems running Motif or Open Look. All of these interfaces collect commands into standard menus that can be browsed and selected by using a keyboard command or a mouse. They put activities on screen into rectangular "windows" that can be moved and sized to the most convenient place and shape. GUIs are generally thought to be easier to learn and use than character interfaces, though sometimes slower to operate—they generally don't require as much memorization or allow quick typing of abbreviated commands. They are popular for multitasking systems, because the various windows can hold the active programs.

Multitasking GUIs make it easy to cut-and-paste words from a word processor page to an E-mail message and vice versa. That's sometimes known as a "Multiple Document Interface" or MDI with a "clipboard." For E-mail programs that can send graphics, multitasking also permits easy graphics viewing and editing.

**Tip:** In a character-screen interface such as those most DOS PC-based programs use, look for the ability to "Exit to DOS" directly from the program, or for a "TSR module" that can handle basic E-mail work. Either of these offers some multitasking ability, but not nearly as much as a full multitasking GUI.

**Tip:** If there is a TSR module with your E-mail program, be sure to use it in the least possible amount of memory. That will boost your chances of running alongside the maximum number of other programs because memory in PCs is often quite limited.

No matter which kind of interface you choose, a good interface should let you read and send messages without quitting whatever other application you use, be customizable, have shortcut keys that will give commands without the use of menus, and offer single-key addressing of messages, for both individual and mailing list addresses.

**Tip:** The flip side of "ease of use" should be "not tedious." Some programs are easy to learn because every command is spelled out in detail on-screen. If there is no shortcut to bypass these explanations and steps later, the program will be slow and tedious after you've learned it. Ideally, you'll be able to use this interface with very little referral to the manual.

### What documentation and support is available?

No matter how easy the interface is, you'll sometimes need to refer to the documentation that came with the program or contact to technical support. The manuals should:

- be clear
- not too weighty
- be complete
- include lots of illustrations and diagrams
- include examples (with screen-shot illustrations)

- include context-sensitive, on-line help (built into the program)
- cover administrative tasks in detail and with tutorials

The support should:
- include access to phone, fax, bbs, and mail service
- ideally be 24-hour, seven-day, and toll-free
- be competent
- be quick

### What performance can or should you expect?

Quick addressing and delivery of mail make an E-mail system easier to use. You'll want a system that quickly:

- switches to E-mail from another program
- finds addresses in a directory
- opens a new message window or file
- gives the cursor back to the user after giving the "send message" command for a single message
- gives the cursor back to the user after giving the "send message" command for a message to a mailing list of recipients
- sends file attachments
- saves received messages and attachments
- searches for archived messages

Some LAN E-mail systems still store their messages as separate files on a server. Most use a single, large database file to store all messages. The single database system is more efficient if your system is used heavily. However, storing all addresses in a central directory can slow addressing and sending of messages. Dividing this work between the server and the client—putting a current directory into each client—can increase performance and reduce access time for the users.

 **Tip:** Make sure you ask what the performance specifications are or test performance yourself. One test could be to evaluate the system when operating under abnormal circumstances such as checking sporadic traffic patterns. Some systems degrade far more quickly than others when encountering lots of traffic. Also look for performance statistics under a variety of network operating systems and network topologies.

### Word processing and printing features

A "text editor" is a program or set of commands for entering and editing text. In the old days—several years ago and more—many E-mail packages ignored the issue of a decent text editor for creating messages. The best they offered would be a simple line editor that behaved much as traditional UNIX systems would—probably because UNIX was the training ground for many program developers. Those developers may have expected each user to have a text editor they preferred anyway.

Now that has changed entirely. Some of the commercial-service E-mail systems use a line editor, but they often supplement this with a more powerful editor built into a front-end program. Typical LAN E-mail programs have powerful text editors—they could nearly be called word processors. The important features in any E-mail text editor are:

- entering and deleting text
- word-wrap at the end of line
- viewing a message while writing a reply
- saving drafts while working
- importing text messages written in other programs and exporting text
- printing a message
- searching for and replacing specified text in the message
- cutting-and-pasting parts of the message, within the message and from other messages
- spelling checking
- underlining and boldfacing text
- mixing fonts and type styles in a message
- including graphics in a message

**Tip:** Spell checking is especially important for formal messages. You may be able to live without some of these features, but viewing a message while creating a new message, cutting-and-pasting blocks of text, and importing text messages are critical.

 **Tip:** The ability to create messages off-line, and then send them when on-line, is critical when using any remote E-mail, most host E-mail, and some network E-mail systems. Without this capability your connect charges and phone bill will be very high.

 **Tip:** Forms could be considered an advanced word-processing feature, where the ability to create, store, share, and fill-in forms would simplify the creation of some messages.

## Messaging options and features

"Messaging" refers to the various methods of receiving and sending a message. The first items on this list are basic; the later items are less common. The more options you have, the better. Your E-mail should offer these:

- sending
- unsending before reading (this is rare but quite handy)
- replying
- forwarding
- carbon copies (CC)
- blind carbon copies (BCC)
- return receipts
- priority sending
- private mailing list
- shared mailing list
- immediate notification (visible or audible)
- hot-keying to reply
- text file attachments
- binary file attachments
- multimedia file attachments

 **Tip:** BCCs, or blind carbon copies, are typically used to send the boss a copy of a memo you're sending a colleague. "Murder by memo" is sometimes the motivation. There are less nefarious reasons for BCCs, though, such as sending yourself copies of a memo to see how they are circulating, and to make it easy to archive the message yourself.

**Tip:** Having a screen-capture utility makes it easier to send quick messages with a file attachment describing some computer action. It also eliminates the need to cut and paste some information into the memo itself.

**Tip:** Ask if your E-mail can disable audible notification of received mail. That could be a pleasant touch if you don't want to hear the notifying sound.

### Mailing lists

One of the great automations in E-mail is the mailing list. This lets you send a single message to many recipients simply by addressing it to the list. A good E-mail system will let you use lists created by the administrator, and let you create and use your own lists as well. Look for support of multiple mailing lists (the higher the limit the better), easy editing of mailing list, and importing mailing lists from other packages or applications.

### File attachments

As mentioned previously, you'll certainly want to attach files to your E-mail messages. Most LAN E-mail let you attach text files. Some commercial-service and host-mail systems do as well. Many systems now let you attach graphics, programs, and multimedia files. This is often referred to as attaching "binary" files. Look for programs that let you:

- attach text files
- attach binary files
- attach multimedia files (including sound, voice, and video)

- easily designate the files to attach
- attach multiple files to a single message (the higher the number the better—a dozen is decent)
- attach large files to a message
- view attached files without opening other applications

 **Tip:** Viewers are a great feature in an E-mail package because they let you see the graphics, fax, spreadsheet, and other files without having to turn-on the appropriate application and open the received or outgoing file.

 **Tip:** One way to attach large files and not devastate network performance is to compress the file before attachment.

## Data compression

There are utilities that will compress files before you attach them, then decompress them again on the receiving end (both sender and recipient need the utility). This puts less of a load on the E-mail database and the network traffic. One example of this is StuffIt Deluxe from Aladdin Systems, which integrates directly with Microsoft Mail for efficient and automatic file compression. You can choose a "Stuff & Send Mail" command. While it works, it provides virus checking and password security.

## Fax capabilities

Sending faxes will probably become a significant part of your organization's outgoing E-mail. To adequately send a fax, you need a fax modem on the network (or a connection to some network with one), a fax gateway, fax addressing ability (from third-party fax software), a fax viewer (to see the fax on screen—these are rare), and fax OCR software (to convert the fax to an editable file—these are extremely rare).

**Tip:** Having a fax viewer isn't necessary, but certainly makes E-mail faxing easier.

 **Tip:** Don't plan to receive faxes via E-mail. Although there are some workarounds, there is no clear scheme yet for routing incoming faxes to a particular E-mail box.

### Conferencing and bulletin board options

Many E-mail systems come with other communications features, such as chatting, conferencing, and bulletin boards. Chatting is immediate messaging back and forth between two conversants. The difference from E-mail is that the link need only be made once; each new comment does not need its own address and send command. Conferencing is like chatting, but is for more than two people at a time. The comments of all participants are immediately relayed and displayed for all other participants. This is like a telephone party line or conference call. Bulletin boards create "topics" over which anyone on the system can read and contribute comments. The comments remain for others to read at any time; unlike conferencing where the comments may be stored but are not kept in a chronological list for later reading.

Look for a bulletin-board facility. For distribution of system and personal news, it will save on sending messages about each subject to every recipient. Also look at conferencing as another way to use electronic messaging to link distant people at the same time, all talking together. This can save time and money over the traditional methods of sending E-mail messages individually and waiting for responses.

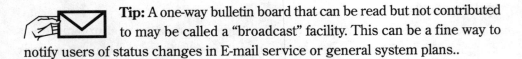 **Tip:** A one-way bulletin board that can be read but not contributed to may be called a "broadcast" facility. This can be a fine way to notify users of status changes in E-mail service or general system plans..

### Voice messaging

Voice is actually a rare element in E-mail, but is becoming more common as:

- more LANs incorporate the ability to move voice messages
- more E-mail packages gain the ability to attach voice files

■ voice-synthesis utilities allow E-mail packages to speak messages
■ voice mail and E-mail move toward integration

The one element that is not yet feasible is turning a voice message into a text message. The software to do so just isn't fast enough or able to handle enough different voices to make it practical. Some computer systems, and some LANs, let you use a special microphone to record messages that can then be attached to messages or sent by themselves across a network. This is in essence another form of E-mail. One example of a third-party voice product utility is VoxLink's VoxVoice. This converts cc:Mail text E-mail messages into speech, which can be played locally or even through a phone connection.

### Reading messages
Received messages are sent to your E-mail address and stay there until you do something such as delete or store them.. Your options for handling them should include:

■ notification of received mail (audible or visual with an option to disable the notifier)
■ viewing a list of received messages, with senders, subjects, and dates
■ opening messages to read them
■ opening more than one message at a time
■ viewing file attachments (see previous section)
■ sorting the In-box by attributes (urgency, sender, subject, date, and so on)

 **Tip:** A rare but handy feature lets a third-party pick up some or all of your mail, temporarily and with a password.

Once you've read a message, you should have the option to keep, delete, forward, print, and save it to either your In-box or to disk.

### Message management

Only a few E-mail programs offer true message management, though this feature will surely spread to others. With message management, you can create rules that will automatically sort received mail by attributes and then take actions based on those messages. The program could reply to messages, forward them, analyze attached files, and take other such actions. BeyondMail is a good example of this. See Chapters 1 and 5.

### Saving messages and archiving

One of the choices for dealing with a received message is to store it. That storage can be temporarily in the main server's mail database, but this is not a good idea. The route would quickly become bogged down by the server and cause delays for everyone. It's better to store it locally on your own disk where you can later recover it for reading, copying, or excerpting.

An E-mail system should offer you lots of ways to store and retrieve your messages, including the ability to:

- create named folders to hold the mail (for logical categories)
- store folders on a local drive (preferably on your own PC)
- store messages in shared folders (for bulletin-board messages)
- save copies of all mail sent
- retrieve messages by individual attributes or combinations of sender, subject, date, and keyword.
- search for messages across all folders
- search for messages through all the text of the messages (a "full-text" search)
- retain message threading—keeping track of which messages were replies to others

### Security features

People won't use E-mail very often if they think just anyone can come along and read their messages, the ones they send or the ones they receive. To protect against such invasions you need security features, such as:

- passwords (to login to mail) including password shrouding and password expiration
- encryption of stored and transmitted messages
- encryption with a tough-to-break code such as the DES standard

### Group scheduling capabilities

A popular add-on utility to E-mail is group scheduling, which creates a calendar and then keeps it up to date with the activities of various members of a workgroup. The members can use the scheduler to identify times when all can get together, find appropriate time slots, and match their schedules. Doing this by sending messages back and forth could take forever. A scheduling feature is often the first step toward groupware.

Ideally, a scheduling utility is integrated with E-mail so you don't have to leave E-mail to use it. Look for scheduling features that:

- are built-in or available as an add-on extension
- include personal calendars, as well as group calendars
- notify members of meetings, and lets them decline or accept
- have appointment alarms
- resolve conflicts and overlaps in schedules
- can schedule resources as well as people

**Tip:** Some E-mail packages don't include a group scheduling package, but you can purchase it as an additional utility. Microsoft Mail and cc:Mail both offer catalogs full of utilities, such as schedulers.

### Built-in utility programs

There are other programs you can get bundled with E-mail packages, often as part of an "office automation" suite. Some typical utilities you can get this way are calculators, notepads, card indexes (simple databases, such as for addresses), and telephone message centers (using a simple database and an E-mail form).

Telephone message centers are common. They let you take a call, pop-up a form for that call, fill-in the form's blanks on caller, reason for the call, and so on. You can then immediately zip that form to the screen of the person called.

### Remote access

It is certain that your E-mail system will at some point, and maybe immediately, need to support some remote users. These people will be either regular users temporarily away from the system or users consistently away. At the very least you'll want to provide them with computers, modems, telecommunications software, an access number connected to a modem and an access server.

 **Tip:** When buying modems, don't get anything slower than a 9600bps modem that follows the V.32 standard. These cost just a little more than modems that are four times slower.

You'll get better performance for remote users if your E-mail has its own remote program. This would include telecommunications abilities and commands for creating and reading mail off-line. It would also save "sent" mail in a queue until a connection was made, and then send it all as a batch.

 **Tip:** It's far easier to use a true remote version of a program than to access your E-mail with only a general-purpose telecommunications program.

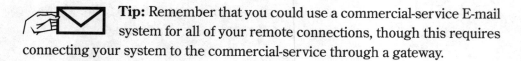 **Tip:** Remember that you could use a commercial-service E-mail system for all of your remote connections, though this requires connecting your system to the commercial-service through a gateway.

## Administration Questions

Every E-mail system has two essential components: use and administration. The administration is often overlooked when choosing E-mail software, both by individuals and by official reviewers. That's a shame because in the long run the administration features may be more important than the user features. E-mail that lacks a particular interface nicety or mailing-list feature may hold users back from their full E-mail potential. E-mail that can't be easily and efficiently managed can fall apart completely and drive users away from the entire idea of E-mail.

Some of the questions you should ask about an E-mail system are discussed in this section. You'll know a good administrative bet when the E-mail program doesn't need constant attention from administrators, automates most of the administrative tasks, keeps a log of use, and analyzes that log to determine how to improve performance. Administration tasks include:

- server maintenance
- directory maintenance
- user addition and deletion
- mailing-list creation and modification
- password setting and changing
- dated-mail purging
- database backup, compression, and restoration
- remote user handling

The more these tasks are automated by the commands or utilities of the E-mail system, the better off you'll be.

### Mail server's architecture

The underlying structure of the mail-server software will be a critical issue to server maintenance. Ideally, the server will:

- store messages in a database (not as individual files)
- store only a single instance of a message (not a copy for each recipient)

■ store only a single instance of each file attachment (not a copy for each recipient)

■ offer a very high limit on the maximum number of users per server (so you can choose the number you assign to the server by performance, not by the limits)

Single-instance storage conserves disk space, using only a pointer to the stored instance for each recipient.

### Ease of administration

This is an overall question. In other words, it asks "What is the E-mail provider's strategy for administration and how seriously does the provider take it?" You should prefer a company that:

■ mentions administration questions before you do
■ is committed to improving and standardizing its administration tools
■ offers powerful tools
■ offers administrator training
■ offers special administrator support

The tools that a company provides should:

■ be extremely easy to use
■ let the administrator easily add and delete users
■ let the administrator easily change forgotten passwords
■ let the administrator propagate user list changes to and from remote post offices
■ be administered and run from any client on the system

**Tip:** When choosing PC-based LAN E-mail, look for programs that don't need lots of drive mapping or CONFIG.SYS changes.

**Tip:** Look for a program that offers lots of reports and diagnostics on system maintenance and performance.

Directory maintenance is the source of a lot of administrative work. This can be eased in systems that have some automatic propagation tools and software that can share the LAN's user database (such as the NetWare Bindery).

### Ease of administrator training

Training comes in at least two flavors: training individual users and training group and regional administrators. The main E-mail administrator is not always responsible for both, but can be. Every bit of work the E-mail provider gives in training is work you don't have to do. Ideally, the provider will offer training classes, support materials, and so on. The minimum requirement should be well-written user and administrator manuals and tutorials. Documentation teamed with classes and sample programs for the users and administrators are very important. All training material should be easy to use and not to difficult to learn.

### Powerful administrative tools

Good software tools will go along way in administrating and troubleshooting your E-mail system. Consider the following questions:

- How do the administrative tools compare within each of the programs?
- How much do they automate routine tasks?
- Do they work on all post-office servers of a network or only on one at a time?
- Do they handle special cases such as remote and gateway connections?
- Do you need to shut the system down to use the tools?

The more automated the tools, the more you'll know about your E-mail's efficiency and the less you'll have to do of the slow and tedious tasks by yourself.

### Security concerns

Security is important to users, who want to know their messages won't be read by anyone but the intended recipient. Security is even more important to administrators, who have the tools to read any unencrypted messages on the system. Some questions to ask potential E-mail suppliers are:

- What provisions does your E-mail make for providing administrator security?
- Can the system be sabotaged by a typical user?
- Are the user directories and administrative directories separate (as they should be)?
- Is there password protection for administrative utilities and commands?
- Are the administrative tools and commands hidden from the users?

### Synchronized platform versions

Most E-mail programs these days run on more than one computer or operating system. In other words, on more than one "platform." As an administrator, your ideal E-mail system would run on multiple platforms—because you'll have users for each and every platform—that look and act the same on all platforms.

"Synchronized" features are those available on all platforms and updated at the same time for each platform. This includes both user and administrator tools. Often there will be more difference in administrator synchronization: The administration tools run only on PC-based DOS or Windows systems or Macintosh.

Having interfaces match as closely as possible from platform to platform is also an advantage. Naturally, they won't match completely: The different types of operating-system software generally won't permit that. But the more they do match, the easier your job will be in training and supporting users and administrators.

### Easy gateway installation and maintenance

Gateways can be the weakest link in an E-mail system. They often come from a different vendor and that vendor may be a small company that is unable to test the gateway as thoroughly as you might like. Also, gateways can be difficult to develop because they attempt to convert information from one environment to another when those environments may be obscured by lack of published details. Information is sometimes intentionally withheld because companies make a lot of money on add-on gateways and want you to continue buying their wares.

The result of inadequately tested gateways is that a message's sender address could be corrupted and the undeliverable message could languish at the gateway. Look for gateways that offer to let you set a preferred hub or host for routing messages with unknown destinations. Also look for gateways that come from the same vendor as your E-mail and have remote access and dial-in capabilities.

Don't buy gateways without carefully considering what you'll need and use most. Each gateway cost thousands of dollars for the software alone, plus the computer to run them and the maintenance expenses. For large volumes of mail moving to and from host-mail systems, you may want to use the Soft-Switch gateway. This is expensive but operates with most E-mail systems.

 **Tip:** A system that can update directories across gateways is nice, but hard to find.

MHS is becoming the most common method for message movement between LAN E-mail systems, connecting software as different as cc:Mail, Microsoft Mail, Higgins, and Da Vinci eMail. Insist on some MHS compliance or support first before worrying about any other protocol, such as X.400. However, if you don't need a LAN-to-LAN connection, then having MHS requirements will mean more difficulty installing and probably more expense for your system.

Any system that supports the X.400 standard should in theory be able to communicate with any other X.400-supporting system. However, X.400 is complex, so expect some deviations from this absolute. X.400 is being adopted much more slowly than proponents suggested, so don't feel that you must use it immediately, nor pay a lot for X.400 compliance. X.500 is still in the exploratory stages—don't put much emphasis into having a system that conforms to it.

**Tip:** European use of X.400 and X.500 is far ahead of U.S. use. If you're communicating to Europe, pay more attention to complying with these standards.

### Service and support issues

Support comes in many, many forms. Most free E-mail programs come without support: You're in charge of figuring it out and keeping it running. Otherwise known as YOYO: you're on your own.

At the other end of the scale, some commercial programs offer:

- telephone support—permanent, toll-free, 24-hours, 7-days-a-week
- fax support—fax a question, they'll call or fax an answer
- BBS support—get on-line with CompuServe or some other bulletin board and type a question; soon you'll see a reply
- in-person support—they'll send people out to train your people and help you troubleshoot problems

 **Tip:** Immediate service and support are more critical in E-mail than in almost any other computer application.

Sometimes the support costs are built into the original price and sometimes they are separate. Sometimes you pay for higher-quality support, such as priority in-calling queues. And, sometimes, you must pay separately for gateway support. Ask what you're getting, and scrutinize the answers carefully.

Support may be the single most critical element. Features are of little use if they can't be used. Administration is worthless if it takes too long. A simple program that's always up and running is worth more than one supposedly loaded with power and performance, but is frequently down for repairs.

## Summary

To choose E-mail:

- start with a strategy (built from your goals, history, geography, and current systems)
- keep the big questions in mind (architecture, host vs. LAN vs. public-service, scalability, and so on)
- compare user features (from basic ease of use through advanced scheduling utilities)
- compare administrator features (to automate the maintenance and optimization of the system)

Look for E-mail that is reliable, scalable, and easy to use, and you'll be in good shape. The most important aspects of E-mail to most buyers fall in about this order:

- easy learning
- basic messaging features
- consistency within and across platforms
- documentation
- gateway support
- file-attachment support
- ease of administration
- security
- easy installation
- price for performance

**Tip:** In practice, most programs offer a fair amount of reliability and few are difficult to use. The biggest differences turn-up in quality and accessibility of product support. Make that a priority in your choices.

Remember that even as you and everyone else wait for exciting advances such as universal directories and transparent multimedia document exchange, what really matters in E-mail is that everyone uses it and that it always is available. E-mail is only effective if it is easy to use and reliable.

# CHAPTER THREE

# Using E-mail

Some estimates suggest that while only 5 percent of the salaries of office workers is spent on word processing, 25 percent is spent by managers and professionals on communications. Although this surely varies from organization to organization, it indicates that great productivity savings could come from E-mail and messaging. The question is, How do you use E-mail to improve productivity? It is also quite possible to spend more time sending messages than before, and messages could be anything but direct contributors to productivity.

E-mail is not just regular mail gone electronic. Its speed, its connection to computers, and its direct link to people of all social and economic levels make it a new medium, a new game. You'll quickly discover that there are some new rules specific to this game, as well as some direct application of old rules that hold for any communication. This section covers such subjects, offering you ideas on making your E-mail as efficient, smooth, and courteous as possible. As Quarterman points out, "Networks have effects on their users beyond their immediate practical uses." There may be social and structural changes from extensive use of E-mail.

 **Tip:** Remember that a new communication channel means more than just a different way to swap memos.

## Efficiency

E-mail will make the maximum contribution to productivity if it is put together the right way. Modeling it only on what the people are already doing, just "electronicating" their current behavior, probably won't reach that end. Certainly you want to observe and ask people how they work and what they want, but often they'll discover new and different uses they had not previously contemplated.

One question is when to use E-mail and when to use conferencing software. Surely most organizations could use a system that provides both, so offer both. Conferences are best for nonurgent communications and for providing details to a group, but they generally lead to private messages between specific members of the conference.

Conference only when there are at least 10 or so users. This minimum, however, can be cut further if a good moderator keeps the conference moving and all the users contributing. Also, if the members of the conference have expressed direct interest, a smaller minimum may succeed. Conference if there are many participants in one discussion, and if they are separated geographically or by different schedules. Computer conferences can handle more people than conference calls or face-to-face meetings. One person can even attend multiple computer conferences at the same time. Conferencing leaves a written record, one great advantage over face-to-face meetings.

 **Tip:** For any messaging technology, encourage its use for all sorts of tasks. People who have successfully used a system will spread it most effectively.

Remember that some work requires face-to-face communication. Messaging can only be used along with other communications media, not as a complete replacement. In fact, telephone calls and paper-mail messages often increase among users of an E-mail system. Although the system brings users into contact with many more people, including some a long-distance call away, people's instinct will be to have some direct, voice, or even face-to-face contact with those people. Paper mail may increase because of a need to send large documents that don't easily fit in an E-mail system, and travel may increase as people want direct contact.

One great advantage of a computer conference, when compared to a face-to-face meeting or even a conference call on the phone, is that no person need be shut out or shouted down. Certainly shyness or fear of appearing stupid can still inhibit people's replies, but they are far more equal than in person where the most glib, largest, and best-looking may exert more influence over who speaks and who does not. In the computer conference, no one must wait a turn to contribute—anyone may contribute at any time. People that are quickest-on-their-feet are rewarded in face-to-face meetings, and even in conference calls, but much less so in computer conferences.

In fact, E-mail and conferencing gain some advantages in the absence of physical cues. The recipients are forced to place more emphasis on the idea than the person. (Some systems even permit anonymity—contributions under assumed names.) This often leads to greater candor from the participants than they might show otherwise, and more willingness to criticize weak ideas.

Some people believe that E-mail and computer-conference members may contribute more without reflecting on their rank in the organization. Some people think this doesn't prove to be true in practice. (Most systems still present the contributor's name, and within an organization others will generally know who people are and where they are in the organization hierarchy.) Lying, which is often reinforced with nonverbal signals, is more difficult in some ways as well. Computer conferences and E-mail also make it easier to both correspond angrily or to ignore such "flames."

Messaging is generally better than face-to-face discussions or even telephone discussions when used among people with different native languages. People working in a new language are more commonly comfortable with written communications, where they can take more time to be sure of their translation.

**Tip:** Learn to quickly scan mail or bulletin-board messages that may contain some information for you, but may also just be junk mail. If you repeatedly receive junk mail from some person or organization, politely request that they stop sending it.

Some companies insist that E-mail be used only for business messages, not for anything personal. The managers think personal messages are a waste of the company's investment in the software and hardware, and a waste of the workers' time. However, those costs will probably be less than the return that comes from having a workforce comfortable and engaged with the E-mail process.

**Tip:** Don't restrict or forbid using the E-mail system for personal messages.

## Ethics

Some E-mail habits you should practice are points of etiquette, for instance, trying to be courteous to others. Some are more serious than that and involve ethics, such as avoiding illegal or harmful acts. E-mail may not seem a likely place to be able to break the law or injure someone, but in fact, it offers many opportunities.

Here are some rules to follow to keep ethical:

- Don't damage property. Avoid damaging any of the software or hardware you use, from your computer or terminal to the communications lines and programs on them. The most probable way you could damage a system is by introducing a virus or worm program.

- Don't damage data. Information can be as or more important than the physical equipment or software. Often it is harder to replace and more critical to an individual's or organization's operation. Certainly don't intentionally view, move, change, or delete anyone's data. Again, avoid viruses and worms—practice safe computing.

**Tip:** Even a "harmless" virus can eat up system performance and cost time to remove from the system. Those harms are just as real as erasing data.

■ Don't steal. Follow the copyright laws. Don't quote something at length if it is copyrighted or covered by some kind of license. Cite your sources; give credit.

■ Don't invade privacy. Don't forward or distribute even part of a private message to you unless you have specific permission. Don't read other people's mail. If you receive a message meant for someone else, forward it to that person and send a message to the sender about what happened.

■ Don't pretend to be someone else.

■ Use the system efficiently. Even in circumstances where you're not charged for each message, someone is paying the freight to keep the system running. The recipients of your messages must spend their time to read your missives. This does not mean to skimp on E-mail, nor to avoid frivolous uses. It just means you should generally stick to the point, whether that's the current work project or the party coming next weekend. Don't send huge messages unless necessary, and don't send copies to people who don't want them.

■ Don't send dangerous information. Of course, you can and should discuss any politics you want. Free speech is a wonderful thing. However, don't post credit card numbers (that's just stealing from the individuals, the companies, the card companies, or the merchants, whomever ends up swallowing the cost). Don't describe how to build a bomb or commit a crime.

■ Notify management of any security holes you happen upon. E-mail is not just a luxury to most people, it is vital to the business, the hospital, and the individual. Work can stop without it and lives can be lost. Help keep it running—and running safely.

■ Choose a good password. You may think your password is only your business. Not true. If someone learns or guesses your password, he'll get access to the system. Then they can send false messages, confuse network traffic, possibly even destroy data, all injuries to others on the system (and possibly to yourself). Choose a password that's not obvious (don't use your middle name, your address, your social security number, your birthdate, the word "password," "sesame," and so on). Then guard that password: Don't give it away to anyone. Finally, change it regularly.

## Privacy and Censorship

Without data encryption it is easy to snoop and read other people's messages. Even with encryption it is possible, with administrative passwords or with a network analysis tool. That means anyone running an E-mail operation will be involved in questions of privacy and censorship.

Privacy is largely a user concern of: Can administrators, and so the organization's management, read our mail? The law in this area is not entirely clear, not having kept up fully with the electronic age. There have already been some cases, including a famous incident at Epson America, where employees accused managers of nefariously reading their mail. Management has countered in such cases with three defenses:

■ We didn't do it.
■ We did it only as much as necessary.
■ We did it and have the full right to do so.

There's not much to say about the "we didn't do it" defense: the outcome will depend on the facts of the particular case. Legally, it isn't clear if the defenses "we did it only as much as necessary" and "we did it and have the full right to do so" are valid. A private E-mail system is not the same thing as traditional mail. Management can argue that it has been set up for the organization's use and benefit, so they have as much right to police its use as they do to police the use of organization automobiles and buildings.

There are two contradictory pieces of advice you'll run into concerning E-mail privacy rights: Some experts will tell managers to state their intentions up front (whether they reserve the right to read mail or not); others will tell managers to not state their intentions, so as not to form a legally binding position. A few experts even advise E-mail managers to not back up E-mail so there won't be any trail to be held against them. This can be implemented automatically, with a kill clock, which erases all E-mail files after a certain time. Your own approach to privacy must be made in concert with your philosophy and your lawyers.

Censorship is also a potent issue for E-mail managers. People may say things on-line to which other people object. If you delete these, you can be accused of censorship, or ignoring the right to free press. If you don't delete controversial items, you can be accused of harboring or encouraging racist, sexist, or even obscene language and thoughts.

A famous case involved the Prodigy commercial-service E-mail system. A Prodigy user made comments that some interpreted as anti-Semitic; others objected. Prodigy caught flak from both sides, either for censorship or for tolerating outrageous behavior.

 **Tip:** Censorship is more of an issue in conferencing than in person-to-person E-mail.

Your administration will need to make some decisions about what language will be accepted and how it will be dealt with:

- Will the unacceptable messages be deleted, without further comment?
- Will conversants or conferencers be told what was deleted?
- Will the contributor of the offending piece be asked to rewrite it?
- Will the contributor be sanctioned in any way?

Post the policies where people can't help but read them, perhaps in an initial sign-on message.

The Electronic Communication Privacy Act of 1986 sets out the privacy rights of users and the guidelines for investigators to use when monitoring E-mail. To tap E-mail, an outside investigator must get a court order and prove to a judge there is probable cause the individual to be snooped has committed or will commit a felony, and that the captured E-mail will give evidence of this.

## Etiquette

Proper etiquette is an important facet of most communications—and that doesn't mean constantly adopting a stuffy attitude. Rather, it means using the form and style appropriate to the occasion. Etiquette is even more important in E-mail than in telephone calls or in-person communication. After all, the E-mail recipient does not have the benefit of voice cues, facial cues, immediate feedback, social situation, and social structures. Those elements can do everything from shade a meaning to completely reverse the intentions of the words used. Remember that though E-mail may seem like a cross between paper mail and a phone call, it isn't either. It has rules of its own.

 **Tip:** A good way to learn E-mail etiquette is to follow the lead of experienced users. They will have already stumbled through discovering what works and what doesn't on-line.

Here are some etiquette rules of thumb to follow when using E-mail:

■ Remember that although E-mail is welcome and vital to some, it is a bother or even frightening to others. Remember too that E-mail flattens corporate and social hierarchies. You can write to anyone, often without the waystation of clearing that person's assistant. (Most people still answer their own E-mail.)

■ Sending messages can be addictive: Don't overdo it because of the thrill of the technology. Every message you send means work for someone else, who must read, consider, and deal with the message. You're threatening them with information overload (or just noise overload, if the messages aren't important enough to be considered real information).

■ Be brief. People probably won't read a long message or they may misunderstand it. Keep your work to a  page or two maximum.

■ Don't copy too much of a previous message. Because it is so easy to cut-and-paste a piece of a previous message into a new one, there's a great temptation to copy paragraphs or even pages to provide context for the reply. If you do this, use as little as possible, perhaps only a title or a line.

■ Supply titles, subjects, and keywords if your system allows. Even if these are officially "optional," you should always supply them. Doing so will help the recipient recognize what messages are about. That means recipients can manage their inbox more efficiently. It will also make the messages easier to dig up later from archives. You'd probably appreciate the same done for you.

 **Tip:** Make reading and considering your messages easy: Always put a subject or title on the message that briefly, but clearly, explains what it is about.

■ Only post messages in a bulletin-board topic or conference where they're relevant. (You'll soon see how annoying it is to see the same message posted many different places, both relevant and completely inappropriate. Each time you end up reading at least part of the message, wasting your time.) In other words, don't "cross-post."

■ Don't make messages "urgent" when they don't need to be. The "Boy that Cried Wolf" story could change in the future to "the Boy Who Labeled all Messages Urgent and Registered."

■ Identify yourself appropriately. If you belong to some organization, have an interest, or have a background or expertise that the reader could benefit from knowing, out with it.

■ Think of the easiest way for your recipients to respond, such as through their favorite E-mail public service, and try to use that when contacting them.

■ Don't send a file when a simple message is enough. Files mean downloading, storing, loading an application, and opening the file—lots of work for your recipient.

■ When you send a file, put your E-mail address into it if possible. That will save the recipient time when replying to you.

■ Don't use receipts and carbon copies unless necessary. Receipts are insulting—they may imply you don't trust the person to read your message. Carbon copies quickly become routine, leading to lots of extra, useless messages in everyone's box.

■ Don't read mail that wasn't meant for you. Normally this won't happen because your mailbox should only receive messages meant for you. However, if someone wrongly addresses a message, or you happen upon a message while on someone else's PC or terminal, use the same consideration you would with traditional mail.

■ Don't ignore messages from all but a fixed set of people, even in your quest to manage your own message overload. You may miss important information if you follow this path too far.

■ Reading messages can be addictive: Don't overdo it. If you're unnecessarily checking your mail 10 times a day, you could be slowing the network for others or bothering others by interrupting more important business.

 **Tip:** Be courteous, even when communicating with someone you know well.

■ Avoid "flaming," sending excited words that could be interpreted as abusive, raving, or rude. Be careful—it is easy to get excited, angry, or otherwise emotional on some topic in E-mail. Flames can scorch the reader, even when you only intend to make a strong statement, not to criticize or harm. Misunderstanding is easy to come by on E-mail because of the lack of physical signals.

 **Tip:** Before you start any sort of excited digression or tirade, you may write something such as "*FLAME ON!*" to warn the reader. This is a rather informal use, however.

■ Don't criticize publicly unless absolutely necessary. Always use personal mail first to clarify, pursue, and if necessary, criticize. Respond to an idea, not to the person sending it. Read any other responses to a message in a bulletin board or conference before adding your own. You may be repeating what has already been said.

 **Tip:** Don't respond in anger. Cool off, then respond.

■ Give anyone the benefit of the doubt. If a message seems outrageous or unfair, quite likely it wasn't intended that way. Even if it was, responding harshly will do little more than escalate emotions.

 **Tip:** Be encouraging and polite to everyone, and especially to new users.

■ Assume that your messages will be around forever. Don't worry about their style and grammar for that reason, only about any negative, insulting, or libelous comments you may make. It is easy for others to copy, store, resurrect, and forward anything you write in E-mail. Only write things you'd be willing to see on the cover of tomorrow's newspaper.

 **Tip:** Remember that people are prone to being far more aggressive in their E-mail than they would ever be face-to-face. Be generous with others because of this tendency.

## Style

Use the appropriate messaging forum: E-mail, bulletin board, or conferencing. Tailor your messages to your recipients. Use a language, style, allusions, and technical terms they'll understand. Avoid subjects that will be taboo with a particular audience. Observe the tradition in your organization and follow it. If E-mail is a replacement for formal memos, you should follow suit, but you might suggest to those in charge that it would be better off as a replacement for meetings in the hallway, quick exchanges of current information and ideas. Don't be too informal—watch how others use it.

Follow the style at your organization, but if possible, feel free to use sentence fragments and very short messages of only a few words. Don't always think of E-mail as business letters, but as a replacement for quick notes in the margin of letters you've received, as quick voice-mail messages, or as correspondence in passing. Though you don't need to worry much about grammar, you should check your spelling. E-mail saves time over traditional correspondence for many reasons, one of them being that you needn't be as careful to make it perfect before sending it.

Be direct. Be brief. Don't overdo off-line composition of long-winded replies. Be spontaneous—reply quickly, that's part of the advantage of E-mail. If possible, avoid official salutations ("Dear So and So") and sign-offs ("Yours whateverly"). Just make your point briefly and courteously and end the message. The recipient will know who it's from—the header tells all.

 **Tip:** Don't add to the message information that is already in the header, such as the sender name, date, time, and subject.

Follow the technical rules of your system. Some limit messages to 80 character widths. If you use more than 80, your lines could wrap to the next line as partial lines, making them difficult to read. Another possibility is that they'll get cut off, making them impossible to read. Similarly, don't use "control characters" or other special information in a file that could confuse the system. They may appear in other systems as unreadable characters or ones you didn't intend.

Avoid tabs when possible. They can be transformed into a different number of spaces in different systems. Avoid proportional fonts when trying to set a right margin. Few E-mail systems offer proportional fonts, so your margins will be changed. Don't add lots of space to a message. That will increase your costs and will take longer for the recipient to read. Do use paragraph breaks to help organize a message. Don't use all capitals. In some E-mail circles it means shouting, but some inexpensive computers only offer uppercase, so the effect may be unintentional. Avoid it if you can.

**Tip:** MESSAGES COMPLETELY IN UPPERCASE are annoying to read.

 **Tip:** Ways to emphasize part of a message that's only in ASCII text:

- *place asterisks around it*
- s p a c e   i t
- add remarks <jokingly>
- add smilies (see following)

## Kawasaki's Laws of E-mail

(My apologies to Guy Kawasaki who does not frame these as laws. They are great ideas, though.)

- First Law: No message longer than 100 words.
- Second Law: No response longer that 1/5 of original.
- Third Law: GIGO—Get in and Get out.

Realize that some people will be put off by the lack of hierarchy in E-mail and that some will be put off by its technology. Label your humor and sarcasm in some way, to make sure others know that's what you're doing.

 **Tip:** E-mail unto others as you would have them E-mail unto you.

## Informality and Smilies

Because E-mail messages only carry text, they are stripped of the information that humans convey with facial expressions and gestures. Even telephone calls can get more across than E-mail because of the variety of pitches, accents, and pacings we naturally use when speaking. Today's more sophisticated E-mail

156

systems can have graphics, sound, or video attachments, but the main message is almost always pure text, with at most a few font changes or text stylings.

How do you get your tone or feelings across then? How do you break E-mail messages out of the cold letters and into a richer communication? How do you convey irony, sarcasm, anger, and other emotional content?

First, you save messages with important emotional content for a telephone call or face-to-face meeting. E-mail won't work for all situations.

Second, you write carefully to make sure the emotions come across in the text. This means reading what you have written before sending it. Read it with another's eye, as if you were coming to it virginal, without any knowledge of the background or context. Remember, even if the original recipient understands what you're getting at, your message may be quickly copied for others who don't know the messages or events that led to it.

Third, use "smilies." These are codes built from text and punctuation. They try to approximate facial expressions. Smilies have a long history in E-mail and are truly beloved by some on-line computer fanatics. They are not kosher in most professional E-mail: Save them for communications with friends you know won't mind or with others who have used smilies in messages to you.

 **Tip:** Only use smilies for informal E-mail. They can look quite amateurish and silly in business communications.

Following are some examples of smilies. If you want more, you can cobble them together yourself or turn to one of the surprisingly long dictionaries of smilies collected by E-mail enthusiasts. For example, Guy Kawasaki, a columnist for *MacUser* magazine, has such a dictionary. Ken Schoenberg has his own on the America Online service.

Most smilies are meant to be funny and start with a colon as a sideways pair of eyes, adding other punctuation to show lips, nose, eyebrows, and other facial elements. Other smilies are abbreviations of phrases.

| Smilie | Meaning | Smilie | Meaning |
| --- | --- | --- | --- |
| :-) | happy | :p | sticking tongue out |
| :-( | sorry | :T | keeping a straight face |
| :-(( | unhappy | :) | smile |
| >-) | irony | :( | frown |
| ;-) | wink | :-(O) | yelling |
| :) | happy | $-) | just won lottery |
| :D | very happy | =:-) | hosehead |
| :( | sad | :-'= | spitting out tobacco |
| (:( | very sad | :D | laughing |
| :/) | Not funny | :* | kiss |
| :" | pursing lips | :X | lips are sealed |
| :1 | smirk | [:-) | wearing a walkman |
| :| | disgusted | :P | sticking out tongue |
| :X | kiss | [] | hug |
| :< | forlorn | LOL | laughing out loud |
| :? | licking lips | OTF | on the floor (laughing) |
| :O | shouting | ROTFL | rolling on the floor |
| :V | shouting (profile) | | (laughing) |
| :v | talking | \V/ | vulcan greeting |
| :J | tongue-in-cheek | RSN | real soon now |
| (:... | crying | | |
| :# | censored | | |
| :w | speaking with a forked tongue | | |

You may use smilies anywhere in a message, but most often they are tacked on at the end of a line, paragraph, or the message itself. Much as a question mark tells you that the sentence just finished is meant as an inquiry, a smilie often comes at the end of a thought to tell you the emotional tone or intent of the words.

## Summary

Using E-mail means more than setting up the hardware and software and letting people swap information. E-mail is a different communication medium from phones or faxes or meetings. People may react to it quite differently from other media: They may send messages that are too informal, too aggressive, or otherwise inappropriate, even if they wouldn't behave that way on the phone or fax. You need to know this when using E-mail or when training others to use it.

# CHAPTER FOUR

# Managing E-mail

This chapter discusses managing your E-mail system and provides answers to many questions. Directions are provided in somewhat the order you should approach them, starting with the overall strategy. Many of the particular suggestions apply to some but not all E-mail packages. For example, many apply only to administrators working with server packages, and so will be superflous to users with client packages.

Even after you choose your E-mail system you'll be faced with many questions:

- What is the best way to install it?
- How do you achieve maximum efficiency?
- How do you train new users?
- How do you control costs?
- How do you protect data security?

## Have a Strategy

Any network installation, including E-mail, requires planning. Individual PCs can be set up somewhat haphazardly, and perhaps the worst result will be inefficient operation. Networking or E-mail management without planning will probably crash, not working at all. So even after you've chosen an architecture and approach, as suggested in Chapter 2, plan how you'll handle all the stages of management and administration.

**Tip:** E-mail management is rarely difficult, but it does require time and expense. Don't ignore it.

Plan so you can make additions with as few changes as possible. Don't think of your E-mail decision as a one-time event. It may seem easier to install some basic E-mail for your group now, and not worry about the future. Don't do it. The decision you make now will affect decisions you will almost certainly be making in the future. Remember how important your choice of an education was—the courses you took and the schools you chose affected the rest of your working life,

Actually, changing your E-mail foundation might not be that extensive or expensive. Computer technology ages so quickly that you can't spend a lifetime with the foundation you choose now anyway. But an appropriate decision now can save you significant money and extra hard work in the future.

What does it mean to have a strategy? Think of more than the initial users and their simple, short messages. Consider such questions as:

■ Who else might want to connect to your users?

■ Do you need to communicate with other colleagues, customers, clients, suppliers, or the world at large?

■ Will users want to connect to a fax, a telex, a public-service E-mail, a company mainframe, or other company E-mail LANs?

■ Do users need access to databases, news sources, conferences for real-time meetings, et cetera? Most complete E-mail systems combine messaging, database access, and bulletin-board features.

■ What else might they want to send? Consider longer messages, word processor documents, spreadsheet files, graphics, sound, voice, images, video, documents, and money?

■ What other technologies may relate to E-mail? Will you want to integrate with voice mail, fax, portable computers, and/or pagers?

 **Tip:** When creating your strategy, keep in mind that you want to work with or from your organization's current culture and structure.

 **Tip:** You may need to create a PC front end such as a menuing system that would allow easy access to the key databases, to E-mail, and to the bulletin boards, for people who did not want to learn all the ins and outs of E-mail, database SQL searches, and bulletin-board commands. It would also let people move information from one location to another, such as finding something in the database and forwarding that in a message to some E-mail recipient.

Architecture is a key word here. You need to think about the "architecture" of the information system you're building as explained in Chapter 2. If you're making a global architecture for an organization with divisions or groups spread widely you may want to use a backbone E-mail network to tie local LAN E-mail and bulletin board systems together. Backbones, a high-speed communication channel for programs and messaging, can make sense even for medium-size organizations. A backbone could be based on the X.400 standard, on IBM SNADS, or on some other well-accepted protocol. You may even choose a proprietary network, but that will limit your choices for gateways and other connections. Even small messaging systems can benefit from planning an underlying architecture. This is because many small systems eventually become part of larger systems, if only to reach telex and fax, and sometimes to link to EDI and other such time-saving, cost-saving ideas.

When planning LAN E-mail, look for a package that can run across many LANs and that can upgrade. Sure, you can make pretty much anything work with anything else, but the questions of cost, difficulty, and gateway maintenance argue for keeping the overall system simple.

## Phasing E-mail In

Unless you're dealing with a very small organization, say only a dozen people on a single-server LAN, you should install E-mail in phases. That will help see you through technical bugs as well as give you insights into user issues such as training.

The first stage could be a trial of some E-mail software or system. Work with relatively few users, perhaps no more than 50. These should be people who are committed to using E-mail, so you don't have the burden at this point of convincing newcomers just to sign on and try it. The goal is to get a feel for what users in your organization need, and for how administration will be delegated and handled.

**Tip:** Be careful, even with the trial stage; warn users that the system may change a little or a lot before it is finished. Users tend to fall in like or even love with whatever they have. If the trial fails or you simply want to try some other approach, taking the trial system away may be tougher than you expected.

After the trial period could come a limited stage phase with more users and more connections to other systems. Finally you would move to a thorough stage phase. I don't call this complete because chances are you'll be continually modifying and enhancing the system—it will never be truly complete.

## Configure It to Balance Speed and Expense

If an E-mail system is large or has servers that are geographically separated from one another, you won't want to have every server exchanging messages or directories with every other server. It's not efficient. You'll want to configure the system so that mail follows certain routes, conserving on long-distance calls and gateways between separate systems.

You have a choice when installing your E-mail: do you want a system where all the post offices are equal or one in which a central post office is a hub?

The most important parts of designing an E-mail network of more than one server is defining the sites and the bridges. It is often best to have all servers within a single Local network be part of the same site. Servers separated by slow, intermittent, or expensive connections should be in different sites. One popular routing method is to connect multiple sites through a central hub. This reduces the number of network connections you need. With a central hub, sites can exchange mail though they have no direct connection between them.

A "site" is a set of servers that will automatically exchange messages and user lists. This could be a single server, or a number of servers within a region. Servers in separate sites do not automatically exchange messages and directories. Instead, bridges between sites carry all the messages and directories between those sites.

## Peer-to-Peer vs Master/Slave

For up to five post offices (servers), a system where all post offices are equal is probably best. This is called a "peer-to-peer" architecture because all of the servers are peers. It has the advantages of quick delivery (only one "hop" is necessary, the message only moves from one server to one other) and simple addressing (no indirect post office names are needed in the address).

For more than five post offices, a system where each post office is connected to only one other—the hub post office—is often best. This "master/slave" architecture cuts down the number of connections necessary, cutting costs and increasing efficiency. After all, as the number of post offices climbs arithmetically (1, 2, 3, 4, 5, etc.), the number of connections or calls for all to reach all others climbs geometrically (1, 2, 4, 8, 16, etc.). With a hub, all connections between the "slaves" are indirect—when a messaged is sent to the hub, the hub sends it on to the recipient slave.

This master/slave or hub architecture can be extended for larger systems, with these pieces:

- *Remotes*— remote individual systems (not connected to a LAN) from a network
- *Local post offices*—single servers
- *Regional hubs*—masters to locals, but slaves to a central hub
- *Central hub*—the master to regional hubs

Some rules of thumb when configuring the system:

- All remotes should be assigned to a single, local post office.
- All local post offices should be assigned to a regional hub.
- Each regional hub should be connected to the central hub.

The central hub carries messages between regions only. It may, in fact, carry only a small amount of mail. But it will also handle many directory-change messages and could handle some system diagnostics and reporting utilities.

 **Tip:** The central hub may have performance and disk space available to handle directory work and mailing list tasks.

 **Tip:** Most messages stay within a post office or region. Only a fraction travel across regional hubs or the central hub.

**Tip:** When you disconnect a gateway or bridge, remember to inform any other system administrators whose system this may affect—such as whoever is responsible for the other end of the gateway or bridge.

Bridging sites permits more complete use of all network operations and provides faster and more immediate transmission of messages than a gateway can. If a site is bridged to another site, and that bridge is set up to import and export directories, your users can send messages directly to recipients on the other site without any special addressing. All they need do is find an address in the directory. Users on the other site can similarly send mail easily to recipients in your site. But if the bridge is not set up to import and export directories, you may need to create a special addressing form and have the administrator handle part of the addressing task. In a configuration such as this, only one copy of the message crosses the bridge, thereby cutting traffic.

 **Tip:** Configuring a system requires the cooperation of the administrators at both ends of the bridge.

## Designing Bridges

Where you put bridges depends on what you want to accomplish in your routing configuration. To put a bridge between two sites you must have a bridge server in each site. Naturally, this means that if you're bridging to a site administered by some other person, you'll need to ask that person which server will handle the bridge. You'll also need that person's cooperation in deciding whether each side will import or export directory information. If not, then you may need to set up some special addressing procedure to get messages to the site.

The bridge server will carry more traffic than other servers in the site, so it's smart to choose either one of the faster servers, or one of the servers with the fewest mail users. If the site has bridges to more than one other site, you may want to choose a different server for each bridge.

Any more than one bridge between two sites will cut efficiency. You rarely need to worry about this. It tends to happen only when sites are merged. In that case, the two sites may both have a bridge to some third site. To keep an efficient system, you'll want to eliminate one of the bridges.

## Gateways

Gateways are almost always separate programs from the server or client portions of LAN E-mail. They'll have their own installation procedures and maintenance needs. For example, gateways have many settings that administrators can fine-tune. One of these is the connection frequency, the number of times and the hours at which the gateway calls other gateways for messages.

A gateway isn't on all the time. Typically it acts as a mailbag, collecting messages headed for the distant system, then calling that system and delivering the messages in a bunch. The administrator determines when that connection takes place and may use several criteria for making that connection such as:

- when a certain number of messages are waiting
- when an urgent message is waiting
- at the same hour of every day
- at regular intervals during the day

or some combination of these factors.

The administrator's choices should balance cost and delivery speed. More frequent connections will increase speed and cost. If the gateway makes a local call, cost may not be significant, but if the call is international, costs could add up quickly. A very expensive connection might even be set for a single, middle-of-the-night call each day to reduce the cost.

 **Tip:** You'll have an easier time getting support for your gateways if you can buy them from the same company that sold you your E-mail.

When setting the connection timing for a gateway, you'll want to follow a few rules of thumb. Start with a single, overnight call. When that's not enough, move to twice a day, then hourly, or twice-hourly as demand proves itself necessary.

It doesn't make sense for a Gateway A (a hypothetical gateway) to call a Gateway B (another hypothetical) for messages if those two gateways just finished a call from B to A. The messages will already have been transferred. You need to coordinate gateway timing with that of gateways on other systems.

 **Tip:** Set some minimum number of messages waiting before a call is made or some calls will be made for no reason at all. You can plan on the other gateway calling you if there are messages incoming. Don't set the minimum too high or the call will not be timely and may be of little use to your user.

Some gateways require that you assign gateway rights for individuals or servers to use that gateway. You may want only some departments or individuals to have access to the gateway.

 **Tip:** Gateways are sometimes run on their own dedicated PCs, computers with no other tasks. Sometimes they are run on access servers, computers also running other programs. If your system is set up to run its gateways on an access server, you should set the various gateways to work at different times, to spread the load on that server.

Naturally each gateway is different, so you'll need to check your gateway's manuals to see what particular settings are allowed. Ask the technical support people what settings they would advise for your situation.

 **Tip:** Most gateways will keep a record of calls tried and calls completed.

## Client RAM

Client systems need a certain amount of disk memory and chip memory to run efficiently; the amount will depend on the size of the E-mail program. It may also depend on the other programs you might want to run at the same time.

In PCs running DOS, for instance, LAN E-mail programs often have a TSR utility—that stands for Terminate and Stay Resident—that needs to fit into memory at the same time as an application program, such as a word processor or spreadsheet. The smaller the TSR, the easier the fit, since the RAM will be limited to at most 640K in a DOS PC.

## Include More Than Computer Expertise

Don't just employ computer experts to find and install the right E-mail. Build a team that includes systems experts, operations people, marketing pros, and engineering personnel. E-mail isn't just a matter of plugging in hardware and installing software. It is also a matter of creating and changing habits, adjusting work processes, allocating costs, and so on.

## Develop a Hierarchy of Administrators

You'll need several levels of administration responsibility on an E-mail system. At the top could be the MIS manager, responsible for all information systems in a company and the overall strategy. Next in the hierarchy could be the System Administrator, responsible for the computer networks in the organization. Then you could identify a network administrator who is in charge of keeping the network running.

Next you would want to identify a local post office administrator, responsible for managing a single server and its E-mail database. This person would be responsible for keeping the mailing lists for that server, and for managing the server's security and use of database space. Last but certainly not least would be the local administrator, who would be responsible for maintaining group mailing lists for a workgroup.

Each post office should have an administrator. This person is responsible for installing, maintaining, reconfiguring, and extending the E-mail network. This job takes time, mostly interacting with users, not handling the hardware and software. The administrator should be chosen from people who show an interest in E-mail, not those who just use it to get a quick message sent.

 **Tip:** When looking for a local administrator, look for a person who voluntarily helps in training, even when it is not part of their job.

The administrator is sometimes also the postmaster, though not necessarily. The postmaster is responsible for maintaining the directory, handling incompletely-addressed mail, and interacting with other postmasters (largely on directory questions).

Here are some typical administrative tasks:

- installing server software (which may include MHS)
- installing client software
- updating server and client software
- creating and modifying the directory
- creating mailing lists
- creating and installing forms
- backing up and restoring the message database file
- maintaining the server disk: defragmenting, optimizing
- protecting the system from viruses
- installing and configuring gateway programs

More detailed tasks may also include:

- starting accounts for users
- creating directory entries
- creating mailing lists
- creating bulletin boards

**Tip:** Have a substitute administrator ready to take charge, in case the regular administrator is out. Someone on site needs to be able to step in and handle emergencies.

 **Tip:** Remember to congratulate your administrator when things are running smoothly. Without problems, the administrator's role is rarely noticed and recognized.

## Include Users in Planning

Include the users, from all levels and vocations, in planning your E-mail system. Do this when first choosing, later when maintaining, and even later when expanding the system. Do this informally through questionnaires, and formally through user representatives on the planning and maintenance team.

## Have a Hero or Champion

Many E-mail systems have started small, with various departments or groups getting their own systems, then MIS eventually deciding to tie them together. Yours may have started that way, or may be starting with a corporate decision to use E-mail. Whether you're tying pieces together or building a framework from scratch, you'll have an easier time if you have an important someone in the organization behind you. And that means having the person behind you in more than authorizing your choices. This person must see the same vision you do for the future. This person must use E-mail actively, setting the standard for others to follow.

To convince Mr. or Ms. Hero you may need two things. First is a graphical user interface that makes the system easy enough to learn and use. Second could be adding direct access to corporate database information, such as personnel, accounting, or sales records. Database features can sometimes persuade a potential hero when messaging alone is not enough.

## Market the Idea of E-mail Internally

Some people will fear the new E-mail system. Others will be too busy to learn it. Some will learn a little and only use it a little. For your E-mail to succeed you need to have all of these people checking their mailboxes every day, and replying through E-mail. You need them looking for ways to cut their use of paper communications and to transfer their communications efforts to E-mail.

To really get these people to support E-mail, an order to "use E-mail" is not enough. You need to see them as "customers" of a new product, and do everything you can to stress its benefits and features. Use your company's marketing expertise, and budget money for an internal product campaign. Your champion or hero, as previously mentioned, will be your celebrity endorsement. You may need to go even farther; for example, offer awards, have news flashes about the service, do all the things you would do to catch the attention of customers outside the company to any other product and more.

 **Tip:** Changing habits can take years.

 **Tip:** Remember that E-mail is only fully successful if everyone uses it.

Some users won't know what took you so long in getting E-mail. They'll take to it immediately. But others will be reluctant, afraid of it or just too busy to learn it. You'll need to market the new system to these people.

 **Tip:** One of the best marketing devices for convincing people in the organization to use E-mail is to get important people to use it.

 **Tip:** Emphasize the efficiency in sending memos and letters via E-mail that are automatically filed, and stress how easy it is to send multiple copies at the same time.

**Tip:** If you're starting with a pilot project, make sure there are enough people on the system to make it practical. If you don't achieve a quorum, the system will be quickly bypassed by whatever other medium offers full reach to everyone in a workgroup or department.

## Connect Everyone

E-mail works best only if everyone uses it. This means that at the very least everyone must have access to it. Be sure to include *everyone*. Certainly you'll connect everyone that has a computer on the network. That's the easiest part. Then connect those with PCs that aren't yet on the network. Network them or give them access to remote connections. Then connect those who don't have PCs but could use them. Perhaps E-mail could be the final advantage to convince you to computerize these people. Then connect those outside the company who need to communicate to those inside. Use gateways, bridges, and public-service connections, whatever you need.

Finally, connect those who don't and won't have their own computers. Assign them mailboxes, and automate the process of printing any mail they get and delivering it to them as hard copy. Look for a way for them to reply via E-mail, perhaps through a postmaster or secretary.

## Remote Usage

Managing remote users means handling both individual dial-in users and gateways. The key is making sure that all such users and gateways are properly listed in the directory. Remote directory updates are often less automatic than those to post offices on the network. Remote changes may need to be manual.

Troubleshooting a remote system can be difficult because you may have only one phone line connecting it. That makes it impossible to talk to the remote user and have the remote system hooked to the E-mail at the same time. When possible, check portable remote systems before they leave the main facility.

**Tip:** You may want to have a gateway regularly make a call to a remote site, if that site is important enough.

## Limit File Attachment Size

Set a limit on the size of the message being transmitted to a remote site. This maximum will depend on the modem speed. Reasonable limits might be 600K for a 2400bps modem; 2.5MB for a 9600bps mode. That's an hour for each. By using data compression a 9600bps modem could move as much as 10MB of data per hour.

 **Tip:** Note that many gateways can also be set to only send or only receive mail.

 **Tip:** Never set the limit below 50K or the typical fax page won't transmit.

## Remote Security

Having remote users that can call into the access server of a network offers a potential security hole. Computer hackers or crackers may try to get into your network by dialing in as if they were remote users. You need passwords at the very least to protect against such attack. You may also want to use dial-back systems. (These don't permit information exchange when the remote calls in, but instead insist on calling the remote user back at his or her agreed-upon number. This makes it more difficult for unauthorized users to dial in using someone else's name and password.)

Your remote users will have more complaints than other users because they will immediately know when something is wrong. If you're remote, any problems will mean that you can't use the mail function at all, not just that you don't get messages.

## Remote Listings

Many E-mail systems leave remote user messages in the user's inbox even after they've been read. Some users who aren't remote may want to be assigned remote status so their mail remains this way as well.

 **Tip:** If a user is remote temporarily, they may be better off keeping their own local mailbox.

## Making E-mail Easy for Network Users

There are a number of steps the administrator can take to make regular E-mail use easier for individuals on the network. Special attention can be given to creating addresses, user directories, and passwords, making E-mail usage more intuitive.

### DOS installation

One such step is to create batch files to automate starting the E-mail program. This batch file would automatically issue the commands to start the E-mail program, to supply the user name, and to set its menus and windows up as desired. (On PCs a batch file is a list of commands in a file. If such a file is named with a .BAT filename extension, you can tell DOS to execute all of its commands in sequence just by typing the file's name.)

 **Tip:** Don't put the password into the batch file. This would make it too easy for unauthorized people to learn the password, just by examining the files on the user's disk.

At the very least you, as the E-mail installer, should enter the path to the E-mail program on the server as part of the DOS or other operating system for each user. This will eliminate the need to remember complicated sign-on commands. This is mainly true for DOS PCs, not for Macintoshs or UNIX systems.

In DOS PCs you may also want to create batch files that will automatically find E-mail, start the program, and log in for the user. Be careful about putting any passwords into these files.

### Windows and DESQview installation

When installing E-mail systems that run under Windows or DESQview, you'll need some knowledge of those programs to configure your E-mail for optimum performance. That means some experience with Windows or DESQview is required and you should have a good idea of how to set their options for the programs.

For instance, in DESQview you'll need to know how much memory to assign each "session." E-mail will run in one of the sessions, alongside other "sessions" running other programs. You'll also need to specify when to let E-mail work in background mode.

In Windows you'll want to be sure that the workstation has enough RAM (2MB is a bare minimum for practical Windows use; 4MB is much better). You'll also want to know something of the WIN.INI configuration file, or ask someone who does for help in fine tuning it for your E-mail and other applications.

Be aware too that Windows application programs have more problems with networking than do the average DOS applications.

### Monitor Performance

You'll need some schemes or utilities to monitor the performance and integrity of your E-mail system. People will only use E-mail if they are sure their messages will get through, and get through in a reasonable length of time.

**Tip:** Here's a quick and cheap way to test your E-mail system. Keep a mailing list with all administrators and deputy administrators. Once or twice a day, send a short message to that list, with a receipt requested. If all the messages go through, and all the receipts come back — the basic E-mail and network system are probably working OK. If possible, include in the list some sample remote sites and gateways.

Although not strictly vital, you should monitor the performance of your E-mail and your network to know when trouble is about to strike. Without monitoring, you won't know when or where to improve the system.

Diagnostic utilities can be quite helpful in this work. Some programs come with them; many do not. There are also some commercial diagnostic utilities available. Diagnostic utilities should tell you about server use, user mailing list use, and group mailing list use.

**Tip:** Data compression can improve efficiency if your network is used for transmitting too many large files. Give a compression utility to anyone who moves large file attachments, and give a decompression utility to everyone on the system. These utilities are usually free or shareware.

Reports on E-mail traffic and server use can help you make the system more efficient. Reporting utilities can tell you:

- the number of messages in each user's mailbox
- the number of unread messages in each user's mailbox
- the number of files in each user's mailbox
- the date of the oldest unread message in a mailbox
- a user's owned space on the server
- a user's shared space on the server

Server space for messages is typically divided into shared space (for messages in transit) and owned space (for messages archived by individuals). You'll recover more useful space if you recover owned space from users.

**Tip:** The date of the oldest unread message in a user's mailbox can tell you how long it has been since the user was active. Long-time inactive users can eat up disk space, and should be notified to read 'em or lose 'em.

**Tip:** One of the best upgrades you can make for any E-mail system is to replace a line editor with a screen or GUI editor. Creating messages or replies with a line editor is too difficult and time consuming.

## Make Backups

Perhaps the single largest maintenance task for E-mail is backing up the post office database. If you don't back up, events such as power loss, virus attack, cracker invasion, and server disk crashes could destroy user mail, system folders, group directories, and user passwords—in other words, everything you need to keep E-mail running except the actual programs.

In most systems backup is a relatively pain-free task, because the mail is kept in one central database. You'll need:

■ a backup process
■ a backup storage device
■ a backup program
■ a backup schedule
■ a backup monitor

For more details you can read many articles on backing up computer files, especially files for a network. General network administration and backup rules apply to E-mail, except that users generally call upon E-mail more frequently and at more hours of the day than they would other network programs. The result is that you'll need to be more careful about when and how you backup E-mail.

The process should specify which files are backed up and where the backups are kept. There should be more than one backup generation, such as the day's backup and the week's. The older backup should be kept offsite, so a single catastrophe (such as a fire or earthquake) cannot destroy all backups at once.

The backup storage device can be another disk drive on the network. A better choice would be a tape drive or removable disk drive which would let you create a backup you could take offsite and lock up. This will be necessary if you follow the wise course of keeping a backup copy at some distance from the original.

The backup program should copy the database files to the backup storage device. It should offer some intelligence, to only copy changed files for example. It should also permit you to set a schedule for the backups. Some E-mail programs come with their own backup utilities. There are also a number of commercial backup utilities.

The backup schedule should balance frequent backups with keeping the system available as much of the time as possible. Backups are typically done in the middle of the night, when the fewest people and programs are likely to be using E-mail. From 2 a.m. to 3 a.m. is a common time to bring a network "down" for maintenance and backup. In most systems, this must be done at least every day. Although some get by with weekly backups, even small organizations can be seriously injured by losing nearly a week's messages and data. More important than keeping the backup time to an absolute minimum is to make it regular and to publicize it. People will be happier if they know why the system is down, and when it is going down. This lets them plan around the maintenance schedule.

The same half-hour or hour that is used for backups should afford time for other maintenance duties as well.

 **Tip:** When scheduling backups and maintenance, keep it as brief as possible, and keep it to the same schedule so people can plan around it.

 **Tip:** Ensure that no one is using the E-mail when you're backing up. Messages sent in that interval can disappear.

The backup monitor is the person responsible for checking that backups are made, properly identified, and secured. This same person could be a network administrator or postmaster.

 **Tip:** One of the advantages of using a public-service E-mail system is that you aren't responsible for maintenance.

Remember to schedule backups to fit the needs of all E-mail users, including those in different time zones.

## Train Users and Administrators

Don't underestimate the importance of training. Efficient use of E-mail is not an inherited ability. You'll need to train:

- all users (at first)
- new users (as they join the organization)
- remote users (who may be current users learning to use a remote facility or users from outside the organization learning to tap into its E-mail)

## Administrators

You may need to create your own training program, or with some E-mail systems you'll find training outside. cc:Mail, for example, runs its own training center. The manufacturer may provide training videotapes, as well as classes.

If you're creating your own lessons for users, the first lesson might last just a few hours and include:

■ how to get help
■ how to sign on
■ starting the E-mail program
■ reading messages

The next step might be:

■ replying to messages
■ creating new messages
■ saving messages

Include training on:

■ attaching files
■ carbon copies and blind carbon copies

Details on faxes and mailing lists could be in more advanced training sessions. Still other classes could cover attaching files, sending and receiving faxes, setting notification preferences (do they want visual, audible, or both kinds of alerts), capturing screens, creating and circulating forms, and even voice integration.

**Tip:** Keep the initial training short and sweet. Get people started quickly, then let them train themselves as much as possible. Have an intermediate class for people to take later, when they show interest in file attachment, gateways, and so on. The single most important part of training is to stress that everyone should check for mail regularly, at least once a day.

Emphasize to your people that it is difficult for them to hurt anything on the E-mail system. The greatest danger is that they'll send a silly message. Even practice messages can accidentally go out to the wrong people, with embarrassing results. Many systems don't allow you to recover a message once it is sent, but this is okay when learning a new system.

When teaching the first lesson to users, don't assume they know anything about networks or messaging. Start at the beginning. Don't assume people know anything about networks or computers, or even about disks. Explain company policy on reading their messages. Tell users how to choose good passwords.

 **Tip:** A good password should be easy to remember but hard to guess.

Don't choose passwords based on birthdays, middle names, initials, or "password." A password cannot have spaces in it on most systems. Explain the security of the system to the users. Explain how encrypted saved messages are different from encrypted transmitted messages. Don't tell users it's OK to forget a password or the administrator will be overwhelmed with requests for new passwords.

Encourage users to train themselves and each other. Encourage them to use the system as soon as possible. Training needs differ. Some people won't need any. Some learn well in groups; others learn individually. Some people will resist using E-mail at all.

 **Tip:** Put a new-user bulletin on the system, perhaps even a welcoming message.

Tell users that blind carbon copies (BCC) can be useful, but that they are often interpreted as being somewhat "sneaky." BCCs can be used, for example, to let a supervisor read a memo that a person has sent to another person. Explain whether the E-mail automatically saves a copy of sent messages or if the users need to use BCCs to keep track of what they said.

 **Tip:** Encourage users to see the E-mail as a post office, not as a library. They should retrieve, read, process, and remove their mail. Otherwise the database will quickly grow too large.

## Maintain the Network

One major aspect of E-mail management is simply administering and maintaining the software and hardware. Much of this is what you'd do with any network. Disk drives can fail, cabling can become disconnected, software may be incompatible, programs may need to be updated, and so on.

**Tip:** You may want to add "fault tolerance" to your E-mail to ensure that it is available as much as possible. This would include redundant hardware and software that could continue operation even if a program crashed or a disk drive lost power.

Maintaining LAN E-mail also means maintaining the network in general. Here's a list of some utilities that can help with that task. Notice that these utilities include logging, backup, and other tools that will be directly applicable to E-mail. LAN metering means tracking how many clients are using a program at once, a necessary measurement if you're to keep legal with the licenses you buy for network software, including E-mail.

- PreCursor is a product from The Aldridge Co. that tracks computer use for time management and billing. It provides log-on and file management utilities for backup.

- StopCopy Plus from BBI Computer Systems offers metering.

- LT Auditor from Blue Lance monitors all network client activities and produces reports and audit trail records. It includes network troubleshooting and automatic archive utilities.

- Caravelle Networks Corp. makes a utility that gives early warning of troubles on TCP/IP and AppleTalk networks. It runs in the background and can warn the administrator through audible or visible alerts, even communicating these alerts to a pager or through E-mail.

- SiteLock from Brightwork Development, Inc. includes virus protection and limits on simultaneous use of network programs.

- Certus LAN from Certus International controls and monitors what network software is used and can recover some data from server crashes.

- Lanscope from Connect Computer Co., Inc. tracks program and network use and reports on network resource use.

- Turnstyle from Connect Computer Co. lets the network administrator see which programs are being used at any time. It reports on the use of metered software, allowing only the licensed number of users to simultaneously use such programs.

- Direct Net from Fifth Generation Systems, Inc. tracks usage and generates usage reports, as well as providing virus protection and password utilities.

- LANShell from LANSystems Inc. meters licensed software.

- NetMenu from NETinc. controls the maximum number of people who can use a network application.

- LANtrail from Network Management Inc. creates an audit trail for NetWare networks, monitoring all network activities and reporting on security and disk use for both network and local disk drives.

- Saber Meter from Saber Software Corp. reports on and even graphs LAN use and activity. It meters software licenses, audits use, and monitors access by user and by application. The results are stored in a dBASE III format. It is available only as part of the Saber LAN Administration Pack, and is not sold as a stand-alone product.

**Figure 4-1.**
**Saber Meter offers a variety of graphs to show network and E-mail performance and status.**

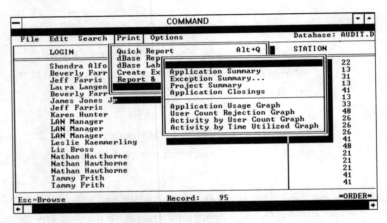

- Argus/n from Triticom tracks client activity and application use.

- Monitrix Network Manager from Cheyenne Software, Inc. tracks the use of file servers, networked printers, and client workstations. It includes an alarm that notifies the administrator when a disk drive's free space drops below a given threshold. It also packs diagnostic tests that analyze in detail the paths between client workstations.

- Outrider from Daystrom Technologies Corp. monitors and logs disk space of up to four file servers at once.

- LAN Command from Dolphin Software, Inc. analyzes and monitors server, client, gateway, bridge, and router use.

- NetCompanion from ETI Software monitors servers and clients for security and performance.

- VigiLAN from EXPERDATA, Inc. lets you use a remote or client PC to view the network's status.

- The Fresh Utilities from the Fresh Technology Group is a collection of utilities for network monitoring and optimization.

- The Frye Utilities for Networks/NetWare Management from Frye Computer Systems, Inc. monitors network use in real-time and collects that data for graphic detailing of network performance.

- STATUS*Mac from Pharos Technologies profiles, inventories, and analyzes all hardware and software components of a Macintosh on a network. It helps verify software license compliance, reports the applications used and their versions, and formats its findings in custom reports.

If software utilities won't do the job you need, then you may need to call in network analysis hardware, such as Sniffer Network Analyzer from Network General Corp. or LANalyzer Network Analyzer from Novell's LANalyzer Products Division. There are also a few utilities aimed precisely at E-mail monitoring, such as Mail Monitor from Soft-Switch, Inc. This program shows you the flow of E-mail.

## Maintaining the Server

The server must be maintained regularly. Both the network operating system and the E-mail software offer variables that can be adjusted to maximize performance.

Most LAN E-mail systems depend on a central database, with a file on one or more server computers. This database holds all the archived and unread messages. As you might guess, the database must be managed, particularly for size. If it is not managed, it can quickly grow too large. At the very least, a large database can hurt system performance, slowing searches for messages. At the most it can fill all available space on the server's disk, restricting further archiving and sending of messages. The most frequent problem with the server hard disk is that it runs out of room. You'd be surprised how many messages relatively few users can save up once they start using E-mail in earnest. Too many saved/archived messages, and your hard disk will fill to capacity. That will hurt performance, and could in some systems crash the network.

Therefore, when installing your E-mail, make sure there's enough room on the hard disk. This may mean you'll have to buy a new disk drive with more capacity. Also, you'll need to regularly check to see how that capacity is holding up. If it is getting too full, you may need to:

- free disk space by encouraging users to delete unneeded messages
- free disk space by deleting messages
- free disk space by moving some archived messages to another storage device
- add more disk space by buying additional disks

When you ask users to delete messages, you might suggest that they delete everything before a certain date. If they still need the messages, they could store them on their own disk drives.

How do you know how much disk space you need? Look at:

- the number of users
- how many messages they send on average
- the typical length of messages
- the size and number of file attachments

Take your estimates for these statistics to the company that sells your E-mail software and ask their advice on optimizing disk space.

 **Tip:** A good rule of thumb when estimating necessary server disk space for E-mail is to calculate what you'll need and then at least double that number.

## Storing E-mail Messages

In the old days of E-mail many systems stored a copy of each message for each recipient. A message sent to a mailing list of people would create many copies of the message. All of those would take up storage space. Attachments would worsen the problem. That approach is now obsolete. Instead a single message or attachment is kept, and all the recipients get a "pointer" to it in their mailbox. This is done "transparently" though. The recipient thinks he or she has the actual message or attachment because a copy of it is made as soon as it is requested.

Attached files can be much larger than typical messages, and can take up significant server disk space. To save server space, many E-mail programs let you restrict the number of files that can be attached to a message, as well as the size of each attached file.

Large attached files can quickly use all of the available space on the server. You may want to set some user limits on such files, especially if they will be moved through a slow modem (2400bps is certainly slow in any context, but 9600bps is still slow when compared to network speeds). You may also want to encourage people to move their attached files to their own disks. But don't set limits too tightly: you want to encourage people to use the system as often as possible.

 **Tip:** Smaller post office databases are more quickly backed up and more quickly fixed.

**Tip:** Make a batch or script to automatically handle all your backup and diagnostic needs.

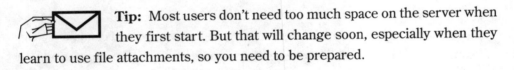 **Tip:** Maintenance and backups are routine processes. You'll set aside regular time every day or week for them. Once you have defined that time, don't give it up on those days when maintenance or backups don't take the full time. Such contradictions will only confuse the users and administrators.

A server for a PC-based LAN E-mail program should have at least a 386sx processor with 640K RAM and a 40MB hard drive for maximum efficiency. PCs that run gateways can get by with far less power—even an original, slow-by-today's-standards PC with only a floppy drive will sometimes suffice. A client workstation probably doesn't need 386 power, unless it is to run Windows or some performance-demanding other program along with E-mail.

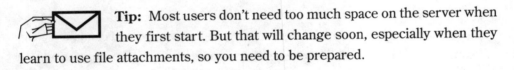 **Tip:** Most users don't need too much space on the server when they first start. But that will change soon, especially when they learn to use file attachments, so you need to be prepared.

Some E-mail server programs can run in the background and don't require a dedicated server. However, the performance of all E-mail on the system and of any other applications you run on that computer will suffer. They won't get the processor chip's full attention nor will they be assured of as much memory as they'd like to operate. Multitasking may be wonderful for users who want to move quickly from task to task, and for small notification utilities that need to be available, but it saps the energy of main programs that would be quicker when run by themselves.

At the very least, you need to choose a server computer that will always be on, or that will be on more than any other computers in the system.

**Tip:** Some manuals call for reserving as little as 100K of disk space per user. For remote users that may be reasonable, because they can store much of their information on their own disk drives. But for network users you can only laugh at such recommendations, and instead plan for at least 512K (½MB) and more likely a full 1MB or more.

A server can fail without warning. If it does, you may be able to start it again without trouble. For instance, power loss may be quickly remedied, or a program conflict may evaporate when both programs crash the server and then only one restarts. But the restart may appear less troublesome than it is. The sudden failure may have damaged the database. Messages may be corrupted or the directory may be hurt.

**Tip:** Ask your E-mail supplier how to save the database from a sudden server failure.

Some databases are designed to withstand such failures and system failures. Others are not. You may need to recover the database from backup copies. If so, notify the users that you have done this, and what duration of messages are considered suspect, what may have been damaged and need to be checked on or sent again. Don't abandon the messages in a corrupted database. Some E-mail companies can fix or at least partially fix recover the information from a corrupted database.

Some E-mail software requires periodic maintenance of the database. How often you need to do this depends on the number of mailboxes, the number of users deleted or added, and other such factors. The result may be a demand for weekly maintenance work, even without any obvious performance loss or other problem indications.

## Maintain the Directory

As E-mail networks grow larger, updating the directory becomes a larger part of the maintenance and management task. Deciding how to keep it current is a complex technological and management process.

The toughest task in maintaining most E-mail systems is to keep the directory accurate and current. Some programs make this easier by updating and displaying a universal user list or directory automatically. They'll search the network for all other servers, even in different zones or sites, and gather user details from them. Many others lack this automation. In either case you'll need to set up processes and assign responsibilities for directory management.

You'll also need to decide a schedule for any automatic or manual directory updates. If you make changes every time any user's name or password changes, and the network is large, a majority of E-mail traffic can be taken up with directory maintenance.

But if you don't regularly purge old names and keep the directory current the server can get overloaded with undeliverable mail. Actually the worst result of this aging directory is the perceived unreliability of the E-mail—people won't trust that a message will be delivered to the correct address.

**Tip:** Directory maintenance is a balance between keeping the most current directory to please users and not spending too much time or system performance on updating the directory changes.

When installing a new directory, there are many different program options. For example, some programs automatically read network operating system directories (that's the best choice). Other programs can read directory lists in tab or comma-delimited format (the second best choice). Still other programs make you manually enter all names (the least desirable).

## Add and Delete Users

One of the responsiblities of the local postmaster or assistant postmaster is to add new users and delete departed users. Adding new users means assigning them a mailbox, assigning them a password, setting them up for training, and making sure they are in the directory.

Deleting departed users means nullifying their password, deleting them from the directory and mailing lists, and setting the system to automatically forward their received mail to that person's replacement, manager, or the post-master (if possible).

When first creating new users, set up a half-dozen or more dummy accounts. These can then be used later for quickly giving someone a mailbox since it's eas-ier in some systems to change the name on a mailbox than to create a new mail-box. Dummy accounts are also useful for a deputy administrator who wants to get into the system to do some work.

 **Tip:** When a name is deleted, make sure all references to it are deleted as well.

## Starting the Directory

Having a LAN E-mail package that automatically reads any user setup infor-mation of your network operating system, such as the Novell NetWare Bindery, not only simplifies setup: it simplifies maintenance. After all, without that automa-tion, the administrator will need to manually change the user setup file.

## Propagating Directory Changes

The directory will be changing constantly, from small changes, such as adding a remote access for one person, to large changes, such as connections to new post offices.

You need to know how you will maintain the directory in the most usable and current form. Ask yourself how will you add, delete, and change directory entries. Some E-mail programs come with utilities for just this work; others don't.

Some E-mail systems automatically "propagate" directory changes from one directory to all others (other post offices). Many do not, requiring that administrators handle that task manually.

You could limit directory propagation troubles by not propagating all changes to all directories on all servers. One way to do this is to have a central post office that routes messages between local post offices. The local post office doesn't need to know all the latest addresses. It could ask the central post office for directory assistance when needed, allowing you to publish the directory monthly.

But you don't want to make it difficult to get an address. That makes it difficult to send a message, and will keep people from using E-mail, weakening the reason to have it in the first place.

There are a few add-on utilities just for E-mail, programs that hope to add the administration features that the E-mail software forgot. For example, Network Corp., which makes its own E-mail program as mentioned in Chapter 5, sells the Post Office Manager utilities for cc:Mail. This program simplifies directory administration by propagating changes made to the directory of one post office to other post offices on separate LANs. It functions something like cc:Mail's own Automatic Directory Exchange feature.

When it comes to administration utilities that are included with E-mail programs, you'll sometimes find that the utilities only run on a single type of computer, even though the E-mail software runs on many different "platforms." Ask your E-mail supplier for details and plans for future multiple platform support.

## Directory Security

You may not want to fully exchange directories with other E-mail systems. For example, you may need E-mail connections to a few individuals in another company. But you may not want to open your system to everyone in the other company. This would increase the network traffic and increase the security risk. In that case, you could limit both traffic and security troubles by limiting who appeared in the other company's directory. You may want to reinforce this plan by specifying that user lists don't move across the bridge.

One way to keep your directory secure and let anyone outside the company—customers, vendors—communicate with your E-mail users at the same time is to use a public-service E-mail system as a gateway. The outside user then joins that public-service system too and uses it like a central hub for moving messages to and from your E-mail. But the outsider does not get any directory privileges into your system.

If a server is to be moved to a different site, zone or network, you'll need to change the directory to reflect that move.

## Changing Post Office Names

Changing a user name or address is easy; changing a mailing list or a post office is tougher.

Your directory will stay organized if you put all post office names at the end of the directory. To do that in many LAN E-mail packages, start the post office name with a symbol such as a tilde (~) or dollar sign ($).

When you assign names to your post offices, think in terms of your full architecture. It will be easier to have a large network, or to expand to a large network later, if you don't use names such as "localpost."

**Tip:** Don't use a name such as "localpost" for a post office, because that name may be repeated in different regions of a large network.

When restructuring a network you may end up with two post offices with the same or similar names. This could confuse anyone sending mail to either of those post offices. At other times you may need to split one post office into two to keep the number of users to a manageable number.

In either case you'll need to change a post office name. This can be a traumatic event because it will affect all sorts of addresses. For example, remote users who dial in or users sending messages from other post offices will continue to use the old name until told to switch. Everyone must get the news. You'll need to personally call other administrators and postmasters to inform them.

 **Tip:** Inform administrators and postmasters of post office name changes before the event.

 **Tip:** When choosing post office names, try to make them ones you won't need to change. Make it both easy to remember and relevant to the location. A city name is good for this, for example.

 **Tip:** When you split a post office, keep the original name for one of the new post offices and name the second something like "name2." This limits the number of changes and will help reduce the confusion.

## Keep All Users Informed

You should keep E-mail users up to date on system facts they need to know. You can do this through a mailing list or a bulletin board. Some systems permit a notice to appear when users first sign on or log in.

System conditions such as unusual system shutdowns must be communicated to users as far in advance as possible.

## Bulletin Boards

Bulletin boards, as explained in Chapter 1, are programs or program features that allow messages to be "posted" in the computer for all users to read. Bulletin boards can help administrators because they are an ideal place to put announcements and answers to common questions without cluttering mailboxes. But a bulletin board also needs its own administration or "sysop" (systems operator) to:

- create topics
- keep discussions on track
- read and possibly edit messages (if they are too long)
- censor materials that shouldn't be on line (such as credit card numbers)

 **Tip:** If your organization doesn't want personal information on the bulletin board, make that known. However, there will be a tendency to do that, so you might want to set up another bulletin board for personal messages (invitations, sales offers, and so on).

## Password Security

Some E-mail systems let you set different passwords for different servers even within a site. This helps prevent unauthorized addition of servers to the network, which would then give full access to the mail. The requirement that a bridge be established at both ends of the connection also helps with this kind of security.

 **Tip:** If a user has a favorite password or code for a credit card, ATM, or online service, they might want to repeat that for use on E-mail.

You can gain more security by using a utility that locks the workstation keyboard. This lets you leave your client PC running, already enabled with the passwords necessary, but not open to someone else's explorations. There's a Public-domain utility called LOCKER that can freeze a keyboard; XTREE's AllSafe is a commercial utility with the same ability.

If someone regularly forgets a password, find out why. Was it too long or maybe too strange? Encourage them not to follow that same pattern again. Set password expiration times to encourage people to change their passwords regularly, but not so often as to annoy them.

 **Tip:** Passwords are sometimes case-sensitive.

Maintaining security is doubly important for administrators because of the power they have to intercept or delete users' mail. Administrators can get into almost any part of the E-mail system because they assign passwords and have system passwords that supercede many of the individual passwords.

## Virus Protection

A virus is a computer program that makes copies of itself. It often moves from one computer to another by "infecting" some file, and then tagging along with that file as it is copied to a floppy disk and then copied to another system. A virus can also travel through a network.

Some viruses are intentionally harmful; they'll make as many copies of themselves as possible and also erase data or otherwise cripple a system. Even a virus that isn't so damaging can cause tremendous trouble by:

- cutting system performance (replication takes up computer power)
- clogging the hard disk (all those copies can take up space)
- fighting with other programs (it may not be compatible with other software)

The administrator is responsible for fighting viruses in three ways:

- installing anti-virus software, for both virus detection and elimination
- setting up anti-virus procedures for users to follow
- training and encouraging users to follow the procedures

 **Tip:** Install virus detection and correction programs and keep them up to date.

 **Tip:** Viruses rarely infect messages, but they can easily ride on attached files.

## Track Projected Costs and Expenses

You'll need some way to keep track of costs, a "billing" system. This should at the very least track and summarize who is using gateways, sending faxes, and using modems to make long-distance calls. Ideally it would track who is creating the most network traffic, such as monitoring who is regularly attaching large files to messages. The billing cost should break charges down by departments and individuals.

## Fax Costs

Sending faxes will probably be one of E-mail's most popular features. And quite possibly one of its most expensive operating costs, considering how much easier it is to send a fax through an E-mail gateway than it is to use a fax machine. In fact, sending faxes on E-mail can become so popular that it can multiply your telephone costs.

Receiving faxes is not yet practical on most systems. Some rudimentary hardware and software currently allow fax reception, but there are too many obstacles to make it practical. The first obstacle is addressing. As explained in Chapter 1, getting a fax to a particular recipient is tough. Also, it takes a lot of power and performance to store and display the 50 to 100K per page that received faxes occupy.

 **Tip:** For receiving faxes, you're better off with some standard fax machines than using E-mail fax reception.

## Create and Register Mailing Lists

One duty of the administrator is to take mailing list suggestions from individuals. The administrator may need to create these lists, and then open access to them for all appropriate users. "Appropriate" could mean everyone, or it could mean just the people in one department. Mailing lists can sometimes be borrowed instead of created, by asking for permission to publicize mailing lists various users have created. For example, one user may have created a mailing list that reaches all mid-level managers handling telecommuting employees. The system administrator may want to make this list available to managers in general.

One of the administrator's tasks is to create public mailing lists. These lists can be seen and used by all, but not changed by anyone. They should appeal to as many people as possible. However, it can be difficult to decide who should be on which list. Some obvious mailing lists to make may be all employees for each manager or all executives for the company.

Watch what lists people want or make for themselves before making too many group mailing lists. Then follow up to see which lists are actually used. Some utilities are available to help you monitor this. For example, the CHK-STAT utility in cc:Mail can tell you which lists are being used.

**Tip:** Always ask for permission before turning a private list into a public list. Don't delete anyone's messages without asking permission. You wouldn't clean out their desk without asking first.

 **Tip:** Huge mailing lists can easily just become junk mail distribution schemes. Keep lists slim and trim.

If you want to build a mailing list that is larger than allowed on your system, you could build a "nested list," sometimes known as "bankshot routing." This means you create a mailing list whose members are themselves are a mailing list.

## Create and Register Electronic Forms

Administrators have similar duties for forms, at least on systems that permit E-mail communication of forms. Forms need to be created or registered, and then users need to be given the proper access.

One of the administrator's jobs is to create and distribute forms that can benefit E-mail users. Some programs can create their own custom forms; others don't have a forms capability.

Use these forms features if they are available for:

■ pre-addressing (putting the most frequently-used names for that form in the "recipients" space—these can be changed if desired, but will save time for the user)

■ tab-order (determining which blanks on the form the tab key will move the cursor to, and in which order)

## Create and Register a Fax Cover Sheet

The administrator of a fax gateway needs to create a fax cover sheet. Your fax gateway may provide one of these or you may need a graphics editor or word processor program to make your own. You could let users send faxes without cover sheets, but that skips an opportunity to both promote your organization (through a logo on the cover sheet), and to neatly and precisely address the fax. After all, it may need to be routed within the receiving organization, and a cover sheet could help with that.

**Tip:** Fax transmissions sometimes get lost. You may not always know that this has happened. For some control or verification, send a blind carbon copy of the fax to yourself as a sort of receipt.

**Tip:** If your E-mail is sending faxes through a shared fax modem you should be aware that many such modems make word-wrapping and pagination mistakes. That could lead to an ugly fax. It's best to send a few to yourself to test how the fax modem works.

You may sometimes have a user who wants to send a message that contains graphics through a service that does not allow graphics. Investigate if the service permits attached binary files. If it does, you could translate the graphic into a PCX or other standard graphics file and attach it to the message. You'll need a graphics conversion program for this. However, be aware that the fax recipient will need to "translate" the converted graphics file they receive before it may be useable again.

## Handle Addressing Mistakes

Some messages sent over gateways will be returned to your system as "undeliverable." Possible reasons for this include:

- incomplete addresses
- incorrect addresses
- out-of-service local server for the recipient
- out-of-service gateway to the recipient

Because the later two reasons are temporary, E-mail programs sometimes let you set a "retry" time for a message, allowing E-mail to try resending the message every 30 minutes.

 **Tip:** Notify users when a server is going down, for regular or unexpected maintenance.

 **Tip:** You can often get the address of someone on a remote system by sending an E-mail query to the postmaster or administrator of that system.

## Establish a Support Relationship

Next to setting up a gateway or expanding your system, installation is the work that requires the most technical support. Look for good documentation and read it. Ask for any walk-through or tutorial guides to installation, and call technical support people for help. Now is the time when you'll be glad for a toll-free technical support line.

Service and support are two of the biggest costs in networks, and will figure prominently in E-mail costs as well. Some estimates are that 50 to 70% of a networking budget is spent on service and support. Only 30 to 50% are spent on hardware and software.

The more of your hardware and software you can buy from a single source, the better your chances for smooth technical support—if that organization provides good support. A mixed network or E-mail system (one with software and hardware from many sources) is more typical, but also harder for any one tech support outfit to diagnose and troubleshoot.

Upgrades to software or hardware are fertile sources for compatibility problems. So are changes or movements of network devices, from client workstations to printers and servers.

Common service problems include:

- disk failures
- cabling disconnections
- power failures

You can buy support contracts from many firms. There are also 900 support numbers now for most popular programs, including network applications. These cost something on the order of $3 per minute and are often available 24-hours a day. To most network administrators these costs are secondary: more important is the response time.

**Tip:** Ask the company that will supply your E-mail what help they give with installation. Ask about free support. Emphasize how you're not just looking for a quick E-mail purchase, but for a partner in creating a long-term, expanding E-mail system for your business.

## Handle Legal Issues

Like many network programs, E-mail is often sold as a server program and a workstation program. You buy a license to use a certain number of copies of the workstation program. If you exceed that number, without buying more license authority, you are stealing the software. That's an important point to make to everyone involved with setting up new users and new post offices.

The Software Publishers Association in Washington, D.C., has been working on a program to help monitor compliance with software licenses. You may wish to contact them for more specific information.

LAN E-mail software is typically purchased as a server package and a client package which you "license" to use on a certain number of workstations. How many licenses should you buy? You need as many as the maximum number of simultaneous users you'll have. That will most often be the number that sign on in the morning: people come to work, grab coffee, and check their mail.

 **Tip:** To know how many license rights to buy, monitor how many people use E-mail first thing in the work morning.

# CHAPTER FIVE

# LAN E-mail Programs

If you have a network built on PCs, typically running the Novell NetWare, Microsoft LAN Manager, LANtastic, or Banyan VINES network operating system, then you can look to this chapter for LAN E-mail program ideas. This chapter covers the programs that run under the PC's typical DOS operating system software. It also covers programs that run under the Windows addition to DOS. (See Chapter 2 for details on these differences.)

Most Windows E-mail programs are recent revisions of DOS client E-mail programs and are part of a family of client programs. A few first appeared for Windows. This chapter mentions both kinds.

It is not a black-and-white matter dividing personal computer E-mail programs into PC, Mac, and other such categories. Many of the programs now appear on more than one system—with versions for PC and Mac. But many began by running on only one kind of personal computer, and most focus their attention on one type of system or the other.

**Tip:** Some of the programs in this chapter will also be useful if you have a network made mainly of Macintoshes and workstations. Some of these programs offer versions for Macintoshes, workstations and PC compatibles.

Software often changes quickly, with new versions full of new features (and new problems) appearing every year. Programs change too often for a book to accurately reflect individual features. The descriptions here just outline the history and trends of the programs. Nor is this a ranking and rating of product features. For current details on a program that looks promising, call the company that makes the program and look for the latest reviews in the computer press (see the Bibliography for names of some of the magazines).

Don't read here either for tips on deciding between DOS or Windows programs. That selection process is covered in Chapter 2.

**Tip:** If you're looking for OS/2 E-mail, check through the listings here. There are too few OS/2 programs to merit an entire chapter. Some of the programs for DOS, however, also come in OS/2 versions.

### cc:Mail

Currently, the most popular PC LAN E-mail program is cc:Mail. ccMail was originally developed by a company of that same name. In 1991, Lotus Development Corporation, maker of the famous Lotus 1-2-3 spreadsheet, bought the company and the program. Lotus didn't pull the company apart—it left the same people and organization in charge of developing and selling cc:Mail. In 1992 IBM agreed to license and distribute cc:Mail to its mainframe customers who were moving to LANs, in place of the mail product that was integrated with IBM's own OfficeVision software. This put a large stamp of approval on cc:Mail.

cc:Mail has a wider range of client versions than any other LAN E-mail program. These include DOS, Windows, OS/2, UNIX, and Macintosh. There's even a memory-card version of the cc:Mail remote being developed for the HP 95LX palmtop and wireless radio E-mail. cc:Mail also offers one of the widest ranges of gateways, for connecting to other E-mail systems.

The Windows, Mac, OS/2, and UNIX versions of cc:Mail are recent developments. The DOS version has been around for a long time. It comes in two forms, the Platform Pack and the User Packages. The Platform Pack for cc:Mail for MS-DOS has both system administrator and server software. The User Packages allow 8 or 25 users, with the larger package having a higher price, naturally.

cc:Mail is easy to install and has lots of security and administrative features. It had some limits on the number of attachments that were lifted in early 1992 and cc:Mail is relatively inexpensive.

Lotus also makes the Notes groupware program, mentioned in Chapter 1 and later in this chapter. Notes has its own E-mail. Lotus has mapped out a plan to offer automatic directory synchronization between cc:Mail and Notes, and then to gradually merge them. Notes users will be able to choose Notes or cc:Mail as their default mail system and let Notes and cc:Mail be resident on the same server. In 1993, Notes and cc:Mail will be integrated.

As a prime mover in the VIM (Vendor Independent Messaging—described in Chapter 1) standard, Lotus is moving quickly toward mail-enabling its own 1-2-3, Symphony (spreadsheet and more), Ami Pro (word processing), and Freelance (chartmaker), all of which will soon have built-in commands for simple mail operations.

cc:Mail's popularity has led to many third-party add-ons and enhancements. Lotus publishes a cc:Mail catalog of these programs and peripherals. For example, the Network Scheduler II program from PowerCore is a calendar and scheduler you can add to cc:Mail. By agreement, the two companies will be developing Scheduler further so it will integrate more closely with cc:Mail.

## Microsoft Mail for PC Networks

Microsoft Mail for PC Networks is the second-most popular PC LAN E-mail program, after cc:Mail. Consumer's Software originally called the product "Network Courier" until Microsoft bought it in 1991, dismantled it, and changed the program's name. This led to confusion because Microsoft already sold a completely different E-mail program for Macintosh AppleTalk networks, calling that "Microsoft Mail," too.

Microsoft Mail for PC Networks now has client programs for DOS, Windows, and Macintosh, but not for OS/2 or UNIX. The three versions are synchronized: each has the same features with the same release numbers.

With Release 2.1, Microsoft Mail's messaging features included most of the basics, though it lacked a few—such as blind carbon copies and advanced word processing. Release 2.1 was really just Network Courier, the original program. By Release 3.0 in mid 1992, Microsoft had time to clearly indicate how it would revamp the program, and those missing features may have appeared. Microsoft publishes a catalog for Microsoft Mail add-on programs. Schedule+, for instance, adds schedule and calendar abilities.

Like cc:Mail, Microsoft Mail offers many gateway options for connecting to other E-mail systems. It is also packed with diagnostic tools for maintenance. As of Release 2.1, Microsoft Mail was one of the most expensive PC LAN E-mail programs.

Microsoft makes both the underlying DOS operating system and the Windows software that enhance Microsoft Mail. These give it a foundation position in most PCs. Microsoft also makes the LAN Manager network operating system, which competes with Novell's NetWare but has only a small part of the market. For now, Microsoft is offering its own API called MAPI (see Chapter 1 for explanations). The company will use MAPI to mail-enable its own applications, such as Excel and Word. For the future, Microsoft suggested in mid 1992 that mail should be part of an operating system. This clearly points toward putting the basics of Microsoft Mail, or a newer back-end Microsoft mail engine code-named "Spitfire", into a combined DOS/Windows operating system. These would compete with whatever mail engine Novell might put in NetWare and would directly attack the need for any mail engine from Lotus or other E-mail companies. Those firms could still try to sell their engines as superior, or turn to selling strictly front-end interface software.

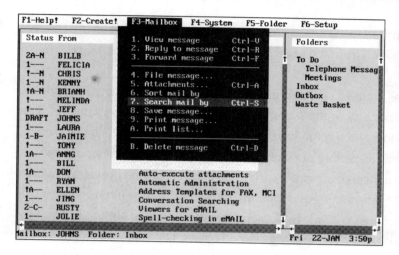

Figure 5-1. DaVinci eMail has all of the standard E-mail features, including a menu to search through archived messages.

## DaVinci eMail

DaVinci is a dark-horse company in the E-mail race, running far behind cc:Mail and Microsoft in the popularity stakes. It still, however, has a solid market share of its own and often wins in side-by-side ease-of-use and features comparisons with those products.

Neither is DaVinci just a small E-mail company getting by on its programs' good looks. Novell, the network operating system company that has beaten Microsoft

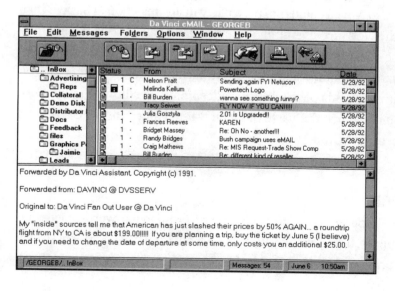

Figure 5-2. The Windows version of the DaVinci eMail shows an inbox list of received messages as shown here, along with a separate window to view or edit messages.

and all others in the NOS market, owns a large share of DaVinci. And the DaVinci E-mail software is built from the ground-up on Novell's MHS technology.

DaVinci eMail comes in DOS, Windows, and Macintosh versions, though the Mac version lacks many of the features of the DOS and Windows clients. The DOS version is widely thought to have the best set of messaging features around. For example, it has a spelling checker and search-and-replace functions, which are nearly unique in mail programs. Its archiving is also renowned because DaVinci lets you keep a "conversation message threading" record so old messages can be sorted and searched not only by subject, keyword, date, or author, but also by their context to other related messages and replies. DaVinci is also famous for its easy-to-use interface and for coming from a company with excellent support.

For administrators, DaVinci email is missing a few gears. It does not , for example, have an integrated directory propagation or synchronization feature. Nor does it offer much in the way of diagnostics, relying on its MHS roots and the tools that MHS has for such work. The MHS foundation makes DaVinci a potent connector to other systems because MHS-compatibility is so widespread in E-mail.

DaVinci's links to Novell could make it a party to any injection of basic E-mail capabilities into the NetWare operating system. Then again, DaVinci could parlay its famous ease-of-use and customer support into a position as a leading seller of front-end software no matter who captures the back-end engine market. In fact, DaVinci is preparing for this possibility by redesigning its software to be more "modular," so you could use the parts of it you wanted and substitute standard or operating system parts, too.

## WordPerfect Office

WordPerfect Corporation makes the world's most-popular word-processing program. The company, however, is trying to branch out from that successful stronghold. One of the programs it offers in this attempt to broaden its market is Word-

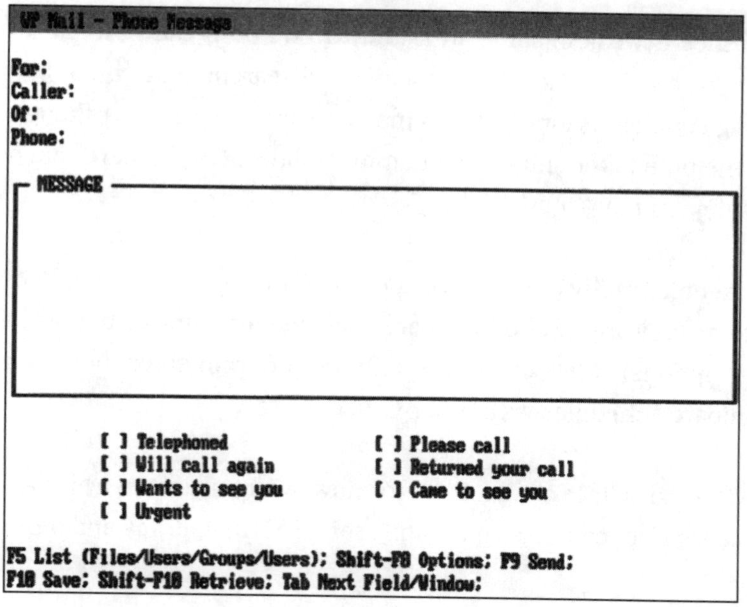

```
┌─────────────────────────────────────────────────────────────┐
│ WP Mail - Phone Message                                      │
│                                                              │
│ For:                                                         │
│ Caller:                                                      │
│ Of:                                                          │
│ Phone:                                                       │
│  ┌─ MESSAGE ─────────────────────────────────────────────┐  │
│  │                                                        │  │
│  │                                                        │  │
│  │                                                        │  │
│  │                                                        │  │
│  │                                                        │  │
│  │                                                        │  │
│  │                                                        │  │
│  └────────────────────────────────────────────────────────┘ │
│                                                              │
│      [ ] Telephoned          [ ] Please call                 │
│      [ ] Will call again      [ ] Returned your call         │
│      [ ] Wants to see you     [ ] Came to see you            │
│      [ ] Urgent                                              │
│                                                              │
│ F5 List (Files/Users/Groups/Users); Shift-F8 Options; F9 Send; │
│ F10 Save; Shift-F10 Retrieve; Tab Next Field/Window;         │
└─────────────────────────────────────────────────────────────┘
```

Figure 5-3.
WordPerfect Office for the PC includes a form for easily and quickly taking telephone messages.

Perfect Office. This package includes E-mail with unique features such as subject security and group scheduling, but lacks many of the messaging features and connectivity options you might take for granted in other E-mail programs. A Windows version appeared recently that contains little more than the E-mail portion.

The foundation of Office is a menuing system. This attempts to make a DOS PC easier to use, by substituting a simple menu for cryptic DOS commands. The menu then encourages using such WordPerfect application programs as the WordPerfect word processor, DrawPerfect (a graphics program), and so on. Finally, the Office includes a set of utility programs: a note taker, a database manager (a simple flat-file manager), a scheduler, and an E-mail program.

The E-mail program has the basic messaging features you'd want. It has some unique features, such as the ability to delete a message even after it has been sent, as long as it hasn't been read (like reaching into someone's mailbox to retrieve a letter they haven't yet opened). Another unique feature is the option to hide the subject of a message, for partial security.

WordPerfect Office is weak in some areas, however. For instance, it has little archiving ability for received messages: sorting and searching are quite limited. Also, the editing commands for creating a message or a reply are few, though you can switch to the note taker and use its editing abilities. Nor is there much security, for encryption of messages.

The built-in Scheduler utility pushes WordPerfect Office beyond a simple E-mail definition into groupware. (Schedulers are available for some of the other E-mail packages as options) It lets each user with the program enter their own schedule, then compare schedules with other Office users.

WordPerfect Office has little connectivity for now, with only gateways available for some public-service mail. It is still waiting for an MHS gateway and other connection options.

## BeyondMail

BeyondMail is a DOS-only E-mail program. There are no Windows or Macintosh versions. It is built on the MHS engine, as is DaVinci eMail. For messaging, BeyondMail provides the basic features you need, from message editing to encryption and mailing lists. It stores received messages and even drafts of your own outgoing messages, if you so choose. It can search through those messages by almost any criterion.

For administration, BeyondMail offers directory synchronization and propagation from built-in utilities. For most maintenance it relies on the MHS foundation. It also uses that MHS core when looking to connect to other systems: you use commercial MHS gateways.

But BeyondMail is not straight E-mail. It has two other features that offer a glimpse of Mail's future.

Forms are one. It comes with some standard forms, and an optional form designer lets you create any sort of form you might want. These forms can then be used for quick entering and sending of information related to such typical transactions as phone calls, meetings, memos, requests, customer support, and so on. (See the Forms section of Chapter 1 for more about the importance of forms.)

Rules are another key to BeyondMail's appeal. This unique feature lets you use a language of rules and commands to do anything from enhancing Beyond-Mail's message security to creating a groupware, work-flow package. Probably the immediate use of rules for most people is to manage incoming mail. You can write rules to sort incoming mail by subject, sender, priority, or other aspects and then deal with the mail in that sorted order.

Because BeyondMail can launch other programs, you can write rules to watch for a particular message or type of message to appear, manipulate the information in that message in some way, then automatically forward the message or its results to another E-mail recipient. That's the essence of work-flow (as explained in Chapter 1). At the least, it lets you cut down on time wasted by junk E-mail. But for the future, it could automate some of your repeated operations, from monthly budget reports to keeping tabs on operating machinery.

## Futurus TEAM

Futurus TEAM used to be known as Right Hand Man II. It starts with E-mail and then adds personal and workgroup utilities. It has rare and unique features for an E-mail package, such as voice messages, scheduling, and a full database-management program.

The voice messaging lets you create a voice record, attach it to a message, and send real voice messages. These attachments travel over the network with the regular E-mail. The recipient can then hear them and record and send replies. To use the voice-messaging feature, you need an Artisoft Sounding Board adapter.

The built-in database handles dBASE files, and can not only view, but also create databases using standard data types (character, numeric, date, memo, and logical).

Futurus has both DOS and Windows versions. It runs under the inexpensive LANtastic operating system as well as the more mainstream Novell and NetBIOS systems.

Beside standard E-mail commands and options, Futurus comes with both individual- and group-scheduling utilities and program features to handle phone messages, calculations, and notes. The scheduling module handles both tasks and resources. The calendar can be your own or open to the group, though you can restrict what details others on the network can see of your personal schedule.

Unfortunately, Futurus's messaging features aren't complete. For example, they lack the ability to link messages in a conversation (threads). Also, connectivity is limited. Futurus does support MHS and can reach other E-mail systems through MHS-compatible gateways.

## Network Mail for VINES

Banyan's VINES network operating system has been a competitor to Novell's NetWare for years. It has a loyal, though small, share of the market. One strength of VINES is the StreetTalk directory technology, a global naming service, which may be adapted to other network operating systems in the future (see Chapter 1 for more on the importance of directory services).

Network Mail for VINES 4.0 is an E-mail program for VINES, naturally. It is available for DOS, Windows, Macintosh, and OS/2 clients. It does not require a dedicated mail server on the network. Gateways for connections to popular mainframe, minicomputer, and standard (X.400) mail systems are optional.

Network Mail's global naming services let you send mail to anyone on the network without complex routing instructions. Each user name has just three components: Name, Domain, and Organization. These naming services also simplify administration of the mail directories.

## Higgins

Higgins, by Enable Software, was one of the first groupware programs, and it continues to combine E-mail with group-organizing utilities.

Available in DOS and OS/2 versions, Higgins can load as a simple TSR utility, using only 50K of memory. That makes it easy to switch back and forth between Higgins and other programs—a boon for an E-mail program. For connection to other systems, gateways to MHS, fax, and X.400 are available as options.

E-mail in Higgins has most standard features, including mailing lists, encryption of stored and transmitted messages, and on-line chatting. It lacks the ability to cancel a sent message and cannot view attached graphics files.

Group utilities include a notepad, a group calendar, a phone-message handler, a calculator, and an expense reporter. The calendar and scheduling functions can also handle personal calendars. Enable also makes Enable Office, an integrated-office software package with E-mail and scheduling. This includes the Enable word processor, spreadsheet, database, graphics, and communications programs.

## Notes

Lotus Notes has E-mail as a natural extension of its ground-breaking groupware abilities. Explained in more detail in Chapter 1, Notes is built around a shared database. The individual computers on the network run a client part of notes that lets them add to, modify, and view the shared database from many different angles. Although Notes offers the ability to quickly and thoroughly collaborate on pro-

Figure 5-4. Lotus
Notes includes its
own E-mail utility,
though this may
soon be a module
that can be
replaced by
cc:Mail.

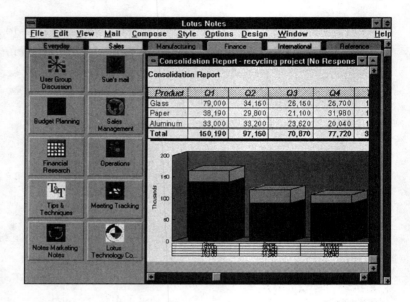

jects across a network, installing, learning, and using Notes is a big job and the program is expensive.

The E-mail portion of Notes does not offer many of the sophisticated features you'll find in cc:Mail or Microsoft Mail, but it does offer the basics.

Lotus plans to merge cc:Mail and Notes. First, the two will share directories. Later, they will be interchangeable, so a Notes user will be able to use cc:Mail instead of the Notes Mail, for example.

## @Mail

@Mail, pronounced "at-mail", is an E-mail program that integrates with the Lotus 1-2-3 spreadsheet. This is probably the first mail-enabled program (see Chapter 1 for details) that lets you send and receive E-mail directly from the menus of an application program. @Mail, however, doesn't use the new VIM or MAPI standards. Instead, it takes advantage of 1-2-3's "add-in architecture," which lets utilities merge with the program, appearing in 1-2-3 menus. (The name comes from 1-2-3's use of the "@" symbol to indicate special functions within the spreadsheet.) @Mail was the first program from Beyond, the company that later produced BeyondMail.

@Mail is ideal only for those who live by 1-2-3. It lets them send and receive annotated 1-2-3 worksheets to one another, depending on MHS as the underlying mechanism. (@Mail also works with Lotus's integrated program, Symphony.)

A surprising strength of @Mail stems from its ability to use 1-2-3 macros (saved command sequences). These let it automatically create and send mail based on changes to the values in a spreadsheet. See BeyondMail for a more robust version of this power.

## Syzygy

Syzygy (pronounced "sizz-a-gee") is not just E-mail. It is a bundle of programs for managing people and projects intended for use alongside a main program such as WordPerfect or WordStar. In fact, it depends on such outside applications for editing messages.

Syzygy, by Syzygy Development, is available only for PCs running DOS. It runs on a variety of networks including NetWare, LAN Manager, NetBIOS, Banyan, PC LAN, and 3Com. It can run in 512K of the server's RAM or as a Value-Added Process (VAP) under NetWare. The E-mail in Syzygy depends on MHS to send and store messages. Through MHS gateways, Syzygy can also connect to other systems.

Syzygy offers standard E-mail features, as well as security through passwords. It lacks such E-mail features as topic folders and bindery reading.

Along with E-mail, Syzygy can handle schedules, calendars, and to-do lists for individuals or groups. It can even produce Gantt project management charts. For use in managing projects, it can import and export 1-2-3 or Excel spreadsheet data and dBASE database information.

## Office Works

Data Access's Office Works teams an E-mail program with a suite of office-organizing programs. It works only on DOS-running PCs, but operates in Novell, Banyan, LAN Manager, IBM Token Ring, PC LAN, or 3Com networks. MHS support is built-in, and there are optional gateways to X.400 and Fax.

The E-mail portion has standard features, including attachments and retrieval by criteria. It also has some unusual features, such as the unique "alternate" ability, which lets someone else attend to your mail with your permission, but without giving away all of your security when you are away. The mail, however, doesn't forward messages easily, nor does it let you cancel a message that's been sent.

The office-organization programs include a scheduler (for individual and group schedules) and a phone message center and phone list (to make notes of incoming calls).

As of early 1992, Office Works had a strange pricing policy, offering a very inexpensive "unlimited user" version for $1995, but charging $8000 for an X.400 gateway.

## Cross+Point

Cross Information's Cross+Point ties a sophisticated personal calendar program to an E-mail program with a number of advanced features. It runs only under DOS, but handles NetWare, LAN Manager, NetBIOS, and (a rare support) the Digital Pathworks network operating systems. Its gateways are quite limited: only Fax, not even MHS.

The personal calendar in Cross+Point lets you handle days, weeks, and months, when managing your time and resources. The E-mail program has separate TSR notification programs for arrived E-mail and phone messages caught by others using Cross+Point on the network. The E-mail also handles bulletin-board information, remote communications, and even conferencing. The stored messages are protected by the necessity for a login password.

Cross+Point is almost free: only $395 for an unlimited number of users.

## OfficeMinder

Century Software's OfficeMinder is a combination of personal-organization, workgroup-organization, and E-mail programs. It runs under DOS and, although it doesn't have a real Windows version, can run under Windows as a DOS program (it is supplied with the appropriate Program Information File).

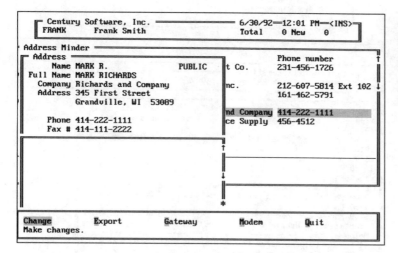

**Figure 5-5. OfficeMinder's E-mail shows a typical window for selecting a recipient's address.**

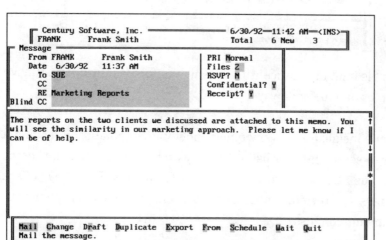

**Figure 5-6. You select the sending priority and copy options in this menu of Office-Minder.**

Figure 5-7.
OfficeMinder
doesn't just have
E-mail. It also
offers a variety of
useful utility
programs.

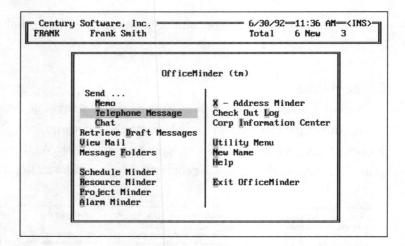

Figure 5-8. You can
schedule meetings
and resources with
this utility of
OfficeMinder.

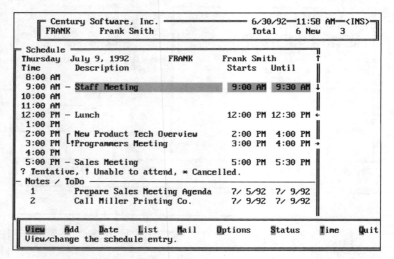

MHS support is built into OfficeMinder, which unfortunately does not have any other built-in or optional gateways.

OfficeMinder's installation is very quick, including automatically reading a NetWare Binder to set up the user list. It has its own menus, set in a line across the screen like Lotus 1-2-3 or Microsoft Word for DOS menus. The E-mail offers file attachment, message receipts, message priority choices, and encryption with password for transmitted messages.

The organization utilities include a notepad, a phone message feature, and a calendar that includes appointment alarms. The group aspect of the calendar lets you check who is in or out. (The other workers must, naturally, let their own copy of the program know when they come and go.) On top of all that is a project scheduler that lets you make outlines, set priorities, check deadlines, schedule resources, and monitor goals.

## NoteWork

NoteWork, by NoteWork Corporation, comes in both DOS and Windows versions. It is famous for being small (occupying little RAM memory) and fast. In fact, it needs only 5K of memory to operate in DOS as a TSR program beside your other applications.

It has the basic messaging features—including mailing lists—but little more. There are no carbon copies or complex archiving schemes. The built-in word processor cannot even move blocks of text.

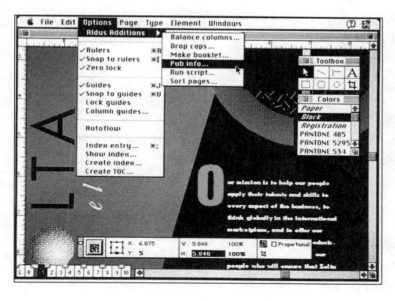

Figure 5-9. NoteWork's E-mail program comes in a PC version that uses its own on-screen windows and menus to show options and messages in progress.

Figure 5-10.
Notework's
Windows E-mail
version provides
similar menus and
windows to the PC
version, but pro-
vides them through
the standard
Windows interface.

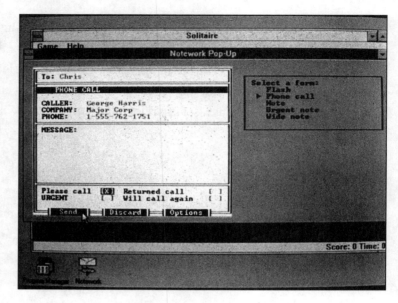

NoteWork does, however, offer quick and useful forms. The Developers Toolkit version lets you create whatever form you might want, and the main program makes it easy to call up, fill out, and send off forms. You can, for example, use a "flash" form to record the details on someone calling in, zip that message to the person the call is for, and get a reply back as to whether they want to take the call or not, all in seconds.

NoteWork also has macros for recording a sequence of actions and automatically playing them back.

The program supports MHS and UUCP as well as sending messages to Fax gateways. There's a remote version that can queue messages the remote system makes and send them as a bunch when dialing into the main network.

## MailMan for NetWare MHS

Reach Software's MailMan is a Windows E-mail program and the company's first step toward the planned WorkMan forms-based, work-flow network software.

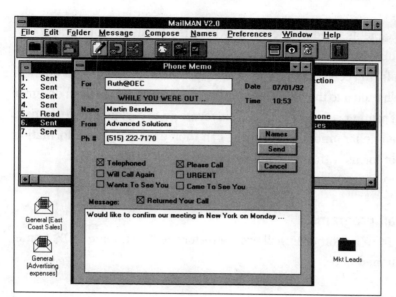

**Figure 5-11.**
**MailMAN** offers a variety of E-mail features including a form for noting telephone msages.

MailMan is built on MHS and can therefore easily exchange messages with other MHS-based programs such as DaVinci's eMail or MHS-supporting programs such as Microsoft Mail or cc:Mail. MailMan supports DDE, the Windows process for exchanging information among programs. MailMan for Windows, for example, could launch Excel to view a spreadsheet attachment or could send a message dictated by a WordBASIC macro in Word for Windows. Future versions will incorporate OLE (Object Linking and Embedding) support.

MailMan's messaging features include all the basics. Some programs use a single window to handle most messaging chores. MailMan uses several, such as a Compose window for creating the message and an Envelope window for addressing it by typing the name or selecting it from a list.

WorkMan is based on object-oriented electronic forms that users create, dictate routes for, and store in a library database. WorkMan automatically routes messages through their predefined paths to recipients. It can keep more than one form moving at a time and track to where the various forms have been sent.

Individual recipients need not decide to whom the forms are forwarded, saving them the trouble and ensuring an orderly flow of information. The people who need to act on a form receive it, have a chance to enter their part, sign off electronically, and then send it to the next person in line. WorkMan lets the form designer set up all sorts of routing rules, such as certain forms go to certain people if a field is over a specified dollar amount. WorkMan can then exchange the information from the filled-out forms with any Windows program that supports DDE.

## Other PC E-mail programs

There are quite a few other E-mail programs for the PC running DOS. Some, not all, are mentioned here.

**Tip:** 3Com made several popular network operating systems and offered E-mail for them. These included 3+Open Mail. 3Com has moved out of the business of network operating systems, so your best bet if you have a 3Com E-mail package is to switch to one of the others mentioned in this book. Microsoft, for example, has at times run special deals, with special conversion software, for 3Com Mail users who want to move to Microsoft Mail. The conversion utilities simplify the move by transferring directories and other such lists to the new mail system.

Televell Sales Mail runs on NetWare, and offers both DOS and Windows clients. It does not require a dedicated mail server. Televell does support MHS and graphics attachments. Gateways are available to PROFS, SMTP, X.400, SNADS, and VMSmail.

Transend makes CompletE-mail/MHS which runs on NetWare, VINES, and NetBIOS. Transend uses MHS and has gateways to PROFS, All-In-One, SMTP, X.400, and VMSmail. Transend's plans for this program include adding the ability to filter messages (message management) and to launch applications from it (like BeyondMail's capability).

Nobel Technologies makes EasyMail 3.0. This program offers mail lists, a mail manager to track incoming and outgoing mail, a built-in editor, message encryption, acknowledgement receipts, and direct printing of messages to a network printer.

Walker Richer and Quinn offers Posthaste which runs on NetWare and VINES and supports DOS, Windows, Mac, and OS/2 clients. It does not require a dedicated mail server and has gateways to cc:Mail, MCI Mail, and Microsoft Mail for PC Networks.

Infinite Technologies makes Express-IT!, E-mail for inexpensive LANs such as NetWare Lite and LANtastic.

Mustang's Brainstorm/MHS combines E-mail and on-line conferencing. It works on most networks and has an MHS gateway. Conferencing lets you set up topics that people can join to follow a single thread of messages.

Network Associates' Netphone is a "chat" utility to let as many as five Net-Ware clients communicate at once.

Photoring's Peer Mail comes in DOS and Windows client versions, runs on NetBIOS and NetWare networks, and uses MHS.

Daystrom's Gallery offers DOS, Windows, and OS/2 clients and runs on LAN Manager and NetWare networks. It depends on a proprietary mail protocol.

PMX/StarMail is E-mail for AT&T's StarLAN network.

Desk Executive from Boston Business Computing performs VAX All-In-1 functions on a PC (see Chapter 7 for a description of All-In-1, an E-mail and office program for minicomputers and mainframes). It provides word processing, filing, time management, and E-mail, along with a central menu. An interface to VMSmail is available.

Connex Systems's Connexion-1 runs only on DOS and uses a proprietary mail protocol. MHS and fax gateways are available.

Datapoint's Vista-Mail runs on NetBIOS and Arcnet network operating systems with clients for DOS and Datapoint's own RMS operating system.

3rd Planet Software's EZ Mail runs on NetWare networks and comes in clients for DOS and Windows. It does not require a dedicated mail server.

Finansa WinMail is a Windows E-mail program. Its forté is using the Windows DLL (Dynamic Linked Libraries) to work interactively or in batch mode with other Windows programs, such as Excel, Word, Ami Pro, and Visual BASIC.

The FidoNet bulletin-board system (BBS) includes E-mail, with the ability to set the time of day for E-mail exchanges and to select routing.

FYI makes a BBS with E-mail, conferencing and real-time chatting.

The Major BBS from Galacticomm is another BBS with E-mail, as well as teleconferencing, classified ads, shopping, and games.

## Integrated packages

There are some integrated programs for PCs which offer E-mail along with many other program capabilities. These are not just equipped with simple notepads or calendars, but have full-blown word processors, spreadsheets, databases and the like. Integrated programs are not a good way to get powerful E-mail. But if you only need basic E-mail, and like the idea of an inexpensive clutch of applications along with it, integrated may be the way to go.

Enable Office from Enable Software, mentioned previously in the Higgins product description, is also an integrated package.

Framework III from Ashton-Tate was one of the leaders in this area. A LAN version added E-mail (with plenty of features and even gateways) to the word processor, database, spreadsheet, and graphics of the original. Now that Ashton-Tate has been swallowed and digested by Borland, Framework's future is in limbo.

### Free E-mail programs

There are some basic DOS E-mail programs you can have for free, though they won't have all the features of commercial programs. Some are truly bare-bones, without carbon copies, mailing lists, and other such features you may need. Then again, your needs may be simple enough to get by with "freeware".

Look to shareware services such as PC-SIG, your local user group, or an on-line software library to find these. Ask the system operator or user-group leader for names of such programs.

One example can be found on the BIX on-line service: PostMan. This E-mail package runs on any NetBIOS-compatible system. It does not require a file server and includes its own text editor. The package includes a small TSR program called Postman that receives and delivers mail, and a larger program called Mail that contains the full set of features.

Another example is Pegasus Mail. This runs on NetWare LANs, supports both MHS and SMTP as well as Internet addressing. You can find it on the CompuServe on-line service in the Novell Library Forum in Library 16, "Public Domain/Text," as PM21C.ZIP. Use the command Go NOVLIB.

## Macintosh LAN E-mail

The Apple Macintosh computer runs operating-system software that is different from what you'll find in the PC. This means anyone using a Macintosh must use different programs from anyone using a PC. A Macintosh E-mail program could come from the same company as the PC program, could even be written to look similar to the PC program, but would be different at its core. Even the disk it is on wouldn't be understandable to a PC.

You don't have to use a Macintosh E-mail program to send E-mail to and receive E-mail from a Macintosh. That is, you can simply use a Macintosh telecommunications program to dial into an E-mail service, and read and write your messages. You could dial into a public service such as MCI Mail, hook up to a mainframe or minicomputer (if your telecommunications program permits the appropriate protocols), or connect remotely to a PC network (see more on this subject in Chapter 1 on WANs).

The Macintosh, however, is famous for its "ease of use," and you won't get the full advantage of that ease if you merely use it as a telecommunications terminal. To fully exploit the Macintosh operating system and interface of pull-down menus, cut-and-paste editing, icons to represent documents and programs, and so on, you need to use a Macintosh E-mail program.

Because the Macintosh is the second-most popular kind of computer—after the PC compatible—it is well represented in the E-mail world. Many of the companies that top the best-seller charts for PC E-mail also offer Macintosh E-mail programs. These programs, however, don't necessarily have the same features and abilities as their PC cousins, even if they sport almost identical names. For example, Microsoft Mail for the PC is quite different from Microsoft Mail for the Macintosh. Even if the real-world programs are quite similar, the administration features may not be equally represented on both PC and Macintosh sides of the fence. Some E-mail software companies, for example, sell both PC and Macintosh versions, but demand that they all be attached to a server running on a PC.

The separate history of the Macintosh—for some years PC software developers didn't consider it a worthwhile market—also leads to some different software choices for you on the Macintosh. QuickMail, for example, is the Macintosh E-mail leader, but is unknown on the PC. cc:Mail, which is the overwhelming leader on the PC, has a Macintosh version, but that program is not nearly as popular as QuickMail.

This section lists some of the most popular E-mail programs for Macintosh networks. You can also find Macintosh client versions of some of the E-mail programs described previously in this chapter.

**Tip:** To make things more confusing, Microsoft sells two different Macintosh E-mail programs, both with the same basic name: Microsoft Mail. One is the Macintosh client of Microsoft Mail for PC Networks (formerly Network Courier) and the other is the Macintosh client of Microsoft Mail for AppleTalk networks.

Remember from Chapters 1 through 4 that the Macintosh doesn't face all the same issues as the PC. Although most features and foundations are the same from one client to another, the difference in operating systems between Macintosh and PC mean different terms about which you should know and ask. PCs might run Windows E-mail software that supports DLLs and OLE. Macintosh E-mail software might run under System 7 and OCE.

## QuickMail

CE Software's QuickMail is the most popular Macintosh E-mail program. It offers clients for DOS, Windows, and OS/2, as well as for the Macintosh. QuickMail requires a dedicated server and uses a proprietary mail protocol. Gateways are available for the current version to link to PROFS, All-In-1, SMTP, X.400, VMSmail, and MHS. Both the server and client software for DOS and Macintosh are included in the same package: a unique selling point.

In early 1992, however, CE Software announced that it was developing a new version built on MHS, which could more easily share messages with other E-mail systems. This new version would run on Novell's NetWare, would not require an

AppleShare system, or a Macintosh as a server. Future gateways might allow direct movement of graphic forms from Macintoshs to PCs.

QuickMail became the Macintosh leader largely because of its use of the Macintosh interface: QuickMail's version was generally acknowledged to be the easi-

**Figure 5-12. Quick-Mail's inbox is typical, showing a list of received mail along with menu commands to handle those messages.**

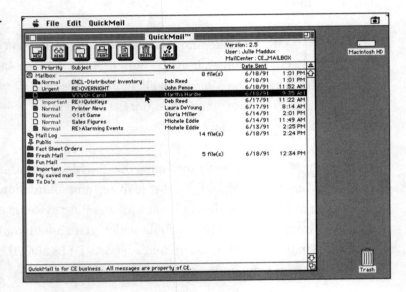

**Figure 5-13. Quick-Mail organizes its screen into easily located areas for message editing, from Subject to the message itself.**

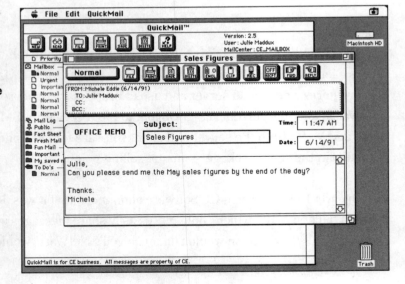

est to use. It did not, however, allow dragging of messages to folders as many Macintosh programs do, but offered pop-up menus with choices for moving messages. For features, QuickMail had all the usual, as well as the ability to attach both graphics and sound files and include them in the messages. Custom forms are possible, though there is no conferencing or searching messages by subject or sender.

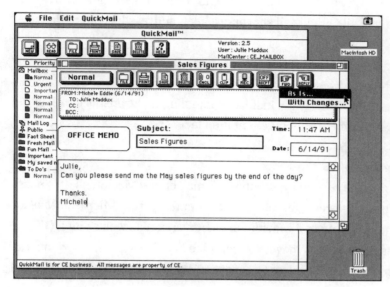

**Figure 5-14.** You can easily forward a message in QuickMail, just by clicking on the icon and deciding whether to send the message as it was received or with some changes.

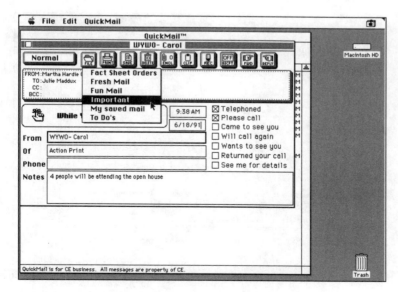

**Figure 5-15.** QuickMail offers a wide variety of options when you save or "archive" a message to disk.

QuickMail differed from many E-mail programs in archiving messages locally instead of on the server which saved server space but also meant tougher administration and more total space devoted to holding messages. The most recent versions are changing this foundation, to work from a server database as most E-mail does. Recent versions also use Apple's Communictions Toolbox instead of CE's own software for remote connections. And for administration, QuickMail offers a facility to poll all QuickMail servers to keep address lists up to date.

OCE will change CE's development strategy. Because OCE will add messaging and directory services to the Macintosh operating system, CE will separate those services from QuickMail. Instead of handling that transport-level work, CE will concentrate on the front-end client interface.

### Microsoft Mail for AppleTalk Networks

Microsoft Mail is the second-most popular E-mail on the Macintosh. It is possibly the most confusing, however, because it differs entirely from Microsoft Mail for PC Networks. That Mail offers a Macintosh client version as well as its DOS and Windows versions. Microsoft is moving to combine Windows and network operating-system features such as message transport on PC networks. That raises some

**Figure 5-16. Microsoft Mail for AppleTalk Networks uses standard Macintosh windows and dialog boxes to present addressing and writing commands.**

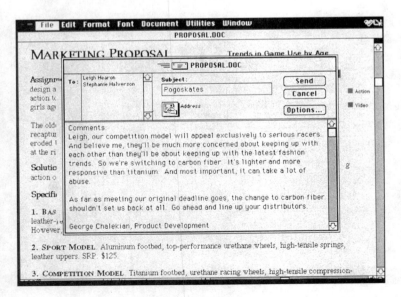

questions about the future of Mail for AppleTalk networks: Will it lose Microsoft's attention as the company focuses on winning the PC networking battle?

Mail for AppleTalk networks is simple to use—a fast program with a relatively short list of features (as of Version 3.0). It offers the basic features as well as some

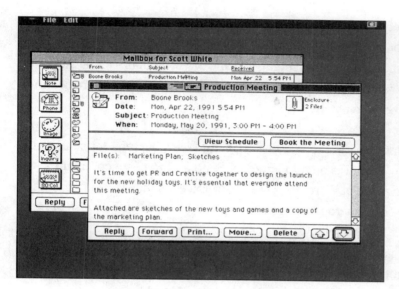

Figure 5-17. Microsoft Mail for PC Networks includes a Macintosh version. From this you can send and receive messages on a PC Network.

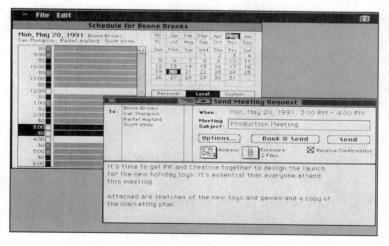

Figure 5-18. The Macintosh version of Microsoft Mail for PC Networks also permits use of the scheduling utility to set and confirm meetings.

unique touches. Sent messages, for example, will automatically be copied to the Sent folder, and messages in the Wastebasket won't be deleted until you turn off your computer. Microsoft Mail lacks some advanced features, such as conferencing or deleting sent-but-unread messages. It comes with typical forms—phone messages, meetings—and lets you design custom forms as well.

You don't need a dedicated server for Microsoft Mail. And for administration, it offers automatic backup to copy the server database to another folder, drive, or backup system. It also permits setting specific days and hours for backup. The database architecture supports client/server computing, which is more common on the PC than the Macintosh.

Microsoft Mail already shows some enabling (see Chapter 1 for an explanation of enabling). If Mail is on a Macintosh, Send and Receive commands will appear in the File menu of Word, PageMaker, or Excel on that Macintosh. In fact, you could use Excel's macros to automate some mail functions. This also permits the program to be a foundation for other network applications such as Status Mac from Pharos Technologies for remote Macintosh management. Optional software-development kits let you build custom mail features in the C programming language for programs such as HyperCard, 4D, and Excel.

Gateways are available to X.400, PROFS, UNIX SMTP, MHS, MCI Mail, AppleLink, and Fax. Alisa Systems and Pacer Software offer programs to run the server portion of Microsoft Mail on a VAX minicomputer, to improve performance.

### cc:Mail

cc:Mail is the world's most popular LAN E-mail program. It is available in DOS, Windows, Macintosh, and UNIX versions. (More details are given earlier in Chapter 5.) The Macintosh cc:Mail client was historically weak in both inter-

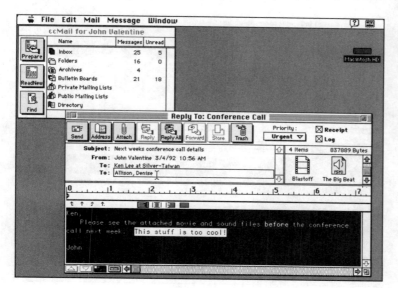

**Figure 5-19.
cc:Mail on the
Macintosh lets you
edit a message
and, uniquely, add
attributes such as
boldface, to the
text in the
message.**

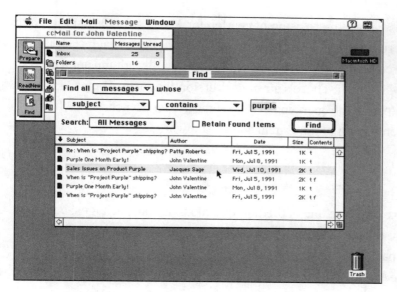

**Figure 5-20.
cc:Mail can search
through the stored
messages by
various criteria
as shown.**

**Figure 5-21.**
**Attached graphics are natural for the Macintosh, and cc:Mail for the Mac permits sending and viewing these.**

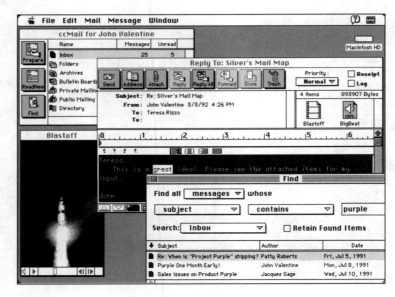

face and features before the revision of cc:Mail for Mac 1.2 in 1991 and then to 2.0 in 1992. These revisions brought it up to par with other Macintosh E-mail clients, and with cc:Mail's other versions. Now you can fully administer a cc:Mail system from a Macintosh. There's a remote version that uses Apple Communications Toolbox (part of the operating system software) for asynchronous, TCP/IP, X.25, or ISDN connection to the E-mail and the network.

### InBox

Sitka's InBox was once one of the hot Macintosh E-mail packages, but it has fallen behind the others in terms of features and compatibilities. It came in two parts: InBox as part of the TOPS network operating system and InBox Plus sold separately for the Macintosh. InBox supports up to 20 users. To route mail between multiple servers or handle more than 20 users, you need InBox Plus.

InBox offers aliases, automatic update of address files, and searching mail by subject or sender. It does not permit sending sound or graphics in messages, has no custom forms capabilities, and doesn't permit remote access to the server. It does not encrypt messages or offer conferencing.

**238**

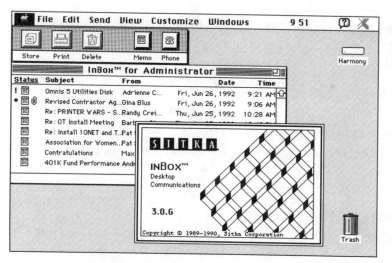

Figure 5-22. Sitka's Inbox has a simple and straightforward mail interface.

There are DOS and UNIX clients for this program. Even the administrative tools will run on a PC. InBox will run on LAN Manager, AppleShare, LAN Server, NetBIOS, Banyan VINES, and Sitka's own network operating system. Gateways to PROFS, SMTP, and X.400 are available.

## WordPerfect Office

WordPerfect Office began as a PC program (see the description earlier in this chapter), and that shows in the Macintosh version. Although it is comprised

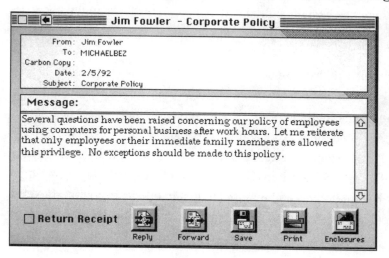

Figure 5-23. WordPerfect Office for the Macintosh has an E-mail component along with other office automation utility programs.

of E-mail and a number of office-management programs, it does not use the Macintosh interface as smoothly as some of the other Macintosh E-mail programs.

In Office you'll find a calendar for group scheduling on the network, a note-taking utility, and a file manager. The E-mail offers some unique features, such as thorough message tracking to see who has and has not read a sent message. It also lets you put a variety of text styles and sizes and multiple colors in E-mail forms.

## Add -on Programs for Managing Mail

Add-on Programs for Managing Mail are available. These programs add to the E-mail programs listed in this chapter. They enhance or extend the powers of those programs.

### BeyondMail

BeyondMail can be used as your main E-mail program or as an addition. As an add-on, BeyondMail brings both forms (through the BeyondMail Forms Designer) and Rules (through the main BeyondMail program).

The user formats information into forms of whatever layout and purpose desired. Once a form has been designed with appropriate labels and blank areas for data entry, it can circulate through E-mail.

Rules let you write programs or scripts to automate any aspect of E-mail operation. The most obvious use of rules is to manage your inbox. You could automatically sort messages by their senders, subjects, or whatever other factor is important to you, and send them to the appropriate folders. You could have Beyond-Mail automatically fax urgent messages to a remote location. Less obvious uses range from automatically forwarding or replying to messages to stripping information from received messages and manipulating it in other programs. (Beyond-Mail can launch other programs automatically.) There are some default and example rules with the program, or you can write your own using the rule commands and Boolean logic.

BeyondMail is certified to work with native MHS programs such as @Mail, DaVinci eMail, Network Scheduler, and the Retix X.400 Open Server and Alcom LAN Fax. Through gateways, it can handle cc:Mail, Notes, Microsoft Mail, MCI Mail, All-In-1, PROFS, and other mail. It comes with administrative utilities for synchronizing its name and address directories with those of cc:Mail, Microsoft Mail for PC Networks, DaVinci eMail, and others.

### JetForm-EMail and JetForm Designer

JetForm EMail acts as a front end to cc:Mail or DaVinci eMail. It lets the user fill out, address, and send forms created with JetForm Designer. The Designer has the commands you need to create and fill out forms and it comes in DOS and Windows versions. It lets you make forms to match current paper versions by drawing boxes, creating fields of set length, and adding any labels (with a built-in word processor). When filling-in forms, you can link data to database files; the program reads and writes Paradox files.

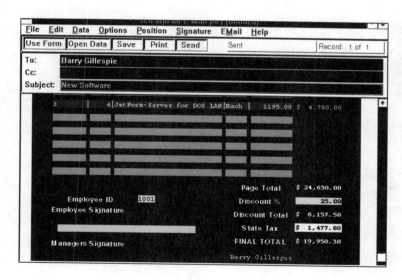

**Figure 5-24.**
**JetForm Mail combines E-mail with form creation functions to let you make and then circulate and fill in those forms.**

### MailBag

MailBag from Folio works with E-mail programs such as DaVinci eMail, Word-Perfect Office, Microsoft Mail, and cc:Mail. After you set it up, you tag messages as you read them. MailBag then uses those tags as it archives and compresses the E-mail messages. When you then want to find and read that archived E-mail, MailBag depends on NetWare's on-line Help Utility to search for and retrieve electronic messages, including their attachments. The Help Utility is a read-only version of Folio's most famous product, Views, an engine for managing "infobases" of text information. Because the messages are compressed and indexed, the searches can be fast and can be "full-text." Full-text search allows you to search through all of every message, not just through their addresses and subject headers as many E-mail programs allow.

# CHAPTER SIX

# UNIX E-mail

This chapter describes the built-in E-mail of the UNIX operating system, the fundamentals of using that E-mail, and some of the programs you can add to simplify and improve it.

The UNIX operating system was invented by AT&T and then improved or adapted by all sorts of companies. In the 1980s, it became the most popular operating system for workstations—desktop computers that are faster and better at networking, though more expensive than personal computers. Sun is the leading maker of workstations, followed by Hewlett-Packard and IBM.

UNIX is also very popular on minicomputers and can be found running on everything from supercomputers and mainframes to personal computers. The most popular personal-computer form of UNIX is called Xenix from the Santa Cruz Operation (SCO). On workstations you'll find AT&T's System V UNIX and the BSD variant developed at the University of California at Berkeley. Because Sun's workstations have been so popular, you'll also encounter plenty of Solaris, the Sun OS, another variation of UNIX.

What your UNIX looks like on screen will depend on the "shell" you're using. The shell is a program that runs on the UNIX kernel, delivers a particular display to you, and accepts a certain set of commands. Most basic commands remain the same from shell to shell. There are even some GUI front ends for UNIX that make it easier for some people to use. Two of the most popular are the Motif GUI and Open Look. Both are extensions of the X Windows GUI standard.

**Figure 6-1. Sun workstations run the UNIX operating system and Sun's own OpenWindows Version 3 graphic user interface. This includes an E-mail utility, built-in.**

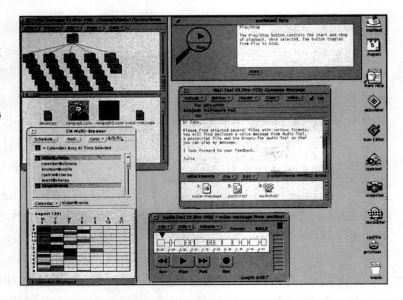

**Figure 6-2. Sun's UNIX E-mail in the OpenWindows Version 3 can handle multimedia messages.**

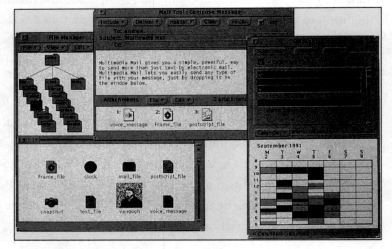

As you login to the UNIX network, you'll be asked to type your password, which will provide some security for your messages: Only someone with the password can read your E-mail.

Most UNIX systems are networked, and many of those networks are connected to Internet (see Chapter 8 for details), which lets them exchange mail with other UNIX and non-UNIX users all over the world.

## Transport and User Agents

The basic UNIX "kernel" (the central heart of the operating system) comes with many utility programs. E-mail is one of these, as are many other communication and networking programs, known collectively as UUCP (for "UNIX-to-UNIX Copy"). Even the SMTP mail protocol is built into most UNIX systems. The UUCP user only needs to know the correct path between UNIX machines to send a message. The more extensive USENET set of programs lets any user read and post articles on "newsgroups," a sort of bulletin-board feature for E-mail.

Because UNIX E-mail is both built-in and consistent in its fundamentals from one system to the next, most UNIX computers can exchange mail with any other UNIX computers.

UNIX E-mail, however, is not monolithic. There are differences in both the mail routing and delivery programs (the MTA or Mail Transport Agents, as explained in Chapter 1), and the front ends or interfaces for sending and reading (the MUA or Mail User Agents, also explained in Chapter 1).

UNIX E-mail has several transport agents. These have names such as: smail, sendmail, and MMDF (Multichannel Memorandum Distribution Facility).

Smail is the simplest. Sendmail which is reliable and flexible is the most common, but not very secure. MMDF is more complex than either and comes with Xenix from SCO.

Most AT&T UNIX systems use the mailx front end, while BSD UNIX systems use Mail.

Both have a command-line interface that is described in detail later in this chapter. You don't have to settle for the bare-bones commands of mail. If you send and receive only a few messages, you probably don't want to bother getting and learning anything more. If you do handle more messages, however, you might want more options for organizing, automating, and customizing your messages.

For this, you can add third-party programs to improve the front-end interface. Some of these are described in this chapter.

The standard UNIX mail interface is line-oriented and harder to create messages with a full-screen driver interface. Third-party interface programs can offer additional features. Elm, Cymail, and Z-mail can all save mail in named folders, for instance, and support group aliases. Product descriptions are given at the end of this chapter. A new interface can shield you from some of the details of your mail transport, which some people prefer. What you want depends on your own style, technical background, and the time you have to spend with the mechanics of mail.

Some third-party interface programs are commercially available—you buy them just as you would PC or Macintosh software package. Some are public-domain (PD); they're free and can be found already on many UNIX systems. Both MH and Elm are PD MUAs (how's that for "acronymese?").

MH or Message-Handling system is a set of E-mail programs that you use from the UNIX-shell prompt, not from a menu inside a single program. Each command is technically its own separate program and can use all shell features, such as aliases, scripts, pipes, and redirection (for directly sending the results of one program to another program). Each message is kept as its own file, with the filename as the message number, which means you can use standard file operations on the messages directly. It uses more disk space, but offers greater flexibility in managing messages.

XMH is a version of MH for X Windows Version 11 Release 4 that runs MH commands from the X Windows graphical interface of windows, buttons, and mouse control. It comes free with X Windows. Emacs mh-rmail and MHE are front ends for MH that run under the GNU emacs text editor. (GNU is another version of UNIX.)

Many MUAs have their own command interpreter, instead of using the shell as MH does. This is the way most PC programs operate, incidentally. They are monolithic, meaning they require that you start the E-mail MUA and then give commands, instead of giving commands from the shell. The mush mail agent is like this. Monolithic agents keep all messages in a single file. This method uses less space than an agent such as MH, but makes it tougher for you to get at the mail because you cannot use shell commands to operate on individual message files.

## Other UNIX E-mail choices

There are a number of other transport and user agents available for UNIX systems. Some of these are mentioned here.

Sun PC-NFS Lifeline Mail runs on NFS (Network File System). It supports DOS client workstations. It is also available in a Windows version for PCs and

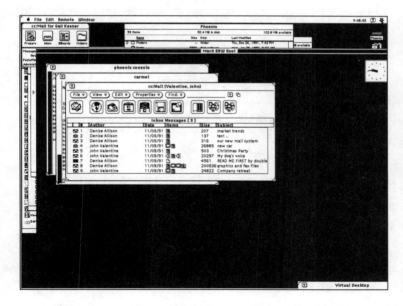

**Figure 6-3. The UNIX version of cc:Mail follows the standard Open Windows GUI for Sun Workstations as shown here, with a graphic desktop for quickly choosing E-mail or other programs**

**Figure 6-4.
cc:Mail for UNIX
offers an inbox list
of received mail
along with icons
for the common
commands.**

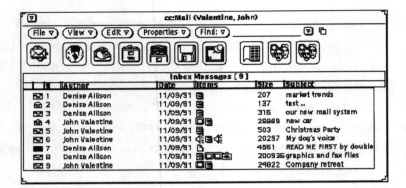

**Figure 6-5.
Creating a
message in cc:Mail
on a UNIX system
means opening a
new message
window and
entering and edit-
ing text.**

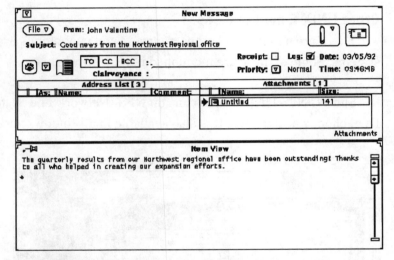

doesn't require a dedicated mail server. It uses the SMTP mail protocol and allows graphics files as attachments.

Wollongong Group's WIN/MHS for SCO UNIX or UNIX System V/386, can be used as a transfer agent or as a gateway supporting X.400. WIN/DS provides the messaging and directory services of the CCITT 1988 X.500 specification.

Developers adapted cc:Mail to UNIX. It runs in Open Look for X Windows on Sun SPARCstations and can handle text, binary, fax, graphics, and sound attachments. Support for SMTP is built-in. Like other cc:Mail versions, it offers message receipts and security.

The Interactive Systems X.400 MTA (see Chapter 1) runs on OSI and TCP/IP. It does not require a dedicated mail server and, naturally, uses the X.400 mail protocol. Graphic-file attachments are a feature and gateways to SMTP are available.

## Using Mail

The popular "Mail" program can send messages and files to other UNIX systems and lets you make distribution lists to send the same message to many recipients. Different versions of "Mail" offer different sets of features beyond these, but most versions are similar to one another.

To notify you of received mail, Mail shows you a simple "You have mail" message each time you logon to the network.

Each Mail user has a mailbox, a file where incoming messages land. This will be in the directory

```
/usr/spool/mail
```

Each user also has a personal mailbox, called mbox, in their home directory. After you've read received mail in your system mailbox you can save it to your mbox. Nobody else can save mail to your mbox.

Finally, each user may have a file called ".mailrc" in the home directory, which contains all special instructions for that particular user's E-mail operation. It will hold mailing lists, command changes, and variable settings. If there is no mailrc file, the Mail program will use defaults for these settings.

**Tip:** UNIX files with names that start with a period are "hidden" files. They don't appear in normal file lists, though they can be found and even unhidden by system adminstrators. Their hidden nature gives them some protection from change.

## Message Structure

Messages have structure. They start with a header that has five parts:

Header Element......................Element Use
To: ...........................................message destination (one or more user-names)
Subject: ..................................description of message
CC:...........................................carbon-copy user names (duplicate recipients)
BCC:.........................................blind carbon-copy user names
Receipt: ..................................user names to which receipts are returned (acknowledgments that the message has been read)

All elements but "To" are optional. (As explained in Chapter 1, both types of CC recipients receive a copy of the message, but CC recipients are listed on the message and BCC recipients are not.)

After the header comes the body text. Simple UNIX mail does not accept graphics or sound in messages, only plain text.

## Reading messages

To read received mail, you type

```
mail
```

at the shell prompt. You'll see a list of heads for received messages, in reverse chronological order (most recent shown first).

If there are no messages, you see a plain "no messages" note and are returned to the shell prompt. If there is more than one page of message headers to show, you may scroll through the headers by typing either of the following two commands:

```
h+
h-
```

You may scan for mail from a particular user with the command

```
h username
```

The list of headers shows what has been done to the messages. Deleted messages don't appear at all; messages marked with an "M" will be saved in your personal mailbox when you leave the Mail program; messages marked with an asterisk will be saved by the Save command; and messages marked "H" are waiting to be held for mail options.

When messages are listed, you'll be in "command mode," with the system ready to accept Mail commands. Press <Return> to show the first message listed and after reading any message to read the next message. Type "P" and a message's number to read that particular message out of order. Type "Top" to show the first five lines of messages in the mailbox.

 **Tip:** You may set the number of lines the Top command will show by editing your .mailrc file.

 **Tip:** With most mail commands, you may follow the command with message numbers of the items you want to process. You may use individual numbers or a range of numbers, such as 1-4. You may also use the wildcard symbol, "*", to indicate all messages listed.

If new mail arrives while you're reading old mail, you'll see a notification on screen. Then you can use the

```
restart
```

command to scan and read it. This checks your system mailbox again and shows a new list of headers.

Press "Q" to quit the Mail program and to delete and save all marked mail. To exit without deleting and saving, press "X."

### Replying to a sender

After reading a message, you may immediately reply to it by typing "r". This will put you in compose mode where you can create a new message. The sender will automatically be the recipient of the message you create. When you're done typing the message, press <Ctrl-D> and it will be on its way.

 **Tip:** Use replies to save time addressing messages.

 **Tip:** If you type an uppercase "R" for replying, you'll be asked for the names of others you want to send the message to, directly or as carbon copies.

### Forwarding messages

If you want to forward a mail message to someone else, you type

```
<<f
```

followed by the user name that you want to receive the message. The last displayed message will move onto the network. You may forward any other message by specifying a message number after the "f" command.

The header will be modified to show that the message was forwarded, not sent as an original, and the text body will also be modified to appear as a forwarded piece. All text will be moved one tab stop to the right.

**Tip:** To avoid moving all text one tab stop right in a forwarded message, use the uppercase F for the command.

### Saving messages

To save mail you've read, use the

```
mb
```

command. This will mark the most recently read piece of mail to be deleted from the system mailbox and saved in your personal mailbox when you quit the Mail program.

You may choose to save a piece of mail in a place other than your personal mailbox by using the

```
s
```

command. Follow it with a filename. The most recently read message will be saved in a file of that name.

### Deleting messages

Delete mail you've read by typing

```
d
```

at the command prompt. This will remove the message from the header list. You can still recall deleted mail with the

```
u
```

command and the message number. You may only do this before you quit the Mail program. (Mail isn't actually deleted until you quit, just marked for deletion.)

Delete all mail with the

```
d *
```

wildcard command.

 **Tip:** A quick way to read and empty a mailbox is to use the <<dp command, which will delete the current message and display the next.

### Sending mail

To send a message using the built-in Mail program, start by typing the mail command at the shell prompt, followed by the names you want to send the message to, like this:

```
mail fred vicky
```

You'll see this appear:

```
Subject:
```

"Subject:" prompts you to enter an optional one-line description of the message. When you have, press <Return>. Then you'll be in "compose mode," where you may type the text body of the message.

Type the lines of the message, pressing <Return> at the end of each line. Unfortunately, the editor is primtive, so you cannot edit completed lines. You can, however, press <Ctrl-H> to backspace while still on a line.

If you think of a person you want to be listed as a CC on the message, type

```
~ c
```

on a line, followed by that person's user name. The tilde character tells Mail to temporarily escape from the compose mode. When that command is done and you press <Return> at the end of the line, you'll be back in compose mode. For BCCs, use

```
~ b
```

 **Tip:** You may send the message to multiple recipients, CCs, or BCCs by typing multiple user names on the line, separating each by a space.

 **Tip:** You may send messages to yourself by including your own user name as a recipient, CC, or BCC.

When you've finished setting up the recipients, CCs, and BCCs, and have completed the text of the message, press <Ctrl-D>. Your message will be sent and you'll see

```
(end of message)
```

and then the shell prompt character.

 **Tip:** BSD UNIX Mail lets you enter your CC and BCC names after you finish the text body. You type the text, then type a period on a line by itself. BSD Mail will ask you for CC and BCC names.

### Sending files

You may send files made with a word processor, editor, spreadsheet, graphics program, or whatever by using the UNIX redirection capability. To do so, type

```
mail username < filename
```

The username is the name of the intended recipient or recipients (several names separated by spaces).

The filename, naturally, is for the file you want to send.

### Mailing lists

A mailing list is an alias or distribution list. That is, it substitutes a single alias name for a list of names, so you need only use the single alias to send a copy of the message to each user in the list. (See Chapter 1 for more details.)

For UNIX mail ,you define your mailing lists in the .mailrc file in your home directory. To create a temporary mailing list, type

```
alias listname user1 user2 user3
```

so the <<alias  command will know to put those user names into the mailing list called "listname".

 **Tip:** You may use "a" for the <<alias  command.

 **Tip:** When you reply to a message sent from a mailing list, everyone on the list will get a copy of your reply.

Any temporary mailing list will disappear when you exit Mail. To make a mailing list permanent, you must use a word processor or editor to add the <<alias command to your .mailrc file. Another possibility is to have the system administrator set up aliases that will work for all Mail users on the system.

## Mail commands summary

Here are the commands for the UNIX Mail program. Type them at the mail prompt, followed by any user names or message numbers you need to specify the command's action. Finish by pressing the Return key.

| Command code | Command effect |
| --- | --- |
| ? | help |
| help | help (though this only works in compose mode if you use the ~ first) |
| * | help (in some mail systems) |
| a | create alias |
| ~b | add names to BCC list |
| ~c | add names to CC list |
| d | delete displayed or specified with numeric argument messages |
| dp | delete displayed message and display next message |
| e | start the editor |
| h+ or h- | scroll headers forward or back |
| f | forward mail |
| F | forward mail without shifting text to right |
| l | print hard copy |
| mb | save message in personal mailbox |
| n | skip n pieces of mail (+ or -) |
| p | display mail |
| q | quit and clean up mailbox |
| r | reply to mail |
| R | reply to multiple user |
| restart | restart mail and check for new messages |
| s | save to file |
| top | display first five lines of specified messages |

u .................................................undelete deleted mail
v .................................................start the vi editor
x .................................................quit without mailbox cleanup
? .................................................display help-screen summary
= .................................................display current message number
! .................................................invoke shell command without leaving Mail

## Addressing

When you're filling in the To, CC, or BCC fields for a UNIX Mail message, follow these general rules as well as any specified for your computer and network:

■ If sending a message to users with an account on your computer, use their username, otherwise known as their login name.

■ If sending a message to users on another computer, start with their username and add the computer name.

There are two forms of this:

username@computername ...........is the form for Internet addressing
computername!username .............is the form for UUCP addressing

Ask the postmaster or administrator of your system for the precise rules to follow.

## MH

MH automates some of the work of Mail. Here's a list of commands for MH:

| Command code | Command effect |
|---|---|
| inc ............................................ | incorporate new messages from system mailbox into MH |
| show ........................................ | show messages |

| | |
|---|---|
| next | show next message |
| prev | show previous message |
| comp | compose new message |
| repl | reply to message |
| forw | forward copy of message |
| dist | redistribute copy of message |
| scan | show summary of messages in folder |
| folder | show summary of folders |
| pick | search for messages |
| sortm | reorder messages |
| rmm | remove messages |
| rmf | remove folder |
| send | send messages |

These MH commands have "switches" for options. For instance, you could use

```
-annotate
```

to annotate the original message to show that it has been replied to or forwarded.

MH keeps track of the current message in each folder and will use that message if you don't specify a message number on the command line. Like Mail, MH can also work on more than one message at a time. Just specify the messages on the command line.

The MH profile, your personal configuration, is like the .mailrc settings for Mail. It is stored in the .mh_profile file in your home directory. It includes paths, signatures, and other details of your mail activity. xmh uses this file as well. MH also keeps an audit log file of your E-mail work.

## UUCP

The UUCP utilities can send mail directly to other UNIX computers on the network. To do so, you need to use the UUCP addressing scheme, as mentioned previously. This is called "bang" addressing, because the exclamation point that separates address elements is called a "bang".

The simplest way to route UUCP messages is to build a path using the names of each successive UNIX computer along the route (each computer has a name). Type the computer names with a bang between names. Ask your system administrator for the computer names. Such an address looks like

```
computer1!computer2
```

To learn your computer's name, you can often use one of these commands (they work with many versions of UNIX):

```
uname -n
```
or
```
uname -1
```

Each time a message moves from one computer to the next, it has made a "hop". You could end up specifying a route with many hops if your computer isn't directly connected to the next. This might entail some serious research to learn routes and computer names. Long addresses could become

```
hostcomputer!computer1!computer2!computer3!computer4!
computer5!remotecomputer
```

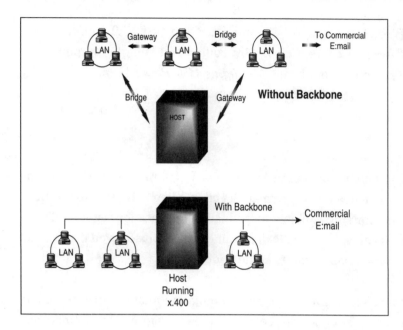

Figure 6-6.
Backbone
Alternative.

 **Tip:** If you have a long or unwieldy address, create an alias for it to make using the address easier. Then you need only type the short alias instead of the full address.

A more efficient method in such a case could be to use a backbone computer in your route. The USENET network for exchanging mail and news, for example, has large computer sites that are connected to yet larger sites, in a hierarchy. The organization is informal, but still useful. If your system adminsitrator can educate you on the organization of the hierarchy, you might find a computer that's a major mail-transfer connection for a particular company or region. Then the long address can be reduced to

```
host!backboneclose!backbonefar!remotehost
```

Again, you can make an alias to cut down on address typing (both for time efficiency and for avoiding typing mistakes).

**Tip:** For more details on UUCP and USENET, see the book *Using UUCP and Usenet* by Todino and Dougherty, published by O'Reilly. The same firm publishes *Managing UUCP and Usenet* by O'Reilly and Todino.

## Elm

Elm is a full-screen, intelligent user agent for UNIX Mail. It works with the transport agents smail, execmail, or rmail. Its addressing conforms to the RFC-822 standard. Elm knows how to use the path alias database for fast E-mail routing, which means it can automatically determine the best path, even if all you do is save someone's login name and machine node.

Elm can automatically save incoming and outgoing mail in separate folders by the name of the sender or addressee. It has a filter program for automatically handling routine mail according to a program you write. You may also customize Elm by changing its .elmrc file.

Elm is free, but you must find it, download it, configure it, and compile it before use. Some of its advanced features can be difficult to learn. Finding Elm means looking on UNIX bulletin boards and in UNIX archive sites, such as any comp.sources.unix site, UUNET.UU.NET.

## Cymail

Cyantic System's Cymail is a full-screen, menu-packing interface for UNIX Mail on Sun SPARCstations and the Commodore Amiga. It comes with a good manual, so it can be easier to learn than a completely free program such as Elm. All commands are shown at the top of the screen. It supports aliases, but forces you to specify the full bang paths for UUCP messages. It does not use the pathalias database and it does not have some security features such as letting you hide message headers.

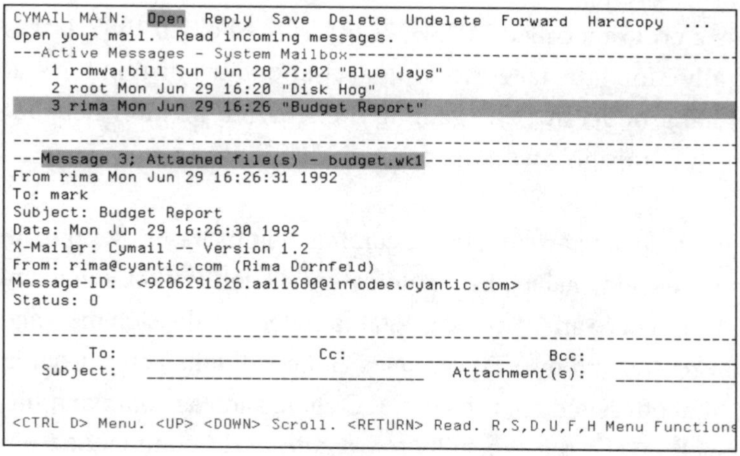

```
CYMAIL MAIN: Open Reply Save Delete Undelete Forward Hardcopy ...
Open your mail.  Read incoming messages.
---Active Messages - System Mailbox-----------------------------------------
   1 romwa!bill Sun Jun 28 22:02 "Blue Jays"
   2 root Mon Jun 29 16:20 "Disk Hog"
   3 rima Mon Jun 29 16:26 "Budget Report"


--------------------------------------------------------------------------
---Message 3; Attached file(s) - budget.wk1------------------------------
From rima Mon Jun 29 16:26:31 1992
To: mark
Subject: Budget Report
Date: Mon Jun 29 16:26:30 1992
X-Mailer: Cymail -- Version 1.2
From: rima@cyantic.com (Rima Dornfeld)
Message-ID:  <9206291626.aa11680@infodes.cyantic.com>
Status: O


--------------------------------------------------------------------------
      To:  _____   Cc:  _____   Bcc:  _____
   Subject: _____   Attachment(s):  _____


<CTRL D> Menu. <UP> <DOWN> Scroll. <RETURN> Read. R,S,D,U,F,H Menu Functions
```

**Figure 6-7. Cymail offers menus and the option of attached messages as shown here.**

Cymail offers a simple method for attaching text or binary files to mail messages, and uses the UUENCODE or UUDECODE facility that most UNIX systems possess. This lets recipients extract the attached files even if they don't have Cymail.

There's a simple text editor in Cymail for creating messages. It is a simple method to attach text or binary files to mail message. You may choose to specify your own text editor as the default. Do so by editing the cymailrc file. You can set other options there as well.

## Z-Mail

Siren Software's Z-Mail has many features. A key to its success is that it has three interfaces: character (command-line), full-screen, and windows (GUI). This interface option lets the individual choose the MUA they like best, but lets large companies use PCs that can run GUI programs and ASCII terminals that can run only character interfaces. The character interface can also be useful for remote connections to the E-mail. When ASCII terminals fade away, replaced perhaps by X Windows or X Terminals, character interfaces may lose their luster. For now, however, they are a real selling point for Z-Mail.

Z-Mail began as a program called MUSH, Mail Users Shell, in 1985. It was meant to be a friendly Mail interface, working at first under SunWindows. It became a commercial product in 1990, gaining the X Windows interface, but remaining backwardly-compatible with the original MUSH product.

You'll find on-line help, custom functions, command-line aliases, scripts, filters, custom message headers, mailing lists, automatic mail notification, and many other features in Z-Mail. There are10 message status codes beside each message header displayed on-screen and over 90 variables and conditions you can set in the zmail.rc file. Z-Mail offers the features of the C shell, such as command history, filename completion, and the capability to execute UNIX commands from inside a program. From archived messages, you can search for mail from a particular person, subject, or date.

Although Z-Mail doesn't have the database-searching ability of Elm, it does have some routing optimization built-in. It can be told which nodes connect directly to a host machine for more direct reply routing.

**Tip:** Sometimes the header of outgoing messages will be wrong if your mail program cannot get your computer's name or "hostname." The system administrator can set the hostname manually using the hostname variable in the system-wide Z-Mail initialization file.

Z-Mail's default interface is the line mode, which doesn't require any graphics display capabilities—just a modem and a terminal. The full-screen and windows interfaces use this as a foundation. Z-Mail is compatible with Mail (it will obey commands used for Mail).

The full-screen mode is like the VI editor: You can press keys or sequences of keys to move the cursor around the screen, which makes editing messages easier. It requires a terminal that would run a full-screen editor such as VI.

The windows mode makes getting at commands and messages easier, but it also loses some features in the line and screen modes, such as pipelines and command-line aliases. This GUI has a main window for most operations, a toolbox, a message display window, and an attachment window. You can get it in both Motif and Open Look versions, which don't differ much. The windows mode depends on using the mouse to point to buttons, menus, and lists of options. It also has icons for frequent commands and lets you show multiple messages at once.

**Tip:** Sometimes messages can't be delivered and are returned as "bounced mail" errors. This can happen immediately or take days. Z-Mail appends these messages to the dead letter folder. To start Z-Mail with its basic line interface, you type

```
mail
```

and press <Return>. For the full-screen interface, you type

```
zmail -fullscreen
```

and press <Return>. To get the graphic interface, you type

```
zmail -gui
```

and press <Return>.

Like Cymail, Z-Mail lets you attach text or binary files to mail messages. It also lets you specify which program will be needed at the receiving end to handle the attached file. This is a courtesy to the recipient, and can also be made part of the scripting process for creating automated applications.

The Z-Script language lets you customize Z-Mail, either for short scripts or for long macros. Many of Z-Mail's own functions are written in Z-Script, which can reach all the regular UNIX Mail functions. Z-Script even lets you create distributed applications based on outside programs. There's a long scripting manual with some examples and sample scripts. For the GUI interface, you may add items to the menus and buttons to the windows.

# CHAPTER SEVEN

# Mainframe and Minicomputer E-mail

Mainframes and minicomputers were the original homes for E-mail and are still used for messaging in many companies. As explained in Chapter 1, they can be the sole site for the E-mail program, contacted by a constellation of terminals around it. That's often referred to as "host mail." Mainframes and minis can also be used as part of an E-mail hierarchy that includes LANs, WANs, and public-service E-mail. (Many of the public-service E-mail systems are, in fact, running on mainframes and minicomputers.)

Many of the makers of large computers offer their own E-mail software for those systems, either for use on its own or as part of a general office-automation package. There are also some third-party makers of such software. Mainframes and minis are sites for gateway programs because they are often centrally located, in a good position to play intermediary between various systems and networks. Soft-Switch, for example, is an electronic mail gateway and interconnection product used by many large corporations. It runs on IBM mainframes with a SNADS gateway. Using the most popular host mail—IBM's PROFS—and Soft-Switch, you can reach 10-million nodes.

This chapter briefly describes some of the most important mainframe and minicomputer E-mail programs. It doesn't go into much detail because the trend is clearly away from building E-mail around mainframes and minis. LANs and WANs are the story today, and mainframes and minis are history—a history that still influences many of today's decisions and that many companies need to recognize, live with, and build upon, but an obsolete way of delivering messaging.

## PROFS and DISOSS

IBM has sold more mainframes than any other company, so it should not be surprising that IBM's PROFS (Professional Office System) should be one of the best-known E-mail packages. IBM's OfficeVision office-automation program, which includes PROFS mail, has the largest user base of any host-based office-automation system, with several million mailboxes in the world.

PROFS runs under VM/CMS and is commonly found on 4341 and 4381 mainframes. It calls for a full-screen 3270 terminal and makes much use of the terminal's function keys. PROFS can be reached in line-by-line mode by IBM 3101 terminals, but that makes the user enter commands directly without using any menus.

PROFS includes other office-automation programs as well, such as time management, calendaring, and filing. When combined with IBM Displaywrite/370, it also includes word processing.

You may send three types of messages in PROFS: messages up to three lines long to deliver to another system in real time, notes created in a full-screen editor and addressed when created, and documents created with a word processor and given predefined addressing.

Simware offers a Macintosh client for PROFS, which uses the Mac's interface of icons and menus. It lets the user create, read, and store E-mail while off-line, connecting to PROFS only to upload and download mail. The same interface can be used to access other OfficeVision functions, such as group scheduling.

IBM does not have a rich source of gateways for PROFS, but most third-party gateway makers accomodate PROFS connections to other E-mail. EasyLink, for example, can exchange telex messages with a PROFS node without any software changes to the IBM system. That happens because EasyLink emulates a PROFS node as part of its service, so PROFS can send messages to it as if it was sending mail to just another node. IBM plans to network PROFS and DISOSS nodes together using SNADS software so that messages and computer files can exchange freely between the systems.

IBM's DISOSS software and its E-mail runs on many 3081 and 3083 mainframes under the MVS, DOS, and OS operating systems. Although once quite dissimilar in appearance from PROFS, it is now much closer in looks and features. IBM's application of its SAA (System Application Architecture) principles pushed the two toward the Common User Interface, which IBM is aiming toward for all of its software.

## All-In-1 and VMSmail

Digital Equipment Corporation, otherwise known as DEC, is the second largest computer company in the U.S. DEC sells a range of computers, but is best known for its VAX line of minicomputers. It offers two E-mail programs for the VAX. VMSmail is the simpler; All-In-1 is an integrated office program for VAXs that includes word processing, database access, E-mail, and decision support (a popular feature in mainframes for analyzing choices, sometimes with weighted choices or charts). All-In-1 runs on DECnet, AppleTalk, MS-Net, LAN Manager, NetBIOS, and TCP/IP and supports DOS, OS/2, Macintosh, and VMS clients. There's even a remote version called Mobilizer for All-In-1 that runs on portable PCs, to let users create, read, store, and send E-mail messages over any modem or other line supporting DEC's Local Area Transport protocol. All-In-1 doesn't require a dedicated mail server, and it separates the transport agent from the user agent. Gateways reach to PROFS, SNADS, Telex, MCI Mail, SMTP, X.400, and VMSmail.

All-In-1 mail can move many different files, including DEC's own file formats. The PC client for All-In-1 can move PC files. You can administer a distributed directory on the network from a central location.

There are several third-party clients for connecting PCs to All-In-1. Boston Business Computing makes Desk Executive, which provides menu management, word processing, E-mail, and time management for integration with All-In-1 or VMSmail. Cappcomm Software makes Mail Call, a program for PCs to send and receive mail from All-In-1 and VMSmail. It has a customizing script language. DEC's own All-In-1 Desktop for MS-DOS lets the PC user access all of the All-In-1 applications on the VAX including scheduling, group conferencing, and E-mail. It also lets them launch applications from All-In-1.

DEC's new TeamLinks distributed-application environment uses the client/server model to let teams or workgroups share, retrieve, and display data. The applications have E-mail, conferencing, work-flow automation, and bulletin-board features. It is built on DEC's PathWorks networking software, integrating PC LANs into DEC's VMS networks. PathWorks is based on Microsoft's LAN Manager. TeamLinks will include a Windows version of All-In-1 mail for PCs. Rumour has it that DEC is planning a Windows NT version of All-In-1. Other companies have announced that they'll develop to TeamLinks. (Lotus is creating versions of 1-2-3, Ami Pro, and Freelance Graphics to the environment.) DEC has announced that it will work with Novell to integrate NetWare services for VAX VMS, Ultrix, and OSF/1 servers.

## AlisaMail

Alisa Systems' AlisaMail runs on DEC VAX minicomputers. It can be used as the heart of a QuickMail or Microsoft Mail for AppleTalk Networks system. It supports all features of those Macintosh E-mail programs. It also lets Macintosh mail users exchange messages with each other and with VMSmail and All-In-1.

AlisaMail can use gateways to reach X.400, PROFS, DISOSS, and UUCP mail. Its directory has a PeopleFinder feature to let users look-up other users to learn addresses, titles, and phone numbers. It even holds scanned photographs of the users. The directory can be edited from a Macintosh and is automatically synchronized from Macintosh to VAX and from VAX to Macintosh. The program has a batch command mode for automating backup and address changes.

## HPDeskmanager III

Hewlett-Packard's HPDeskmanager is an integrated office program for HP 9000 minicomputers. It includes filing, time management, and E-mail. Related modules include HPWord and HPDraw. There are gateways to connect it to Telex, X.400, and other E-mail systems.

HPDeskmanager can transmit ASCII messages and formatted files from many different applications, including PC files. It has unique features such as letting a designated colleague edit and send messages.

The central directory can be searched to find the name and nodal address of any user. There's a General Delivery Mail Box that lets you leave messages for a recipient without a known address. The messages are then forwarded to a printer, other software such as HPTelex II, HPWord, HPDraw, and general E-mail tools.

## ADR/eMail

ADR/eMail from Applied Data Research runs on IBM mainframes under the MVS, DOS, and OS operating systems. It needs either IBM's CICS or ADR's own ROSCOE teleprocessing monitor.

ADR/eMail includes E-mail, scheduling, and activity tracking. It can send messages both to mailboxes and to other application programs as well as move its own files and ASCII PC files. You can buy a PC/eMail program as a front end for PC access to ADR/eMail.

A unique feature of the E-mail in ADR/eMail lets you view a message and all its associated replies and comments, to follow one full thread of messaging. The package also includes an eMail System Interface (ESI) for customizing mail transmission to other programs. A built-in accounting system provides departmental bill-back. Directories are kept synchronized automatically.

## CEO

Data General's Comprehensive Electronic Office (CEO) is an integrated office-automation program. It runs on Data General's minicomputers with the AOS/VS operating system. Gateways reach to X.400, MCI Mail, DISOSS, and other mail systems.

CEO includes E-mail, word processing, decision-support, business-graphics, and database-access tools. The E-mail portion operates on three different kinds of messages, something like IBM's PROFS. These include short messages of up to nine lines made using the built-in editor, documents of unlimited length created with the CEO word processor, and files from any system source. CEO also lets you move PC files through the system.

## MEMO

Verimation's MEMO is one of the most popular host E-mail systems in Europe, with more than a million mailboxes, but it wasn't even available in the US until 1987. Verimation is a joint subsidiary of Sweden's Volvo and L.M.Ericsson companies. MEMO was originally created as an internal system for Volvo. But other companies expressed interest and Volvo decided to make it a commercial product. MEMO runs on IBM mainframes under the MVS operating system and uses IBM's Virtual Telcommunications Access Monitor.

A program called MEMO/PC lets you read and create messages offline. Verimation is developing a LAN version of MEMO in conjunction with Action Technologies. The LAN version will include MEMO's existing work-flow capability to automatically route forms. These forms can have sophisticated elements such as protected fields and calculations.

MEMO can reach other E-mail systems through gateways to Telex, Fax, Quik-Comm, SNADS, and X.400. It includes an API for building custom gateways to other systems and programs. Other E-mail programs could use this feature to employ the work-flow capabilities of MEMO.

**Figure 7-1.**
**Verimation's**
**MEMO E-mail**
**program looks like**
**this when viewed**
**on a 3270 terminal**
**attached to**
**the mainframe**
**computer**
**running MEMO.**

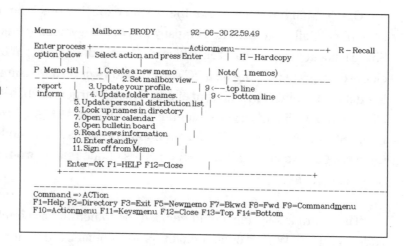

**Figure 7-2.**
**The LAN version**
**of Verimation's**
**MEMO can use the**
**menus and icons**
**of Windows on**
**a PC display,**
**as shown here.**

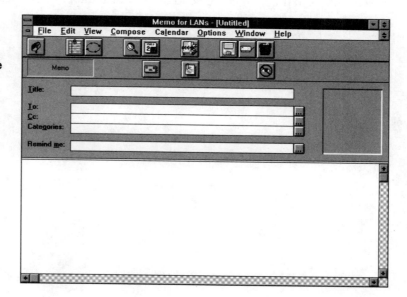

## OracleMail

Oracle is one of the world's largest database software companies. Its database programs run on a wide range of computers, from personal systems to mainframes.

Oracle Mail has been one of the first to explicitly reach out to wireless and portable E-mail systems. The company has been developing PalmLink, a link to Sharp's pocket-size "organizer," Wizard. PalmLink connects Wizard to the OracleCard program running on a PC with Windows or on a Macintosh. OracleCard is a data-entry-and-retrieval front end to Oracle's larger database programs—the client end of a client/server system. PostCard is an API (Applications Programming Interface) for OracleCard. Programmers can use it to add E-mail functions to OracleCard to automatically send copies of documents from the database to others on the network.

The PalmLink system could be used for something as simple as loading an address list into Wizard or as complex as an automatic order-entry system, where Wizard users in the field could send their information back to headquarters. See Chapter 1 for more details on portable E-mail.

# CHAPTER EIGHT

# Public E-mail and the Internet

You can use E-mail even if you don't set up your own LAN, mainframe, or minicomputer. Instead, you can turn to one of the public E-mail services mentioned in this chapter.

Many public E-mail services are remote computer systems running E-mail software. You connect to them through dial-up phone lines or through a packet-switching network. (As explained in Chapter 1, a packet-switching network provides a local phone number you can call. The network's computers then take your local call and bundle it with other calls, sending the bundle through high-speed phone lines to distant computers. The distant computers then respond to you over the same packet-switching network. This arrangement permits high-speed communications at low prices—because the calls are local instead of long distance.)

When you connect, you may upload (transmit from your terminal or computer to the remote computer) any messages you've created and download (receive from the remote computer to your computer or terminal) any messages intended for you. Other users of the service will similarly connect to upload their created messages and download waiting mail. Like most other E-mail systems, public service E-mail uses a "mailbox" scheme. Each user has a mailbox that holds any mail addressed to that user. Once the mail is read, it may be replied to, deleted, or stored (the storage options depend on the E-mail service). In these systems, you pay according to the number and length of messages you send. Many of these sages you send. Many of these commercial services offer gateway connections to Fax, to other commercial E-mail, and to the Internet.

Some public E-mail services are not paid, commercial endeavors. Instead, they are byproducts of the LANs and WANs (see Chapter 1) set up by government, academic, and research institutions. The premier example of such a WAN is the Internet, a network of networks reaching around the world. Any computer on a network that is connected to the Internet can exchange mail with any computer on any other network of the Internet. Typical Internet users are students, teachers, and researchers. Commercial use of the Internet is growing.

## The Current Market

There are dozens of public E-mail services in the United States. They include:

- the Internet
- telecommunications services
- timesharing services (which rent computer time and have E-mail as one feature)
- commercial services (which offer only E-mail)
- on-line services (which offer database, shopping, financial, and conferencing as well as E-mail)
- bulletin boards (which offer E-mail along with conferencing and file exchange features)

**Tip:** Packet-switching makes it relatively easy for a new, small company to provide E-mail services to anyone, anywhere. Gateways between mail services also help the small and startup firms, because you don't have to be on a particular mail system to send messages to others on that system.

A 1991 Link Resources count put the U.S. E-mail market at:

- EasyLink (AT&T) 30%
- Dialcom (BT Tymnet) 18%
- SprintMail (US Sprint) 17%
- Quik-Comm (GE Information Services) 12%
- MCI Mail (MCI) 7%
- Infoplex (CompuServe) 5%
- Notice (Infonet) 3%
- Other 8%

Prodigy E-mail is quite popular too, but was not counted because it was considered a videotext service, not an E-mail service. Definition conflicts often skew the results. Results may also change if you look at different countries. Canada's most popular system, for example, is Telecom Canada's Envoy 100, with nearly 90 percent of all users.

To further add to the confusion in E-mail popularity suppliers often repackage their wares for particular vertical industries. Many companies that advertise bulletin-board support of products along with E-mail actually use a sliver of the CompuServe on-line service, for instance. Or Apple Computer's AppleLink is a part of Quik-Comm. These repackaged E-mail services are, at other times, bundled with a database service and front-end client software for the PC. You may want to find your public E-mail in this guise, because bundled packages tend to be more focused, and could have better service for your particular industry.

**Note:** Remember that surveys and percentages may be skewed by the definitions, and you may not be getting a very accurate listing of how many people are using each E-mail service.

## The Internet

The Internet is not an individual service or organization. It is a term for the collection of many interconnected backbone, regional, and local data networks around the U.S. and the world. There are more than 5000 networks in 33 countries on the Internet with about 500,000 computers and about three million users. This is the result of more and more computers joining networks, networks joining WANs, and WANs cross-connecting with gateways, bridges, and routers. The roots of the Internet are in the Arpanet and other research and academic networks in the U.S. For that reason, the heart of the Internet is still the many networks at universities and major research institutes.

Anyone on the Internet can send mail to anyone else on the Internet, often very inexpensively, because most of the Internet computers share standard protocols and software such as UNIX and TCP/IP. They also abide by similar addressing rules in most cases, as explained in Chapter 1. Sometimes messages are sent directly from one Internet member to another, routed through regional or backbone systems. Other times the mail moves through the Internet only as part of its trip, branching off to private networks or public-service E-mail. The low cost comes from the economies of scale of the Internet, such as the 56Kbps (Kilobits per second) and multi-megabit links in place of dial-up connections. They also come from the original nonprofit status of the net.

Through the Internet you can also reach many databases, news services, on-line library catalogs, and so on. There are conferences and bulletin boards where virtually any subject is discussed, with many devoted to computers.

More companies are using the Internet as part of their WAN strategy. This has become a more practical step now that the Internet Activities Board has begun adding new security and authentication features to the network. That protects E-mail, a necessary step for commercial uses.

For an Internet Resource Guide and a list of Internet service providers, you may write E-mail to NSF Network Service Center (NNSC) at:

```
<<nnsc@nnsc.nsf.net>>
```

## EasyLink

AT&T's EasyLink is the most popular E-mail public service in the U.S. Originally owned by Western Union, it now carries around eight million messages a month for AT&T, or about 30 percent of the public market. EasyLink gives access to a variety of databases including the OAG Official Airlines Guide for travel reservations and the FYI news service. Its links to the Infocom information databases include sophisticated searching commands. EasyLink has been improving its on-line directory to provide white- and yellow-page listings of subscribers.

EasyLink used to be famous for its great connections to Telex and Mailgram services and for its feeble interface. For example, it had no built-in editor—you needed to use your own editor or word processor to create even simple messages.

One IBM PC front-end program for EasyLink is called Instant Mail Manager. It offers the editor that EasyLink doesn't have on-line. Like many other front-end programs, it lets you read and create messages off-line, connecting only to send and receive the messages. There's also an Instant Forms Manager program to make custom business forms you can fill in off-line and then send through EasyLink. AT&T Access Plus for Windows is yet another automating front-end program. It supports Windows DDE and so can directly exchange information with other Windows applications, such as Word for Windows and Excel. Theoretically, PC owners could send and receive E-mail directly from their spreadsheet and word-processing programs.

To reach EasyLink from the Internet, use this address:

```
<<accountname@attmail.com>>
```

To reach the Internet from EasyLink, use this address:

```
<<internet!subdomain.domain!user>>
```

## MCI Mail

MCI Mail from MCI International provides only messaging, not the databases, shopping, or other features of many on-line services. Started in 1983, it offers E-mail mailboxes for individuals and companies, with gateways to many other messaging systems. You may send an MCI Mail message for regular E-mail delivery, and for urgent delivery, for delivery with receipt as a Fax message (by just typing the fax phone number), as a Telex message (just type the telex number), as hardcopy (type the address and specify postal delivery), or as an express hardcopy (which costs more than postal delivery but arrives within a day). You may register a graphics letterhead for an additional price, and then have that printed each time you specify a hard-copy delivery. You may do the same for your signature, placing that on file with MCI Mail and then having it printed as part of a hard-copy letter.

You pay for using MCI Mail by the number, size, and types of transactions, not by the month or the time spent on-line with it. There's an 800 number for contacting MCI Mail.

MCI originally aimed MCI Mail at individuals, and recent pricing deals such as the family plan indicate that individuals are still a priority. However, the service is also trying to capture corporate interest by adding features such as bulletin boards, where a company can post and update information that all of its people need to find and read.

There are several personal computer programs to automate MCI Mail use. Lotus Corp. makes Lotus Express, for instance, a PC program that presents simple menus for creating, reading, and storing messages. Desktop Express is a similar program for Macintosh computers. Unfortunately, it was sold by Dow Jones to Solutions Inc., and then orphaned by the failure of the latter. MCI picked up Desktop Express from Solutions but has not yet updated it. Both programs let users work off-line on their messages, then upload outgoing and download incoming messages in a batch operation. The interface of windows and buttons makes these programs easier for most computer users than the strict menus of MCI Mail's on-line help. An additional advantage of using these programs is that they can send formatted and binary files through MCI Mail, as long as both sender and recipient have the same Express program. There are other MCI Mail front-end packages that operate as scripts for popular communications programs. MCI Mail Management is one of these, from Future Soft Engineering.

## CompuServe

CompuServe, from CompuServe Inc., is both a general on-line service with E-mail as only one of many features. It lets you upload and download files and programs, read news, check financial statistics, search databases, join conferences on a myriad different subjects, make travel reservations, get technical support for computer products, shop, play games, and more. It is perhaps the largest network connecting personal computers in the world, with about a million subscribers. CompuServe also offers the InfoPlex E-mail system for corporations, aiming CompuServe more at individuals.

CompuServe E-mail is linked by gateways to other services, including the Internet and Fax. An MHS hub on CompuServe lets any MHS-supporting E-mail system exchange mail with any other.

You can reach and use CompuServe's E-mail with any personal computer or terminal equipped with a modem. The service provides plenty of menus and on-line help to explain the various services and commands, but there are also several personal computer programs to automate and simplify CompuServe use.

The Compuserve Information Manager, or CIM, is from CompuServe. It runs on PCs and presents a more flexible menu system than plain CompuServe. It

**Figure 8-1.**
**CompuServe has**
**its own E-mail as**
**well as scores of**
**on-line database**
**and information**
**services.**

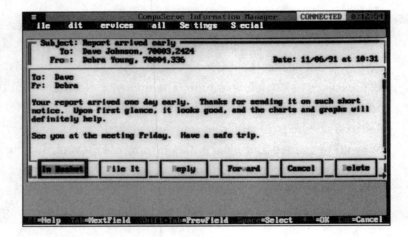

adds search and retrieval options. It also has unique features, such as allowing resumption of an interrupted file transfer and automatic scanning of the news services. You tell it what to check and the program does so in the least possible time. You can create E-mail with the editor, have it sent automatically and receive incoming mail at the same time, then disconnect and read the new mail off-line.

**Figure 8-2.**
**The CompuServe**
**Information**
**Manager (CIM)**
**program gives a**
**neatly organized**
**set of menus to**
**simplify use of**
**the online service.**

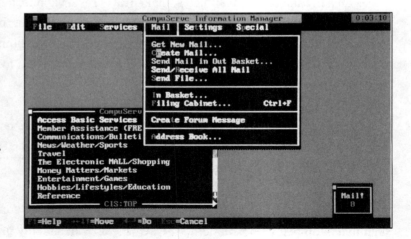

Cisop is a popular front-end for CompuServe. You can find it in CompuServe by giving the command "Go XTALK". It's a script for the Crosstalk telecommunications program. TAPCIS, from the Support Group, is available as shareware you can download from CompuServe and try for three weeks before paying. It is best for automating repetitive acts on CompuServe. Navigator is a Macintosh program for automating CompuServe work, both E-mail and access to the other services.

## Prodigy

Prodigy, an on-line service, is a joint venture of Sears, Roebuck & Co. and IBM (also called Prodigy). It is intended to be easier to use for the many home users and small-business owners who operate computers, but aren't necessarily computer experts. It was intentionally billed as a single charge per month, of about $13, to make it affordable for such users. (Those using services that cost $5 an hour or more were sometimes running up charges of thousands of dollars per month. Even those who are charged per message on systems such as MCI Mail can run up large bills in a hurry.)

Prodigy offers many services. Some are shopping, bill paying, financial news, general information, advice (famous columnists write for it and answer subscriber questions directly), games, travel recommendations, weather, sports news, headline news, and an on-line encyclopedia.

It also offers E-mail, with connections to other E-mail systems including MCI Mail, EasyLink, DialCom, and others. Prodigy carries about 30,000 messages a day, according to its managers, with about two-thirds of its million users sending at least one message a day.

Prodigy's popularity has grown quickly, and the service has managed to garner a lot of publicity, largely for its E-mail. For example, Prodigy E-mail was popular with military families communicating with soldiers in the Persian Gulf during the war of 1991. Then it was the conduit for messages between Earth and the Space

Figure 8-3.
Prodigy's E-mail
is aimed at the
home market,
and is presented
on a computer
screen with large,
easy-to-find
command buttons.

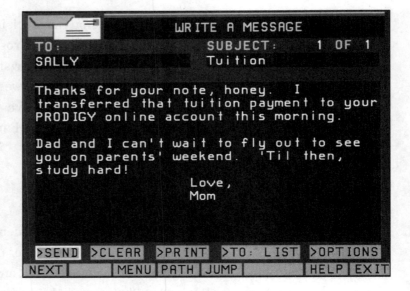

Shuttle astronauts. The Wall Street Journal even featured Prodigy as the focus for messages among members of a particular family during a serious illness.

Unfortunately for Prodigy, some of the press coverage has been negative. A remark, made in Prodigy, that was interpreted as anti-Semitic led to charges and countercharges about it's privacy and censorship policies (see those sections in Chapter 1 for details). Also, in mid 1990 the Prodigy company announced it would charge 25 cents for each mail message beyond a monthly limit of 30. This led to a rebellion by groups who felt defrauded: The original contract with Prodigy mentioned no such messaging limit. The Cooperative Defense Committee (CDC) and the Member Outreach Committee (MOC) tried to organize subscribers to write to Prodigy executives protesting the new charges, to post protest messages on Prodigy's bulletin board areas, or to ignore the on-line advertisements. Prodigy officials countered that it was necessary to create the new surcharge because of a few subscribers who were abusing the system. The mail system, they said, had been made for people who sent relatively few messages. In fact, while 95 percent of the members sent 360,000 messages, a mere 5 percent were sending 3.7 million messages. (The huge number was made possible in part by those sending the same message to many recipients.) The brouhaha continued when the Prodigy staff censored some of the protest messages—raising issues of free speech. Newspapers covered the story, following Prodigy's defense that company policy was "not to post bulletins that advocate campaigns or boycotts—contrary to the interest of the Prodigy Service.

## AppleLink

Apple Computer set up its own E-mail and software dissemination service called AppleLink. General Electric Information Services (GEIS) runs it on the QUIKComm mail system. AppleLink runs 24 hours a day anywhere the X.25 network can reach, using dial-up lines.

Originally just for Apple employees, dealers, developers, customers, and suppliers, AppleLink has been opened more recently to some interested outsiders. AppleLink also shares mail with other E-mail services, including the Internet.

On AppleLink you'll find bulletin boards, technical databases (particularly with information on Apple products and projects), E-mail, and technical updates on Apple publications. You will also find the latest versions of some Apple software—calling AppleLink and downloading these programs can be the fastest and least expensive way to obtain them.

A $56 startup fee and a charge of $9.60 per hour doesn't make AppleLink one of the least expensive, but it is one of the best if you're an avid Macintosh user. The software for reaching it uses the Macintosh interface, as previously shown.

Many AppleLink users depend on Internet-style addresses, such as:

```
<<user@applelink.apple.com>>
```

In UUCP-style addressing, you'd use:

```
<<apple!applelink.apple.com!user>>
```

The user is the AppleLink user identification number. AppleLink E-mail can reach Internet, BITNET, and UUCP recipients. It first goes to the Apple Internet host. That computer runs a smart mailer program to route UUCP mail.

To reach AppleLink from Internet you can use addresses such as:

```
<<comments@applelink.apple.com>>
<<postmaster@apple.com>>
```

## GEnie

GEnie is an abbreviation of General Electric Information Services, sort of. It's the on-line service of General Electric company. It offers bulletin-board conferences, software, news, financial information, games (to play against others or against the computer), travel information, and of course, E-mail. When used at off-hours, GEnie is a very inexpensive service, costing as little as $4.95 a month.

## America Online

America Online is an on-line service with E-mail as one of its features. It used to be known as Quantum Computer Services. It offers news, access to databases, direct communications to computer-magazine editors (from PC World and MacWorld magazines, for example), financial information, an encyclopedia, traveling reservations, conferencing forums to discuss issues, software you may download to your own computer, and even buyers guides of computer hardware and software.

America Online's E-mail can send messages to other services, such as AppleLink and CompuServe, and was scheduled for an Internet connection as of early 1992. The E-mail comes with on-line help and a hotline for questions. The PC client software for America Online comes with an interface of pull-down menus and icons so you can work it with a keyboard or mouse.

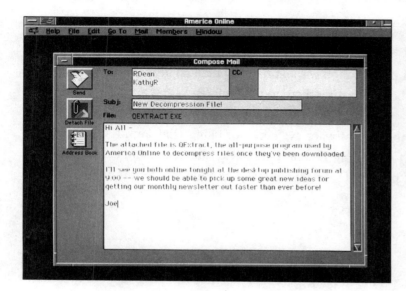

**Figure 8-4.**
**America Online's**
**E-mail allows**
**users to not only**
**exchange**
**messages but**
**to move attached**
**files, such as**
**the program file**
**mentioned in**
**this display.**

You can sometimes get special deals on joining America Online through promotions of the magazines mentioned previously.

## BT DialCom

BT DialCom was one of the first public E-mail services. It began as a time-sharing service for the federal government and is famous now for both its integration with databases and its strong international networking presence, including telex connections and licenses with many of the PTT (Postal, Telephone, and Telegraph) authorities in various countries.

The international reach of DialCom lets people make local calls to packet-switching networks, and thence to DialCom, to send E-mail between countries. The costs end up as only about $1 for the first 1000 characters and 50 cents for each additional 1000 characters.

DialCom also offers private databases for clients, often by setting up gateways from its host computer to external database systems. You can search the databases via keywords and have the results appear in your mailbox as messages. File transfer is possible, but as a separate module from mail. You may upload and download ASCII files, though with a relatively manual procedure, moving them first to the host before moving them to the recipient.

UpFront is the PC software available for using DialCom. It can connect a PC to DialCom for sending E-mail, Fax, telex, mailgram, and cablegram messages. UpFront provides tutorials to learn and macros to automate mail and news features.

## TeleMail

Telenet is one of the two largest packet-switched networks in the U.S. Its Tele-Mail is one of the most popular public-service E-mail systems. Around since 1979, TeleMail was initially most popular with corporations. Since 1988, it has also encouraged individual subscribers.

TeleMail has many features, including bulletin boards, forms creation, and hard-copy delivery. There's a PC front-end program called PCTelemail. This makes the system easier to use, especially for file transfer. Connections to telex permit lower costs than direct telex messages. Gateways to X.400 and other E-mail systems permit exchange of E-mail.

## Freedom Network

Graphnet's Freedom Network is one of the oldest message networks. It offers an unusually potent hard-copy delivery option. For example, it can send messages with full-color logos and electronic signatures. It can even include business-reply envelopes.

## Quik-Comm

General Electronic Information Services, or GEISCO, began Quik-Comm in the 1970s as a messaging system for timeshare customers. It let the customers send Telex messages internationally at much lower prices than they would otherwise find. Quik-Comm has since moved beyond those timesharing customers. For example, it is used by companies linking their internal E-mail systems to the outside through gateways. Some use it as a central connection between remote offices and headquarters. Many of these are multinational companies.

GEISCO offers custom PC software for file transfer and off-line message editing. Quik-Comm has a bulletin board, Telex access, and hard-copy delivery of messages via the U.S. Postal Service. It can also send messages to other applications on the GEISCO system, such as databases.

## Notice

This messaging system from Computer Sciences (CSC) started as part of a service for timesharing customers. Now it offers special abilities in data collection, order entry, automatic price distribution, and other forms-oriented messaging. It can be accessed by IBM 3270 terminals and standard ASCII terminals. CSC also has a PC program to automate Notice work, including file transfers. The PC program is popular with companies that send international messages—it consolidates the messages and sends them during reduced-rate times.

## AT&T Mail

AT&T owns EasyLink, the most popular E-mail service in the U.S. Before it bought EasyLink, however, it was already offering AT&T Mail. This service has standard E-mail features as well as connections to a network of laser-printer sites (for hard-copy delivery of messages) and to the domestic and international Telex network. AT&T sells telecommunications programs for PCs and Macintoshes to use AT&T Mail. These let you send mail as text messages and as attached files.

The software lets you prepare messages off-line, and then transmit messages in batches. Costs of AT&T Mail are based on the number of transactions, though a distinction is made between messages created off-line and those created using AT&T Mail's on-line editor program.

## OnTyme II

McDonnell-Douglas offers OnTyme II as well as the Tymnet packet-switching network, one of the two largest in the U.S. (Telenet is the other). OnTyme has most public network E-mail features. It is used by some companies to move information to and from databases. It does not have many connections to other mail systems, public or in-house. The costs come from a mix of time spent and characters transmitted.

## Envoy 100

Telecom Canada is an organization of all the major telephone companies in Canada. It was created to develop cross-company services. Envoy 100, Telecom's E-mail software, is the most popular public E-mail in Canada. It is licensed from Telenet.

Envoy is interconnected to Canada Post. It has all the normal E-mail features and offers through Canada Post some of the lowest cost next-day, hard-copy letter delivery in North America. It is also connected with Telemail in the U.S. and to other private mail systems through X.400 gateways. Costs are based on the number of characters and recipients of a message.

Both individuals and companies use Envoy. At first it was focused on transferring corporate forms. Now it is used for all sorts of messaging, and even has a published paper directory of subscribers. There are third-party PC software packages for automating its use.

## BIX

BIX was known as the BYTE Information Exchange, an on-line service started by BYTE Magazine. Although it had conferences devoted to thousands of subjects, it was most famous for its computer-information conferences. Just as BYTE is well-known as a source of highly-technical computer information, BIX became a forum for the discussion and debate of such information.

In 1992, General Videotex Corporation bought BIX. This is the same company that operates the DELPHI consumer on-line service, with more entertainment features than found on BIX.

BIX has its own E-mail and links to some other on-line E-mail networks.

## The Well

The WELL is the Whole Earth 'Lectronic Link, a computer bulletin-board system created by the people who also founded the Whole Earth catalogs and magazines. On the WELL you'll find E-mail and many different discussion conferences on subjects ranging from computer programming to the music of the Grateful Dead. You can reach the WELL through dial-up phone lines.

## AMIX

American Information Exchange makes AMIX, a new on-line service in 1992. It is a subsidiary of Autodesk, Inc., which develops AutoCAD, the most popular computer-aided design (CAD) program for PCs.

AMIX is as a marketplace specializing in on-line documents, software, and consulting services. In other words, it is a place to buy and sell information. Producers of information and brokers offer their stuff, buyers search for information, the two negotiate prices and payments, and the service shows the profits and expenses on monthly reports.

Much of the information concerns technical subjects, such as AutoCAD, LANs, desktop publishing, multimedia, engineering, architecture, and manufacturing. Programs will be offered for sale and evaluation, as complete programs or as components in languages such as SmallTalk, C, C++, and Windows. However, more diverse subjects such as science, politics, and art and fiction will appear. Also, business experts will offer marketing and management services as well as data on computer trends and market analysis.

AMIX will include an E-mail facility that will handle file attachments. You may dial-in through direct lines or through local and long-distance packet-switching networks.

# Addresses

**3Com Corp.**
3165 Kifer Rd.
Santa Clara, CA 95052-8145
800-638-3266
408-562-6400
Fax 408-970-1112

**AAC Associates, Inc.**
8470 Tyco Rd., Ste. C
Vienna, VA 22182
703-448-8666
Fax 703-893-1911

**Action Plus Software**
935 E. 7220 South, Ste. D108
Salt Lake City, UT 84047
801-255-0600

**Action Technologies, Inc.**
2200 Powell St., 11th Fl.
Emeryville, CA 94608
800-624-2162
415-654-4444
Fax 415-547-2190

**Advanced Concepts, Inc.**
4129 N. Port Washington Ave.
Milwaukee, WI 53212-1029
800-222-6736
414-963-0999
Fax 414-963-2090

**Alcom**
2464 Embarcadero Way
Palo Alto, CA, 94303
415-493-3800

**Aldus Corporation**
411 1st Ave. South
Seattle, WA 98104-2817
206-622-5500

**Alisa Systems, Inc.**
221 E. Walnut St., Ste. 175
Pasadena, CA 91101
818-792-9474
800-628-3274
Fax 818-792-4068

**Aladdin Systems, Inc.**
Deer Park Center, Ste. 23-171
Aptos, CA 95003
408-685-9175
Fax 408-662-8418

**All The Fax, Inc.**
917 Northern Blvd.
Great Neck, NY 11021
516-829-0556
800-289-3329

**America Online**
8619 Westwood Center Dr., Ste. 200
Vienna, VA 22182-9806
800-827-6364
703-448-8700

**American Information Exchange Corp.**
(AMIX)
2345 Yale St.
Palo Alto, CA 94306
415-86-1234
Fax 415-856-4123

## Association of PC User Groups
1730 M St. NW #700
Washington, DC 20036
408-439-9367
BBS 408-439-9371 at N-8-1

## Articulate Systems, Inc.
99 Erie St.
Cambridge, MA, 02139
800-443-7077
Fax 617-661-3278

## Artisoft, Inc.
575 E. River Rd., Artisoft Plaza
Tucson, AZ  85704
602-293-6363
Fax 602-293-8065

## Asante Technologies
404 Tasman Dr.
Sunnyvale, CA  94089
800-662-9686

## AT&T (American Telephone & Telegraph Co.)
295 N. Maple Ave.
Basking Ridge, NJ  07920
800-346-3288

## AT&T Computer Systems
100 Southgate Pkwy.
Morristown, NJ  07960
800-247-1212
201-898-8000
Fax 201-644-9768

## AT&T EasyLink Services
One Lake St.
Upper Saddle River, NJ  07458
800-321-6747
201-818-5000
Fax 201-818-6611

## Avalan Technology
Timothy Fiske House
747 Washington St.
Holliston, MA  01746
800-441-2281

## BBI Computer Systems
14105 Heritage Ln.
Silver Spring, MD  20906
301-871-1094
Fax 301-460-7545

## Banyan Systems, Inc.
120 Flanders Rd.
Westboro, MA  01581-1033
508-898-1000
Fax 508-898-1755

## Baranof Software
479 Washington St.
Brighton, MA  02135
617-783-0800
Fax 617-254-1412

## Beyond, Inc.
38 Sidney St.
Cambridge, MA  02139
617-621-0095

## BIX
General Videotex Corporation
1030 Massachusetts Avenue
Cambridge, MA 02138
617-491-3342
800-695-4005

## BLAST/Communications Research Group
5615 Corporate Blvd.
Baton Rouge, LA 70808
800-242-5278
504-923-0888
Fax 504-926-2155

## BICC Data Networks
1800 W. Park Dr., Ste. 150
Westborough, MA 01581
800-447-6526
508-898-2422
Fax 508-898-3739

## Blue Lance
P.O. Box 430546
Houston, TX 77243
713-680-1187
Fax 713-622-1370
Boston Business Computing, Ltd.
Three Dundee Park
Andover, MA 01810-3743
508-470-0444
Fax 508-474-9244

## Bravo Technologies, Inc.
P.O. Box 10078
Berkeley, CA 94709-0078
415-841-8552
AppleLink D1380

## Brightwork Development, Inc.
766 Shrewsbury Ave.
Jerral Center West
Tinton Falls, NJ 07724
800-552-9876
201-530-0440
Fax 201-530-0622

## BT Tymnet, Inc.
2560 N. 1st St.
P.O. Box 49019
San Jose, CA 9161-9019
800-872-7654
408-922-0250
Fax 408-922-7030

## Bulletin Board Systems
Capital PC User Group Software Library
P.O. Box 1785
Bethesda, MD 20827-1785
301-762-6775

## Calera Recognition Systems
475 Potrero Ave.
Sunnyvale, CA 94086
800-544-7051
408-720-0999

## Campbell Services, Inc.
21700 Northwestern Hwy., #1070
Southfield, MI 48075
800-345-6747

## Cappcomm Software, Inc.
26 Journal Sq., Ste. 1003
Jersey City, NJ 07306
800-262-4522
201-795-1500
Fax 201-795-0244

### Carrier Current Technolgies, Inc.
9600 Southern Pine Blvd.
Charlotte, NC 28217
800-222-0377
704-529-6550
Fax 704-523-7651

### Castelle
3255-3 Scott Blvd.
Santa Clara, CA 95051
800-359-7654
408-496-0474
Fax 408-496-0502

### Cayman Systems, Inc.
26 Landsdowne St.
Cambridge, MA 02139
617-494-1999
Fax 617-494-9270

### cc:Mail, Inc.
A division of Lotus
2141 Landings Dr.
Mountain View, CA 94043
800-448-2500
415-961-8800

### CE Software
P.O. Box 65580
W. Des Moines, IA 50265
515-224-1995
800-523-7638
Fax 515-224-4534

### Century Software
310 N. Wilson Ave.
Hartford, WI 53027
800-437-4492

### Certus International
13110 Shaker Sq.
Cleveland, OH 44120
800-722-8737
216-752-8181
Fax 216-752-8188

### Chesapeake Computing, Inc.
8401 Corporate Dr.
Metroplex I #560
Landover, MD 20785
800-899-2255

### Cheyenne Software, Inc.
55 Bryant Ave.
Roslyn, NY 11576
800-243-9462
516-484-5110
Fax 516-484-3446

### Chronos Software, Inc.
555 De Haro St., #240
San Francisco, CA 94107
415-206-0580
Fax 415-206-0587

### Clark Development Co.
3950 S. 700 East #303
Murray, UT 84107-2173
800-356-1686
801-261-1686

### Coker Electronics
1430 Lexington Ave.
San Mateo, CA 94402
415-573-5515

**CompLink**
1419 Ave. J
Brooklyn, NY 11230
718-338-9646

**CompuServe, Inc.**
5000 Arlington Centre Blvd.
P.O. Box 20212
Columbus, OH 43220
614-457-8600
800-848-8199
614-457-0802 for international

**Computer Associates
International, Inc.**
201 University Ave.
Westwood, MA 02090-2198
617-329-7700
Fax 617-329-1134

**Concept Development Systems**
P.O. Box 1988
Kennesaw, GA 30144
404-424-6240
Fax 404-424-8995

**Connect Computer, Inc.**
9855 W. 78th St., Ste. 270
Eden Prarie, MN 55344
612-944-0181
Fax 612-944-9298

**Connex Systems**
9341 Courtland Dr.
Rockford, MI 49351
800-748-0212
616-866-5678
Fax 616-866-1250

**Coordination Technology, Inc.**
35 Corporate Dr.
Trumbull, CT 06611
800-292-7755
203-268-4045

**Cross Communications**
1881 9th St., Ste. 302
Boulder, CO 80302
303-444-7799

**Cross Information Co.**
1881 9th St., Canyon Center, Ste. 212
Boulder, CO 80302-5181
303-444-7799
Fax 303-444-4687

**Crosstalk Communications**
1000 Holcomb Woods Pkwy., Ste. 440
Roswell, GA 30076-2575
800-241-6393
404-442-4930
Fax 404-442-4361

**Cyantic Systems**
101 Subway Crescent, Ste. 2103
Etobicoke, Ontario
Canada M9B 6K4
416-234-9048
Fax 416-234-0477

**D-Link Systems, Inc.**
Five Musick
Irvine, CA 92718
714-455-1688
Fax 714-455-2521

**Dale, Gesek, McWilliams & Sheridan, Inc.**
1025 Briggs Rd., Ste. 100
Mt. Laurel, NJ 08054
609-866-1212
Fax 609-866-8850

**Data Access Corp.**
14000 Southwest 119th Ave.
Miami, FL 33186
800-451-3539
800-331-3960
305-238-0012
Fax 305-238-0017

**Datacom Technologies, Inc.**
11001 31st Pl., West
Everett, WA 98204
800-468-5557
206-355-0590
Fax 206-353-9292

**Datapoint Corp.**
8400 Datapoint Dr.
San Antonio, TX 78229-8500
800-733-1500
512-593-7000
Fax 512-593-7355

**Data Race, Inc.**
11550 I-10 W., Ste. 395
San Antonio, TX 78249
512-558-1900
Fax 512-558-1929

**DaVinci Systems**
4200 Six Forks Rd., Ste. 200
Raleigh, NC 27609
800-328-4624
919-881-4320
Fax 919-787-3550

**Dayna Communications**
50 S. Main St., 5th Fl.
Salt Lake City, UT 84144
801-531-0600
Fax 801-359-9135

**Daystrom Technologies Corp.**
405 Tarrytown Rd., Ste. 414
White Plains, NY 10607
914-896-7378

**DigiBoard**
6751 Osford St.
Minneapolis, MN 55426
800-344-4273
612-922-8055
Fax 612-922-4287

**Digital Communications Associates, Inc.**
10NET Communications Division
7887 Washington Village Dr.
Dayton, OH 45459
800-358-1010
800-782-1010
513-433-2238
Fax 513-434-6305

**Digital Equipment Corp.**
146 Main St.
Maynard, MA 01754-2571
508-493-5111
Fax 508-493-8780

**DMA**
1776 E. Jericho Turnpike
Huntington, NY 11743
516-462-0440
Fax 516-462-6652

ADDRESSES

**Dolphin Software, Inc.**
6050 Peachtree Pkwy., Ste. 340-208
Norcross, GA 30092
404-339-7877

**Dowty Network Systems, Inc.**
555 Twin Dolphin Dr.
Redwood City, CA 94065
415-508-2500
Fax 415-508-2501

**Edge Systems, Inc.**
1245 Corporate Blvd., 4th Fl.
Aurora, IL 60504-6420
708-898-0021
Fax 708-898-5406

**Edify Corp.**
2840 San Tomas Expressway
Santa Clara, CA 95051
408-982-2000
Fax 408-982-0777

**Enable Software, Inc.**
Northway Ten Executive Park
Ballston Lake, NY 12019
800-888-0684
518-877-8600
Fax 518-877-5225

**Enable Software/Higgins Group**
1150 Marina Village Pkwy. #101
Alameda, CA 94501
800-854-2807
510-865-9805
510-521-9779 Fax

**Epic Systems Corp.**
5609 Medical Circle
Madison, WI 53719-1228
608-271-9000
Fax 608-271-7237

**Ericsson GE**
100 Park Ave., Ste. 2705
New York, NY 10017
212-685-4030

**eSoft, Inc.**
15200 E. Girard Ave. #2550
Aurora, CO 80014
303-699-6565

**ETI Software**
2930 Prospect Ave.
Cleveland, OH 44115
800-336-2014
216-241-1140
Fax 216-241-2319

**Ex Machina, Inc.**
45 E. 89th St., No. 39-A
New York, NY 10128
212-831-3142
Fax 212-534-3716

**Experdata, Inc.**
10301 Toledo Ave., South
Bloomington, MN 55437
612-831-2122
Fax 612-835-0700

**Farallon Computing, Inc.**
2000 Powell St., Ste. 600
Emeryville, CA 94608
415-596-9000

**Fido Software**
164 Shipley St.
San Francisco, CA 94107
415-764-1688

**Fifth Generation Systems, Inc.**
10049 N. Reiger Rd.
Baton Rouge, LA 70809
800-873-4384
504-291-7221
Fax 504-295-3268

**Finalsoft**
3900 N.W. 79th Ave., Ste. 215
Miami, FL 33166
800-232-8228

**Finansa, Ltd.**
Dunstable, Bedforshire, UK
011-44-582-662268
F:662461

**Folio Corp.**
2155 N. Freedom Blvd., #150
Provo, UT 84604
800-543-6546
801-375-3700

**Fresh Technology Group**
1478 N. Tech Blvd., Ste. 101
Gilbert, AZ 85234
800-545-8324
602-497-4200
Fax 602-497-4242

**Frye Computer Systems, Inc.**
19 Temple Pl.
Boston, MA 02111
800-234-3793
617-247-2300
Fax 617-451-6711

**FTP Software, Inc.**
26 Princess St.
Wakefield, MA 01880
617-246-0900
Fax 617-246-0901

**Futurus Corp.**
211 Perimeter Center Pkwy., Ste. 910
Atlanta, GA 30346
800-327-8296
404-392-7979
Fax 404-392-9313

**FYI, Inc.**
P.O. Box 26481
Austin, TX 78755
512-346-0133

**Galacticomm, Inc.**
411 S.W. 47th Ave., Ste. 101
Ft. Lauderdale, FL 33314
305-583-5990
Fax 305-583-7846

**GammaLink**
133 Caspian Court
Sunnyvale, CA 94089
408-744-1430
Fax 408-744-1549

**GE Information Services**
401 N. Washington St.
Rockville, MD 20850
800-433-3683
301-340-4000
Fax 301-340-4251

**Hayes Microcomputer Products, Inc.**
P.O. Box 105203
Atlanta, GA  303438
404-449-8791
Fax 404-441-1238

**Hewlett-Packard Co.**
1000 NE Circle Blvd.
Corvaillis, OR  97330-4239
503-757-2000

**Hewlett-Packard Limited**
Pinewood Information Systems Division
Nine Mile Ride
Wokingham
Berkshire RG11 3LL  U.K.
44-344-763184

**IBM**
Old Orchard Rd.
Armonk, NY  10504
800-426-2468
914-765-1900

**ICL Business Systems**
9801 Muirlands Blvd.
Irvine, CA  92718
714-458-7282
Fax 714-458-6257

**ICL Networks Industry**
ISDN Systems Group
777 Long Ridge Rd.
P.O. Box 10276
Stamford, CT  06904
800-446-4736
203-968-7222

**IDR UniCom, Inc.**
400 Stenton Ave.
Plymouth Meeting, PA  19462
215-825-8181
Fax 215-825-8188

**Infinite Technologies**
Owings Mills, MD
410-363-1097
Fax 410-363-3779

**Information Research Corporation**
P.O. Box 7644
Charlottesville, VA  22906
804-979-8191
Fax 804-977-1949
AppleLink D6222.

**Infralink of America, Inc.**
6525 T Corners Pkwy., #400
Norcross, GA  30092
404-449-7858

**Innosoft International, Inc.**
250 W. 1st St., Ste. 240
Claremont, CA 91711
714-624-7907
714-621-5319

**Intel**
5200 N.E. Elam Young Pkwy.
Hillsboro, OR  97124
800-538-3373
503-629-7000

**International Intergroup**
1777 S. Harrison St., Ste. 500
Denver, CO  80210
303-692-9090
Fax 303-756-0678

**International Resource Development, Inc.**
New Canaan, CT
203-966-2525

**Interpreter, Inc.**
11455 W. 48th Ave.
Wheat Ridge, CO 80033
800-232-4687
303-431-8991
Fax 303-431-9056

**Intran Systems, Inc.**
7493 N. Oracle Rd., Ste. 207
Tucson, AZ 85704
602-797-2797
Fax 602-797-2799

**Invisible Software, Inc.**
1165 Chess Dr., Ste. D
Foster City, CA 94404
415-570-5967
Fax 415-570-6017

**ISDN Technologies Corp.**
1940 Colony St.
Mountain View, CA 94043
415-960-1025
Fax 415-960-1029

**JetForm Corp.**
560 Rochester St., Ste. 400
Ottawa, Ontario K1S 5K2
800-267-9976
613- 594-3026
Fax 613-594-8886

**LanQuest Group**
1251 Parkmoor Ave.
San Jose, CA 95126
408-283-8900
Fax 408-283-8989

**LANsmith Corp.**
406 Lincolnwood Pl.
Santa Barbara, CA 93110
800-522-4567
805-687-1271
Fax 805-687-2401

**LANSystems, Inc.**
300 Park Ave. South
New York, NY 10010
800-LAN-STEL
212-995-7700
Fax 212-995-8604

**LCS/Telegrpahics**
150 Rogers St.
Cambridge, MA 02142
617-225-7970
Fax 617-225-7969

**Lotus Development Corp.**
55 Cambridge Pkwy.
Cambridge, MA 02142
800-635-6887
617-577-8500

**Magnum Software Corporation**
21115 Devonshire St., Ste. 337
Chatsworth, CA 91311
818-701-5051
Fax 818-700-8225.

## Management Systems Designers, Inc.
(Systems Engineering Division)
131 Park St., NE
Vienna, VA 22180
703-281-7440
Fax 703-281-7636

## McCarty Associates, Inc.
929 Boston Post Rd.
Old Saybrook, CT 06475
203-388-6994
Fax 203-388-6826

## MCI Communications Corp.
1650 Tysons Blvd.
McLean, VA 22102
800-888-0800

## MCI Mail
1111 19th St., NW, Ste. 500
Washington, DC 20036
Fax 800-677-3303

## MCTel, Inc.
5070 Parkside Ave., Ste. 1300
Philadelphia, PA 19131
215-879-3819

## Meridian Networx, Inc.
14044 Ventura Blvd., Ste. 303
Sherman Oaks, CA 91423
818-501-7410

## Microsoft Corp.
One Microsoft Way
Redmond, WA 98052-6399
800-426-9400
206-882-8080
Fax 206-883-8101

## Microsystems Software, Inc.
600 Worcester Rd.
Framingham, MA 01701
508-626-8511
Fax 508-626-8515

## Mitek Systems Corp.
2033 Chennault Dr.
Carrollton, TX 75006
214-490-4090
Fax 214-490-5052

## MMB Development
800-832-6022

## Modem Controls, Inc.
432 N. Clark St., Ste. 202
Chicago, IL 60610
800-266-8765
312-321-0018
Fax 312-321-1276

## Motorola
Paging Division
1500 N.W. 22nd Ave.
Boynton Beach, FL 33426
800-247-2346

## Mustang Software, Inc.
P.O. Box 2264
Bakersfield, CA 93303
800-999-9619
805-395-0223
Fax 805-395-0713

## NCR Corp.
1700 S. Patterson Blvd.
Dayton, OH 45479
800-544-3333
513-445-5000
Fax 513-445-2008

**NETinc.**
P.O. Box 271105
Houston, TX 77277-1105
713-974-1810

**Network General Corp.**
4200 Bohannnon Dr.
Menlo Park, CA 94025
415-688-2700
Fax 415-321-0855

**Network Management Inc.**
19 Rector St.
New York, NY 10006
800-LAN-USER
212-797-3800
Fax 212-797-3817

**Network Software Associates, Inc.**
39 Argonaut
Laguna Hills, CA 92656
714-768-4013
Fax 714-768-5049

**Network Technology, Inc.**
215 Kindswood Dr.
Fayetteville, VA 30214
404-461-2622
404-461-6883

**Norton-Lambert Corp.**
P.O. Box 4085
Santa Barbara, CA 93140
805-964-6767
Fax 805-683-5679

**Notework Corp.**
72 Kent St.
Brookline, MA 02146
617-734-4317
Fax 617-734-4160

**Novell, Inc.**
122 E. 1700 South
Provo, UT 84606
800-453-1267
801-379-5900
Fax 801-429-5775

**Novell, Inc.**
LANalyzer Products Division
2180 Fortune Dr.
San Jose, CA 95131
800-243-8526
408-434-2300
Fax 408-435-1706

**Now Software, Inc.**
520 S. W. Harrison St., Ste. 425
Portland, OR 97209
503-274-2800

**OAZ Communications, Inc.**
1362 Bordeaux Dr.
Sunnyvale, CA 94089
408-745-1750
Fax 408-745-1808

**OMM Corp.**
4200 Wisconsin Ave. NW, Ste. 106
Washington, DC 20016
202-234-2117

**Omni Computer Systems, Inc.**
P.O. Box 162
Chestnut Hill, MA 02167
617-522-4760
Fax 617-522-2793

**O'Neill Communications, Inc.**
100 Thanet Circle, #304
Princeton, NJ 08540
800-624-5296
609-497-6800
Fax 609-497-6801

**ON Technology, Inc.**
156 2nd St.
Cambridge, MA 02141
617-876-0900
Fax 617-876-0391

**Oracle Corp.**
500 Oracle Parkway
Redwood Shores, CA 94065
800-633-0598
415-506-3228
Fax 415-506-7103

**OST, Inc.**
14225 Sullyfield Circle
Chantilly, VA 22021
800-OST-9678
703-817-0400
Fax 703-817-0402

**Pacer Software, Inc.**
7911 Herschel Ave., Ste. 402
La Jolla, CA 92037
619-454-0565
Fax 619-454-6267
AppleLink: PACER

**Palindrome Corp.**
710 E. Ogden Ave., Ste. 208
Naperville, IL 60540
312-357-4600
312-355-0779

**Paradox Development Corp.**
7544 Trade St.
San Diego, CA 92121
619-586-0878

**Performance Technology**
7800 I-10 W.
800 Lincoln Center
San Antonio, TX 78230
512-349-2000

**Pharos Technologies , Inc.**
4243 Hunt Rd.
Cincinnati, OH 45242
800-548-8871
513-984-9273 for international callers

**Polaris Software**
17150 Via Del Campo, #307
San Diego, CA 92127
800-722-5728
619-674-6500

**PostMaster**
432 N. Clark St.
Chicago, IL 60610
312-321-0018

**Powercore, Inc.**
P.O. Box 756
Manteno, IL 60950-0756
800-237-4754
815-468-3737

**Prodigy**
445 Hamilton Ave.
White Plains, NY 10601
800-776-3552

**Public Software Library**
P.O. Box 35705
Houston, TX 77235-5705
800-242-4775

**PureData, Inc.**
200 W. Beaver Creek Rd.
Richmond Hill, Ontario
Canada
L4B 1B4
416-731-6444
Fax 416-731-7017

**Quadratron Systems, Inc.**
141 Triunfo Canyon Rd.
Westlake Village, CA 91361
805-494-1158
Fax 805-494-1721

**Quantum Computer Services, Inc.**
861 Westwood Center Dr.
Vienna, VA 22182
703-893-6288

**Rainbow Software International Corp.**
Atlanta, GA
404-612-0500
Fax 404-612-9100

**RAM**
212-373-1930

**Reach Software Corp.**
330 Potrero Rd.
Sunnyvale, CA 94086
800-624-5356
408-733-8685

**Remote Control**
5928 Pascal Ct., Ste. 150
Carlsbad, CA 92008
800-992-9952
619-431-4000
Fax 619-431-4006

**REMS, Inc.**
5632 Van Nuys Blvd., Ste. 375
Van Nuys, CA 91401
800-388-0204

**Retix**
2644 30th St.
Santa Monica, CA 90405-3009
800-255-2333
213-399-2200
Fax 213-458-2685

**Riverbend Group**
1491 Chain Bridge Rd.
McLean, VA 22101
703-883-0616
Fax 703-893-9858

**RTI USA**
7603 1st Avenue #C2
North Bergen, NJ 07047
201-861-1259
201-861-0084

**S&H Computer Systems, Inc.**
1027 17th Ave., South
Nashville, TN 37212
615-327-3670
Fax 615-321-5929

## Saber Software Corp.
P.O. Box 9088
Dallas, TX 75209
800-338-8754
214-361-8086
Fax 214-361-1882

## Shana Corporation
Advanced Technology Center 105
9650 20th Ave.
Edmonton, Alberta
Canada
T6N 1G1
403-463-3330
Fax 403-428-5376
AppleLink CDA0004

## Sharp Electronics Corp.
Sharp Plaza
Mahwah, NJ 07430
201-529-8200
800-321-8877

## Shiva
800-458-3550
617-252-6300
Fax 617-252-4852

## SilverSoft, Inc.
1301 Geranium St., NW
Washington, DC 20012
202-291-8212

## Simpact Associates
9210 Sky Park Ct.
San Diego, CA 92123
800-488-4188

## Siren Software Corp.
750 Menlo Ave., Ste. 200
Menlo Park, CA 94025
800-457-4736
415-322-0600
Fax 415-322-4023
info@siren.com

## Sitka Corp.
950 Marina Village Pkwy.
Alameda, CA 94501
510-769-9669
800-495-8677

## SkyTel
800-456-3333

## SofNet, Inc.
380 Interstate N. Pkwy., Ste. 150
Atlanta, GA 30339
404-984-8088
Fax 404-984-9956

## Soft*Switch, Inc.
640 Lee Rd.
Wayne, PA 19087
215-640-9600
Fax 215-640-7550
telex 6502803762

## Software Engineering of America
2001 Marcus Ave.
Lake Success, NY 11042
800-272-7322
516-328-7000
Fax 516-354-4015

**Software Products International**
9920 Pacific Heights Blvd.
San Diego, CA 92121
800-937-4774

**Source Data Systems, Inc.**
950 Ridgemount Dr., NE
Cedar Rapids, IA 52402-7222
319-393-3343
Fax 319-393-5173

**Sprint Data Group**
10951 Lakeview Dr.
Lenexa, KS 66215
800-736-1130
913-541-6876

**SprintNet Data Network**
(U.S. Sprint Communications Co.)
12490 Sunrise Valley Dr.
Reston, VA 22096
800-736-1130
703-689-6000

**StarNine Technologies, Inc.**
2126 6th St.
Berkeley, CA 94710
415-548-0391
Fax 415-548-0393

**Strategic Marketing Associates**
2785 Pacific Coast Hwy. #251
Torrance, CA 90505
310-378-7632
Fax 310-378-8285

**Sun Microsystems**
2550 Garcia Ave.
Mountain View, CA 94043
415-960-1300

**SuperOffice Corp.**
One Cranberry Hill
Lexington, MA 02173
617-674-1101

**SuperTime, Inc.**
2025 Sheppard Ave. East #2206
Willowdale, Ontario
Canada
M2J 1V7
416-499-3288
Fax 416-499-6462

**Surf Computer Services, Inc.**
71-540 Gardess Rd.
Rancho Mirage, CA 92270
619-346-9430

**System Enhancement Associates**
21 New St.
Wayne, NJ 07470
201-473-5153

**Syzygy Development**
5555 Triangle Pkwy., Ste. 320
Norcross, GA 30092
404-662-5362

**Teleos Communications, Inc.**
Two Meridian Rd.
Eatontown, NJ 07724
908-389-5700
Fax 908-544-9890

**The Aldridge Co.**
2500 City West Blvd., Ste. 575
Houston, TX 77042
800-548-5019
713-953-1940
Fax 713-953-0806

**The Complete PC**
1983 Concourse Dr.
San Jose, CA 95131
408-434-0145
Fax 408-434-1048

**The Electronic Mail Association**
1555 Wilson Blvd., Ste. 300
Arlington, VA 22209
703-875-8620

**The NTI Group**
3265 Kifer Rd.
Santa Clara, CA 95051
408-739-2180
Fax 408-739-4847

**The Support Group, Inc.**
Lake Technology Park
McHenry, MD 21541
800-872-4768

**Touch Communications, Inc.**
250 E. Hacienda Ave.
Campbell, CA 95008
408-374-2500
Fax 408-374-1680

**Transend**
884 Portola Rd.
Portola Valley, CA 94025
415-851-3401
Fax 415-851-1031

**Traveling Software, Inc.**
18702 N. Creek Pkwy.
Bothell, WA 98011
800-662-2652
206-483-8088
Fax 206-487-1284

**Triticom**
P.O. Box 11536
St. Paul, MN 55111
612-937-0772

**Triton Technologies, Inc.**
200 Middlesex Turnpike
Iselin, NJ 08830
800-322-9440
201-855-9440
Fax 201-855-9608

**Tymnet Global Network**
(BT North America, Inc.)
2560 N. 1st St.
San Jose, CA 95161-9019
800-872-7654
408-922-0250

**Ultinet Development, Inc.**
9724 Washington Blvd., Ste. 200
Carver City, CA 90232
213-204-0111
Fax 213-287-2447

**UniPress Software, Inc.**
2025 Lincoln Hwy.
Edison, NJ 08817
800-222-0550
201-985-8000
Fax 201-287-4929

**Vadis, Inc.**
1201 Richardson Dr., Ste. 200
Richardson, TX 75080
214-690-2481
Fax 214-996-0370

**Ventana Corp.**
1430 E. Fort Lowell, Ste. 301
Tucson, AZ 85719
800-368-6338
602-325-8228

**Verimation Inc.**
P.O. Box 154
6 Volvo Drive
Rockleigh, NJ 07647-0154
201-767-4795
Fax 201-767-4885

**Walker Richer and Quinn, Inc.**
2815 Eastlake Ave. East
Seattle, WA 98102
800-872-2829
206-324-0350
Fax 206-322-8151

**Wang Laboratories, Inc.**
One Industrial Way
Mail Stop 014-A1B
Lowell, MA 01851
800-835-9264
508-459-5000

**Wollongong Group, Inc.**
P.O. Box 51860
1129 San Antonio Rd.
Palo Alto, CA 94303
800-872-8649
800-962-8649
415-962-7200
Fax 415-969-5547

**WordPerfect Corp.**
1555 N. Technology Wy.
Orem, UT 84057
801-228-5000

**XcelleNet, Inc.**
Five Concourse Pkwy., Ste. 200
Atlanta, GA 30328
404-804-8100
Fax 404-804-8102

# Glossary

**administration.** Handling some or all of E-mail system tasks such as: assigning user IDs, deleting users, creating and changing public mail lists, setting up bulletin boards, diagnosing system troubles, keeping enough hard disk space free for the post office, dictating routing, and maintaining gateways.

**administrator.** Person who manages all or part of the E-mail system.

**AFP.** AppleTalk File Protocol, Apple Computer's network protocol to give access between file servers and clients on an AppleShare network.

**alias.** A single word or number that stands in for one or more E-mail addresses, used to simplify addressing.

**ANSI.** American National Standards Institute, the U.S. organization for collecting and publishing agreed-upon standards for industry.

**API.** Application Programming Interface, a set of standardized software rules that let different programs communicate with networks or with other programs. Each Network Operating System, each E-mail program, can have its own API.

**AppleTalk.** The original name for the Apple Computer networking system that is built into every Macintosh computer. Now it is called LocalTalk. See that glossary definition.

**application layer.** The seventh or highest level of the OSI model of computer networks.

**ARPANET.** Advanced Research Projects Agency Network, the network created by a branch of the U.S. military to connect universities and government research sites. Many of the popular protocols used in E-mail and the Internet were created for ARPANET.

**ASCII.** American Standard Code for Information Interchange, a standard way to represent any numeral, character, or symbol in 7 bits (and an extra parity bit). Because computers only deal in bits, they need a code such as this to store words, numbers, and other information. ASCII is the most commonly used code. However, because the 7 bits allows only 128 different combinations, the ASCII code doesn't have room for fancy formatting or text fonts. So files from word processors, spreadsheets, and databases, that are stored in "ASCII-only" form (also known as "Text-only" or "Plain-text") have been stripped of any such formatting and fonts. That preserves a file's core information and makes it the most universal for importing into other programs.

**asynchronous.** Data transmission without time synchronization of the sending and receiving systems. See synchronous.

**background processing.** Although some computers allow more than one program to run at a time, typically they only show one, or focus on one, on the display screen. Any programs running "behind" this "top" (focused) program are "running in the background". For E-mail, this is important because you may want to have an E-mail program running constantly in the background, checking for incoming mail for instance, while you work on other software you have—word processor, spreadsheet, or whatever. See multitasking.

**baud.** A measure of data-transmission speed, often confused with bps (bits per second; see glossary definition for that). Baud is generally an obsolete term for computer users, who should use bps. (Baud is still useful for technicians and system designers.)

**BB.** Bulletin Board, a combination of software and hardware that allows people to post messages and read posted messages from others. A one-to-many communication scheme that differs from the one-to-one or one-to-a-few communications of typical E-mail. Some E-mail programs have BB features. There are also BB programs with some E-mail capabilities.

**BBS.** Bulletin Board System.

**bindery.** A database in Novell's NetWare network operating system that holds information on the users and servers of the network. E-mail systems typically need to know such information, so one that automatically reads the bindery is easier to install and maintain than one that requires manual entry of bindery details.

**bit.** The smallest piece of computer information, representing only a single 1 or 0. To represent numerals, characters, symbols, and other usable information, bits must be clumped together into bytes using a code such as ASCII. See "byte".

**body.** The part of the E-mail message that contains all of the message text (see header and attachments).

**bps.** Bits per second, a measure of transmission speed. Modems typically operate at 2400, 9600, or 19,200bps. Networks operate at 250Kbps (K = 1024) to 10Mbps (M = 1,048,576 or roughly a Million).

**bridge.** A device that connects two networks. The bridge automatically reads and filters data packets and frames while passing them from one network to another.

**bulletin board.** See BB.

**button.** A small area on the computer screen that is graphically outlined to look like a physical "button" you could push. Typically such "buttons" offer options or commands in a graphical user environment (see GUI). You choose a button by "clicking" it with the mouse (place the mouse cursor on it and press the mouse button).

**byte.** 8 bits together, the minimum number of bits it takes to represent useful information such as a numeral or character. See bit and ASCII.

**C.** A computer programming language, the most popular for commercial program development, though challenged by C++.

**C++.** A form of the C computer programming language that follows the rules of "object-oriented programming," a new philosophy of programming that hopes to make programs more modular and therefore more easily maintained or changed.

**CCITT.** Comitè Consultatif Internationale Tèlègraphie et Tèlèphonie, the international standards-setting group that has created many computer and communications rules, such as the X.400 and X.500 standards.

**client/server.** A computer system that distributes work to "client" computers from a central "server" computer. The server typically stores data and programs. Client/server computing is becoming more popular as time-sharing (all processing on a central computer connected to outlying terminals) and stand-alone computing (processing only on individual computers) recede. Client/server takes advantage of both the centralized information of a server and the distributed processing power of many desktop computers.

**command line.** The typed string of text that tells a computer what to do from a single line of the display.

**common carrier.** An information transmission company serving the public.

**CPU.** Central processing unit, the main brains of a computer, typically a microprocessor chip.

**current message.** The message you're working on (reading or writing) in an E-mail system.

**DECnet.** A set of networking protocols from Digital Equipment. DECnet is compatible with Ethernet.

**default.** The automatically assumed setting for a protocol or format in a computer program.

**dial-up line.** Communications via a dialed phone number on the commercial phone network.

**directory.** List of all users in the E-mail system.

**DISOSS.** Distributed Office Supported System, an IBM program for mainframe computers that includes E-mail abilities.

**EBCDIC.** Extended Binary Coded Decimal Interchange Code, a code like ASCII for representing numerals, characters, and symbols as bits. EBCDIC is used on all IBM computers except the PC line, which uses the more popular ASCII.

**EDI.** Electronic Data Interchange, moving financial and business documents as electronic information instead of as paper.

**Ethernet.** A network protocol and cabling system originally developed by Xerox.

**elm.** A UNIX E-mail user agent.

**facsimile.** See fax.

**fax.** A method for sending pages of information through the telephone system. A fax can operate independently of computers and E-mail, or can be tied to it so that its information appears on computer screens.

**file.** A single unit of computer information stored on disk. A file can be part of a program, a word-processing document, a database of many documents, a graphic image, or even a sound.

**file server.** A computer devoted to "serving" files to other computers on a network.

**folder.** Used different ways in various E-mail programs, but always referring to a logical storage place for E-mail messages.

**gateway.** A connection from an E-mail system to another post office on the same system or to another E-mail system.

**GUI.** Graphical User Interface, a scheme for using graphic images on the computer screen to represent commands and options, instead of the more traditional "command line." The Apple Macintosh first made the GUI popular, but it is now available on PCs through Microsoft Windows and on workstations through Motif or Open Look.

**header.** The first part of an E-mail message (see also Body and Attachments). The header contains address information such as To, Subject, and so on.

**inbox.** The storage area where all received E-mail messages are kept in your computer's "mailbox."

**interface.** 1) A connection between two parts of a computer's software or hardware; 2) the connection between you and the computer—the display shown on screen along with the keyboard or mouse you use to control it.

**Internet.** A collection of networks and gateways that encompasses the world, including ARPANET, MILnet, NSFnet, and many other networks. Internet is probably the largest international network. It uses TCP/IP protocols.

**IP.** Internet Protocol, the Internet's software protocol for tracking node addresses, routing messages, and recognizing incoming messages.

**IPX.** Internet Packet Exchange, the protocol for network communication used on Novell's NetWare.

**ISDN.** Integrated Services Digital Network, the standard for handling all telephone communications digitally. Traditional phone-line communications are analog. ISDN is faster and so allows not only voice but also data and images to travel through the phone.

**ISO.** International Standards Organization, the international group that develops standards such as the OSI model for networks.

**k.** "Kilo" or "thousand", typically referring to 1000 of something (such as a "kilometer" as 1000 meters). In digital work, though, including E-mail, "k" means 1024, a multiple of two that is close to 1000 (digital systems work in multiples of two).

**LAN Manager.** A network operating system from Microsoft that competes with Novell's NetWare for handling the fundamental tasks of local area networks of PCs.

**local.** Disks, files, and other computer resources that are within the computer at hand, not located in other computers on the network.

**LocalTalk.** The networking system built into every Macintosh computer which is based on the AppleTalk protocols. LocalTalk is easy to set up but slow to move large amounts of information when compared to common PC networks such as Ethernet and Token Ring. It is commonly used to connect small- to medium-size workgroups.

**mailbox.** The location within your computer E-mail software that holds all incoming mail. Some mailboxes also hold copies of sent mail.

**mainframe.** A large, central computer.

**message.** A communication, typically built of a header, a body, and optional attachments.

**MHS.** Message Handling Service, a program for message handling (a message transport standard) that comes free with Novell's NetWare network operating system. MHS has become a de facto standard in E-mail because of the huge popularity of NetWare. Two E-mail programs that both support MHS should theoretically be able to exchange message with one another without any special gateways.

**modem.** A device that connects a computer or network to a standard telephone line for communicating computer information through the phone to another computer or network.

**multitasking.** Running more than one program at a time, a feature that only sophisticated operating systems allow. Apple Macintosh and PC DOS permit some multitasking, Windows allows more, and OS/2 and UNIX have full multitasking.

**mush.** Mail User's Shell, a user agent in UNIX systems.

**NetBIOS.** Network Basic Input/Output System, the software that links a network operating system with a piece of computer hardware. Originally developed by IBM and Sytek, there are now many compatible versions of NetBIOS.

**NetWare.** The most popular Network Operating System, NOS, for handling the fundamental tasks of linking personal computers into a local area network, LAN. From Novell Corporation.

**network.** A continuing connection between two or more computers. Networks let computers share peripheral devices, files, programs, and other resources.

**node.** A single connection or computer on a network.

**OCE.** Open Collaboration Environment, an Apple Computer software specification and API (Applications Programming Interface) for standardizing the interaction of directory services, authentication, and other such fundamental messaging services.

**OMI.** Open Messaging Interface, a specification or standard for exchanging messages between application programs. Originally created by Lotus, IBM, Apple, and others, OMI has been superseded by VIM.

**OSI.** Open Systems Interconnection, an ISO standard for computer connections and networks.

**OS/2.** A computer operating system developed in a joint venture of IBM and Microsoft, and that has multitasking and networking like UNIX. Meant to succeed the less-capable DOS operating system, OS/2 has had little market success so far.

**packet switching.** Sending digital information by collecting it into "packets" and sent at high speed, which maximizes the use of the transmission channel.

**PBX.** Private Branch Exchange, a piece of telephone equipment that connects lines within a company or department.

**PDN.** See Public Data Network.

**polling.** The process software uses to regularly inquire for something, such as an E-mail user agent program checking to see if new mail has arrived.

**postmaster.** A person or address you may send questions and reports to on the E-mail system.

**post office.** The main database in an E-mail system that stores all of the messages. The post office is typically located on the server.

**PROFS.** Professional Office System, an IBM program for mainframes running the VM/CMS operating system. PROFS includes its own E-mail.

**protocol.** A set of rules or a specification that tells how hardware or software should operate. By following a protocol, a program or network can communicate with another program or network that follows the same protocol.

**public data network.** A packet-switched network that is open to the public as a commercial service.

**queue.** A line or list of items.

**RAM.** Random Access Memory, the main memory chips in a computer. A certain amount of RAM is necessary for the operating system, more for utility programs, more for network connection software, and yet more for running main application programs.

**receipt.** An option in some E-mail programs. When you ask for a receipt, the program will notify you when the recipient of a message "opens" that message. This is the electronic equivalent of certified mail.

**redirector.** A piece of software in each computer on a network. That takes requests from programs for peripherals and files on the network and sends them to the network operating system software.

**remote client.** A computer that accesses the network from outside the physically cabled system. Typically a remote client uses a modem instead of a LAN adapter, calling-in to another modem that is cabled to the network. This permits use of the E-mail system, and other network capabilities, from a distance. Because modems are much slower than LAN adapters, the communication of large attached files can be much slower to and from remote clients.

**router.** A device that connects networks. It is similar to a bridge, handling packets and frames and moving them from one network to another. Bridges and routers are easily confused, but the differences are less tangible than they used to be, and aren't too important for E-mail discussions.

**server.** A computer dedicated to managing the shared files and resources of a network, providing printer or file services to client workstations.

**shell.** A piece of software that sits between the operating system and the computer user, presenting a command line, menus, or a GUI.

**SMF.** Standard Message Format, dictates how a message is built from addressing information, an ASCII message body, and any attachments. Used by MHS.

**SMTP.** Simple Mail Transfer Protocol, a common protocol for computers running the UNIX operating system. It describes how an E-mail system operates between host and user.

**SQL.** Structured Query Language, a computer language for retrieving information from databases. This is a well-accepted standard, and is pronounced "Sequel."

**store-and-forward.** The fundamental structure of most E-mail programs, which offer no specific and immediate path between sender and recipient, but instead depend on intermediate servers or hosts that accept incoming messages, store them temporarily, and then forward them to another server or host closer to the final recipient.

**string.** A piece of text information, from one character to many.

**switch.** An optional command code you add to a command in a program, to tell that program to behave in some particular way.

**synchronous.** Information transmission with a common, synchronized clock between sender and recipient. This is typically faster but more expensive than asynchronous communications.

**TCP.** Transmission Control Protocol, a popular software specification, especially in UNIX systems, for managing information packets on a network.

**TSR.** Terminate and Stay Resident, a type of PC program that stays in memory even when it is not operating. This occupies memory—a disadvantage—but makes the program quicker to respond—an advantage. Many E-mail programs have a TSR notification utility, so that they can always and quickly alert the user to recieved messages.

**TCP/IP.** Transmission Control Protocol/Internet Protocol.

**Telex.** An international electronic-messaging technology that has largely been superseded by E-mail. There are still millions of Telex machines in the world, and many E-mail systems can send messages to them via gateways.

**Token Ring.** A network cabling and protocol specification made popular by IBM. It competes with the Ethernet specification.

**transport agent.** E-mail systems can be, and increasingly are, broken into two components: transport agents and user agents. The transport agent software is responsible for moving messages from sender to recipient.

**UNIX.** An operating system for computers that is popular on workstations and minicomputers. UNIX has built-in E-mail abilities.

**user agent.** E-mail systems can be, and increasingly are, broken into two components: transport agents and user agents. The user agent software presents the messages and commands to the user.

**V.32, V.32bis, V.42, V.42bis.** CCITT standards for modems, specifying modem speeds and compression schemes. Modems that support the same specification should be able to communicate with one another.

**VIM.** An API standard for E-mail programs developed and promoted by Lotus, IBM, Apple, Novell, Borland, and many other companies. It replaces the older OMI standard. VIM competes with Microsoft's proposed MAPI standard API. Programs that support VIM should be able to communicate with one another. APIs such as VIM and MAPI are necessary for mail-enabled applications and other such advanced E-mail software.

**VAN.** Value-added network, a private packet-switched network. Sometimes VANs sell their services publicly.

**VAP.** Value Added Process, a piece of software that can add to Novell's NetWare to give it some additional function.

**Vines.** A network operating system from Banyan.

**WAN.** Wide area network, a network that connects computers over a wider geographic region than a LAN can. Sometimes a WAN is made up of interconnected LANs.

**window.** An area on the computer display devoted to a particular program or a part of a program—used in GUIs.

**X.400.** CCITT standard for E-mail message structure. Two programs or systems that support X.400 should be able to exchange messages. X.400 is complicated and has not become as popular as originally expected, but is popular in Europe and is growing more important in the U.S. There are new X.400 specifications every four years, with a 1984 spec, a 1988 spec, and an expected 1992 spec.

**X.500.** CCITT standard for E-mail directories. Only in the initial stages of testing, this specification is intended to allow all supporting systems to direct mail to anyone on any X.500 supporting system.

**X Windows.** A GUI and communication scheme for UNIX and related computers.

# Resource List

## Magazines

For news of E-mail standards and specifications, for examples of current E-mail use, and for reviews of E-mail programs, read:

*PC Magazine*
*PC World*
*BYTE*
*InfoWorld*
*MacWorld*
*MacUser*
*MacWeek*
*PC Week*
*PC/Computing*
*PC Resources*
*ComputerWorld*
*CIO*

## Books

Naturally, what you're holding is my favorite general book on E-mail. There are some other volumes that hold more specific information, however:

*Delivering cc:Mail*, Eric Arnum, M&T Books, 1991.
*Using cc:Mail*, Stephen Caswell, M&T Books, 1991.
*E-mail*, Stephen Caswell, Artech House, 1988.
*The Complete MCI Mail Handbook*, Paul Schindler, Bantam,1988.
*MH & xmh: E-mail for Users & Programmers*, Jerry Peek, O'Reilly & Assoc., Inc., 1991.
*The Z-Mail Handbook*, Hanna Nelson, O'Reilly & Assoc., Inc., 1991.
*!%@:: A Directory of Electronic Mail Addressing and Networks*, Frey and Adam O'Reilly & Assoc., 1990.

*The Matrix: Computer Networks and Conferencing Systems Worldwide,* John S
Quarterman, Digital Press, 1990.

## Newsletters

*EMMS Electronic Mail & Micro Systems* from International Resource Devel
opment is a bimonthly newsletter covering technology, user, product, and
market trends in electronic mail, facsimile, advanced networking (LAN
and WAN), and microcomputer communications.

## Groups

The Electronic Mail Association helps establish E-mail standards and brings
E-mail users and developers together to discuss relevant issues.

Microcomputer Manager's Association
Association of PC User Groups (ACPUG) is an association of associations, a
central point for all the various PC user groups in the world devoted to various PC hardware and software. APCUG offers an E-mail communications
hub for more than 200 user groups around the world. The $25 annual mem-
bership includes a free Tymnet account for group officers and the rights
to use the APCUG BBS.

## Conferences

There are several conferences and conventions you can attend to see the latest E-mail software and systems demonstrated.

EMA Annual Convention (The Electronic Mail Association)
NetWorld (biannual)
Comdex (biannual)
PC Expo (biannual)
MacWorld (biannual)

# Index

# A Library of Technical References
# from M&T Books

### Delivering cc:Mail
### Installing, Maintaining, and Troubleshooting a cc:Mail System
### by Eric Arnum

Delivering cc:Mail teaches administrators how to install, troubleshoot, and maintain cc:Mail, one of the most popular E-mail applications for the PC. In-depth discussions and practical examples show administrators how to establish and maintain program and database files; how to create and modify bulletin boards, mail directory, and public mailing lists; and how to diagnose and repair potential problems. Information on using the management tools included with the package, plus tips and techniques for creating efficient batch files are also included. All source code is available on disk in MS/PC-DOS format.  234 pp.

| | | |
|---|---|---|
| Book | $29.95 | 1-55851-185-7 |
| Book/Disk (MS-DOS) | $39.95 | 1-55851-187-3 |

Level:  Advanced

### The NetWare User's Guide
### by Edward Liebing

The essential guide for NetWare users working with, or considering upgrading to version 2.2.  Covers all changes and additions found in version 2.2. Presents network printing information, detailed tutorials, and descriptions of every NetWare 2.2 menu and command-line utility.  662 pp.

| | | |
|---|---|---|
| Book | $29.95 | 1-55851-235-7 |

Level: Beginning - Intermediate

# ORDER FORM

**To Order:**

Return this form with your payment to M&T books, 501 Galveston Drive, Redwood City, CA 94063 or **call toll-free 1-800-533-4372 (in California, call 1-800-356-2002).**

| ITEM # | DESCRIPTION | DISK | PRICE |
|--------|-------------|------|-------|
|        |             |      |       |
|        |             |      |       |
|        |             |      |       |
|        |             |      |       |
|        |             |      |       |
|        |             |      |       |
|        |             |      |       |
|        |             |      |       |
|        |             |      |       |

Subtotal

CA residents add sales tax ____%

Add $3.75 per item for shipping and handling

TOTAL

NOTE: **FREE SHIPPING** ON ORDERS OF THREE OR MORE BOOKS.

**Charge my:**
- ❏ **Visa**
- ❏ **MasterCard**
- ❏ **AmExpress**

- ❏ **Check enclosed, payable to M&T Books.**

CARD NO.

SIGNATURE                          EXP. DATE

NAME

ADDRESS

CITY

STATE                              ZIP

**M&T GUARANTEE:** If your are not satisfied with your order for any reason, return it to us within 25 days of receipt for a full refund. Note: Refunds on disks apply only when returned with book within guarantee period. Disks damaged in transit or defective will be promptly replaced, but cannot be exchanged for a disk from a different title.

1709

## 1-800-533-4372 (in CA 1-800-356-2002)

# Tell us what you think and we'll send you a free M&T Books catalog

It is our goal at M&T Books to produce the best technical books available. But you can help us make our books even better by letting us know what you think about this particular title. Please take a moment to fill out this card and mail it to us. Your opinion is appreciated.

## Tell us about yourself

Name_____

Company_____

Address_____

City_____

State/Zip_____

## Title of this book?

_____

## Where did you purchase this book?

☐ Bookstore
☐ Catalog
☐ Direct Mail
☐ Magazine Ad
☐ Postcard Pack
☐ Other

## Why did you choose this book?

☐ Recommended
☐ Read book review
☐ Read ad/catalog copy
☐ Responded to a special offer
☐ M&T Books' reputation
☐ Price
☐ Nice Cover

## How would you rate the overall content of this book?

☐ Excellent
☐ Good
☐ Fair
☐ Poor

## Why?

_____

_____

## What chapters did you find valuable?

_____

_____

_____

## What did you find least useful?

_____

_____

_____

## What topic(s) would you add to future editions of this book?

_____

_____

_____

## What other titles would you like to see M&T Books publish?

_____

_____

_____

## Which format do you prefer for the optional disk?

☐ 5.25"     ☐ 3.5"

## Any other comments?

_____

_____

_____

☐ Check here for
M&T Books Catalog

M&T BOOKS